Boat Building Techniques Illustrated

Richard Birmingham

ADLARD COLES NAUTICAL
London

This book is dedicated to everyone who takes a big bite and keeps chewing.

Published by Adlard Coles Nautical
an imprint of A & C Black Publishers Ltd
38 Soho Square, London W1D 3HB
www.adlardcoles.com

First edition published by Adlard Coles 1984
Reprinted 1985, 1988
Reprinted by Adlard Coles Nautical 1992, 1994
First paperback edition 2005
Reprinted 2008

ISBN 978-0-7136-7621-1

A CIP catalogue record for this book is available from the British Library.

A & C Black uses paper produced with elemental chlorine-free pulp, harvested from managed sustainable forests.

Printed and bound in Great Britain by The Cromwell Press, Trowbridge, Wiltshire

Note: While all reasonable care has been taken in the publication of this book, the publisher takes no responsibility for the use of the methods or products described in the book.

Contents

LIST OF TABLES

Acknowledgements

Many people have given me advice, assistance, and encouragement in the preparation of this book, and I would like to express my gratitude to them all, even though only a few are mentioned here by name.

The International Boatbuilding Training Centre at Oulton Broad was expecially co-operative, giving me complete freedom to photograph when and where I liked, and kindly allowing the staff and trainees to help me set up particular shots. In fact without the unhesitating help of John Parker, the chief instructor there, this book would have been very incomplete. It was he who originally gave me a basic understanding of boatbuilding, and I continue to heed his advice, and value his friendship.

Cliff Patchett, another friend who has taught me much about boatbuilding, checked over the draft of part of the 'Materials' section, and helped me with photographs at his Martham Ferry Boatyard in Norfolk, as did Whisstock's Boatyard in Woodbridge. Photos were also provided by Denise Phillips, Ford Jenkins, Duncan Birmingham and Gilbert Oltramare. Mick Sparksman gave useful tips on preparing the drawings.

Both TRADA (Timber Research and Development Association) and the Building Research Establishment kindly allowed me to reproduce some of their material in the tables concerning timbers.

Sue did all the typing, patiently converting my often scruffy manuscript into a form fit for the publishers. I want to thank her for that, and also because while I have been writing, she has kept us solvent.

Introduction

There is a fascination in the intricate shapes and curves of a boat under construction that is like the fascination of the sea itself. For those involved in the work, the pleasure of creating a boat's shape, giving it strength, and eventually finishing it with an attention to detail that will enhance the vessel's natural grace, is matched only by the satisfaction of a successful launch. The cumbersome object is transformed: the dead weight that was agonisingly awkward to move to the water nods and dances on it with astonishing ease, like a young animal taking the measure of its first moments of life. Her beauty, that was incongruously striking in the angular confines of the boatshed, is now seen to be what nature dictated: no longer remarkable, but simply right.

There is pleasure for the boatbuilder in making something that is pleasing to the eye, but the moments spent tasting that pleasure are few and widely spaced in many months of work. Much of that work is of a very unromantic nature: the boatshop is leaky, draughty, and unheated; the materials (whether modern resins or old-fashioned recipes) are both toxic and messy, with an unpleasant habit of getting everywhere. The immediate task, whether demanding or simple, is usually made unreasonably difficult by its ridiculous situation, perhaps underneath the hull, or at the back of a locker. During most of the work the perspective is too close to give any concept of the project as a whole, and the only satisfaction that can be gained is that of overcoming the obstacle that is often literally just in front of one's nose.

The boatbuilder, or shipwright, was traditionally a specialist in the broad field of carpentry. Even today, despite the advent of many other materials for hull construction, the boatbuilder is still primarily concerned with working in wood. Even hulls of fibreglass, ferrocement, steel, or aluminium alloy, are all fitted out using plywood and solid timber. But if the boatbuilder is essentially a woodworker he must also be familiar with a wide variety of other materials, as is reflected in the 'Materials' section of this book.

In addition, to complete a boat, many other skills are required, including those of the draughtsman, welder, engineer, mechanic, plumber, electrician, rigger, sailmaker, and upholsterer. An understanding of the technology and terminology used in any of these trades is a useful asset and will speed the resolution of many headaches.

Headaches, — that is what boatbuilding is really all about. The image of the boatbuilder as a craftsman, at one with nature, his work a therapy for the twentieth century, unfortunately just does not ring true. To enjoy boatbuilding one must be ready to take on an endless stream of problems, and solving them must be considered part of the fun. But if it is to be fun, they have to be solved, and that is where I hope this book comes in.

It is not intended to be a description of how to build a boat, which starts with the laying of the keel, and finishes with the launch, but rather an aid to solving the problems every builder will encounter, whether starting from scratch, working from a kit, or restoring an old hull. Following the preliminary discussions of decisions that have to be made when setting up a boatbuilding project, the main body of the book is divided into three sections that reflect the constituent parts of any problem: which method, material, and tool are best suited to the job. Little is contained in this book that cannot be found elsewhere, but the information needed by the boatbuilder is of such a diverse nature that it is inevitably spread out among many sources, and requires time and patience to find in odd corners of specialist books and manufacturers' catalogues. The pertinent facts from several fields are brought together in this single volume, while for those who require more detailed information a bibliography is included that is arranged subject by subject, in parallel with the text.

Of course every problem has several solutions, and where possible, alternatives are included. Further possibilities will be discovered by asking, or simply looking: a walk along the quay, examining one detail of each boat in turn (perhaps the rudder fittings, none of which will be the same) can produce some interesting ideas. Which of several solutions is most suitable on any occasion has to be decided by the builder himself, but if available, the advice of someone with considerable experience is well heeded. An old boatbuilder who is willing to part with his knowledge is a rare find, and his friendship more valuable than any number of books. Listen to him attentively but do not irritate him by asking 'why?' too often. The answer was worked out long ago in his apprenticeship, or perhaps his father's, and may be almost forgotten.

Preparatory Considerations

When setting up a boatbuilding project, the first and obvious decision that has to be made is a choice of design. Much advice has been given in cruising handbooks and design manuals on the various merits of different designs, and the prospective boat *owner* will no doubt give due attention to these counsels. The intending *boatbuilder* should also take into account some other aspects that have been less widely discussed.

Careful consideration must be given to the size of the project, the construction method, the building site, and even the source of plans, each of which is a separate strand in the boatbuilder's calculations, though all are intertwined and influence or limit the design. Ultimately this is a personal choice, but the following discussion may provide some guidance, and also instil a little caution.

A Sense of Scale

Boats look small in the water, and they feel small to anyone only used to shoreside accommodation, so when considering owning and cruising a boat, the tendency is repeatedly to decide that it should be a little bit larger. Dreams easily grow more and more grandiose, but even if the scheme does get off the ground, the boat unfortunately never reaches the water. Set up in the boatshop, a boat looks big, and if it has to be built single handed, enormous. When considering building a boat, the wise person asks if it could be a little bit smaller.

'Little bits' make a surprising amount of difference. If a 25 ft (7.6 m) boat, for example, seems a feasible proposition it is tempting to think that a 30 ft (9.1 m) boat will only be a fifth more work. But boats are three dimensional and an increase in length produces an increase in work (and expense) proportional to the cube of the lengths. So the ratio is not 25:30 but $25^3:30^3$ or 15625:27000. Not one fifth more work, but four fifths! The calculation may be rough and ready, but it does help keep a sense of scale when assessing

1

both labour and expenses.

A larger boat may be possible if some of the work or expense can be avoided, perhaps by buying a moulded hull, or by building one from a cheaper material. In these cases a sense of proportion is provided by this old rule of thumb: in a traditionally built boat half the work is in the hull, and half in the fitting out; financially one third is the hull, one third fitting out, and one third the rig, sails, and other major equipment. Modern construction methods may speed up hull construction, but fitting out remains extremely time consuming. In practical terms this means that there is likely to be as much work in fitting out a 32 ft (9.7 m) hull, as in building and completing a 25 ft (7.6 m) one. Similarly the financial saving obtained by using a cheaper hull material is not necessarily as large as it first appears to be: ferrocement is often said to save about half the cost of a hull, but if the hull is only one third of the total cost, the final saving is in fact only one sixth.

When trying to calculate how long the job will take, a hefty allowance should be made for time spent organising, ordering, chasing, and purchasing materials. On average, in a week's work, one full day will be spent on administration of this sort. This is one of the great savings achieved by building a boat from a kit; all the material estimating is avoided, and all the purchasing is achieved in one session. A financial allowance should also be made for purchasing and hiring of necessary tools and equipment, which could quite easily be as much as ten percent of the total cost of the project.

Estimating costs, both in time and money, is difficult even for a professional continually involved in such assessments. For others it is almost impossible. The usual advice is to work it out as accurately and realistically as possible, then double it! This may work if undivided attention can be given to the project for the duration, but if distractions are likely to creep in (perhaps irresistible offers of sailing, even accidental breeding, or the inevitable need to restart earning) then better advice is: double all estimates again.

Construction Methods

Boatbuilders are inventive people, so there have always been many ways of building a boat. Technological advances have increased the scope even further such that now there is a bewildering number of choices. Choosing the construction method goes hand in hand with choosing the design, as plans are always drawn with one method in mind. Often they can satisfactorily be used for an alternative system, but this should be done with caution as different construction methods require different internal strengthening. In some cases it is physically impossible to change the form of construction.

The main types of construction method, using timber, are set out and illustrated here, but a more detailed description of the different processes involved with each will be found in the 'Planking' section in Part 1 of this book.

One way to classify the many wooden boatbuilding methods is to differentiate between the traditional and modern, the use of glue being the distinguishing characteristic. Before the arrival of modern resins an effective marine adhesive did not exist; fastenings had to be mechanical and watertightness ensured by good craftsmanship combined with an understanding of the behaviour of timber. The arrival of modern glues has opened up a whole new range of boat-building methods, which characteristically produce monocoque hulls that are strong and watertight, their only drawback being that they are perhaps more difficult to repair.

The two methods that are normally considered traditional are clinker (or lapstrake) and carvel, shown in Plates 0.1 and 0.2. On a clinker hull the planks overlap each other, the very visible run of the planking being a distinguishing feature. This ancient type of construction produces a strong hull which is lighter than a carvel planked hull of the same strength and size. The lapped planks add strength, allowing both the omission of internal stringers and the

Plate 0.1 On *Tirrick's* clinker hull the visible run of the planking is an attractive feature.

3

Plate 0.2 *Tara* shows the smooth hull produced by carvel planking.

use of thinner planking material than would be necessary on a similar size of carvel built boat. Carvel construction, like most other building methods, produces a smooth hull as the planks simply butt up to each other, a tight fit and caulking cotton or timber splines keeping the water out. Carvel planks are easier to fit than clinker ones, but time saved planking is lost because of the additional stages involved preparing for planking and cleaning up the hull afterwards. Today clinker hulls are rarely built over 30 ft (9.1 m) in length.

Both carvel and clinker methods produce the compound curves properly associated with a boat. In contrast the cross-section of a chined hull, illustrated in Plate 0.3, has angular corners (the chines) and comprises two or more flat sections on either side of the hull

Plate 0.3 The angular shape of a chined hull is still noticeable even though *Naja* has three chines.

which makes construction comparatively straightforward. Originally each flat section was planked by conventional carvel techniques, but the use of plywood simplifies things even further. Chined designs bridge the gap between traditional and modern, as the original carvel planked types could be classed as a traditional method, while those constructed from plywood, and probably using glue and ring nails, must be classed as modern. Although similar in appearance, plans for a chined hull must be drawn with plywood in mind, if that is to be used, for the plywood sheets will not bend to the shapes incorporated in the older designs.

Plate 0.4 *Sandyloo* combines a flat plywood bottom with four clenched planks either side.

Both carvel and clinker construction demand considerably more skill than for a plywood built chined hull, which is often considered to be the amateur's method. However, two methods can be combined. The boat illustrated in Plate 0.4 is a flat bottomed skiff which has four clenched planks either side; it is technically within the capability of a complete beginner. He would learn a considerable amount about boatbuilding techniques while producing an attractive, traditional looking boat.

Other combinations have been used in the past, including the construction of barges on the East Coast of England which were clinker planked from the keel up past the turn of the bilge, then carvel planked for the remainder.

Modern boatbuilding methods all take advantage of the truly remarkable performance of today's marine adhesives, laminating the complete hull shape from thin strips or veneers of timber. There are many different patterns, but the terms 'strip planking' and 'cold moulding' (illustrated respectively in Plates 0.5 and 0.6) differentiate between the two basic systems. Strip planking uses narrow planks sprung fore and aft around a minimum of moulds, then glued and nailed edge to edge, while cold moulded hulls require a complete hull-shaped jig to which several layers of veneers are stapled. The grain of each veneer is orientated at an opposing angle to the one below, and glued to it.

Plate 0.5 Modern construction methods: *Crestadonna* is strip planked.

Plate 0.6 The two tenders to *Arethusa* are cold moulded.

Plate 0.7 *Arethusa* herself combines the two methods — only the internal strip planking is visible here, but further layers of diagonal planking are cold moulded onto it.

As with traditional methods, a combination of these modern ones can also be found, for example a lightly strip planked hull can be covered with three cold moulded layers of veneer. This produces the multi-directional strength of a cold moulded hull, without the need

7

to build a complicated jig, and is proving to be a commercially viable building method that can compete successfully with the cost of a standard glass fibre moulding.

Both strip planking and cold moulding can be used to produce the shapes of most designs, but another recently devised method called 'Constant Camber' can only be used on designs drawn specifically for it. It involves cold moulding several panels on a single jig; each looks like a huge sheet of curved plywood, but two are combined to form a single hull. It is most suited to the construction of the long lean shape required for multihulls, where it has the advantage that one jig can be used to produce panels for all the hulls.

Well-known proponents of modern boatbuilding methods which lay such great emphasis on the properties of today's resins are the Gougeon Brothers of the USA. The WEST System is linked with their name, but WEST (an acronym derived from Wood Epoxy Saturation Technique) is not itself a construction method, but a resin system that is an adhesive, filler, and protective coating, and can be used on any of the modern construction methods, and has even been used to simplify clinker building. But if the techniques developed and promoted by the Gougeon Brothers are not a construction method in themselves, it is unfair to call them a mere gluing system for they are much more than that — practically a philosophy of boatbuilding!

At the heart of their system is the use of very dry timber, every piece of which is coated with epoxy resin, effectively sealing it and preventing the reabsorption of moisture. If this can be successfully accomplished, a number of advantages are gained: the dry timber has a better strength to weight ratio, is no longer susceptible to decay, and will not shrink or swell.

The more widely acknowledged part of the WEST System which is not really so remarkable is that the gap filling properties of the glue are so good that fitted joints are unnecessary. R. D. Culler in *Skiffs and Schooners* says something to the effect that he has no time for gap filling glues as they encourage bad workmanship. The Gougeon Brothers would no doubt say that commercially there is no time for fitted joints, let the resin do the work. Well, both produce good boats.

Although the boatbuilding methods discussed above have been divided into the categories of traditional and modern, this is only for clarity and in reality no such precise division exists. Today the strength in a traditional boat may well take the form of frames laminated using modern adhesives, while the builder of a cold moulded hull may equally well choose to strengthen his with the traditional steam bent timbers. The boatbuilder uses whatever method or substance suits his purpose best, and this is reflected in this book by the juxtaposition of old and new in both materials and techniques.

The Building Site

Boats always seem to be built under adverse conditions. Poor lighting, no heating, cramped space and minimum security are considered normal. Just how adverse those conditions are should affect the choice of construction method.

Modern synthetic materials often require controlled temperature and humidity. While this may be easy to achieve for the construction of individual members, if the entire hull is a laminated structure, the boatshop should resemble a factory rather than a barn. If it is proposed to build a boat to the Gougeon Brothers' principles just discussed, it is no good having kiln dried timber which has been stored in the open air until use (even if well protected from rain), as by then its moisture content will no longer be at the low levels required.

Conversely a hull that is to be built from air dried timber will not survive in an excessively heated environment as the timber will continue to dry after it is fitted causing checks to open in the wood and gaps to appear in the joints. Boatshops in the past had earth floors as these did not entirely dry out, ensuring a more even humidity during the construction of each boat. Old-fashioned materials like pitch and linseed oil were found to work effectively in these environments, and this is worth remembering when the latest super-something-composition does not live up to expectations in the less than space age environment of the backyard in midwinter.

Assuming a small workshop is available for prefabricating and laminating individual members, the minimum requirements of the actual building site are that the wind and rain can be kept at bay. The wind saps moisture from timber unacceptably quickly; while rain through a leaky roof saps morale from the workforce even faster. A third basic requirement of a building site is a secure tenure: it will take much longer than anticipated, and a quarter finished boat with the moulds set up and attached to roof beams is impossible to move.

The next requirements are good lighting (preferably natural), a good power supply, and good neighbours, or better still no neighbours. Noisy power tools worked late into the night test the closest of friendships.

Finally life is made easier if the site has easy access, is close to home, and can be heated during the winter. Access should be considered primarily from the point of view of delivery drivers with timber, masts etc. Actually getting the boat out never seems to be a problem. After the struggle of building, a minor difficulty like taking down a wall, or hiring a crane to lift the hull from the back garden over the house seems quite straightforward! Building the boat close to home is certainly an advantage as it means that calculations can be done more easily in the evenings, popping out as necessary to take a few measurements. In many boatshops heating is virtually impossible, in which case it is a matter of long-johns and woolly hats, but if some sort of heater can be installed, the number of hours spent on the site during the cold months, and the amount accomplished in those hours, will increase enormously.

The larger the working area the better, of course, but minimum requirements must be these:

(1) Room for the boat itself with adequate space each side to bend the planks and gunwales, and preferably with scope to stand back and check that lines are fair.
(2) Storage space, particularly for timber, both planking stock and plywood.
(3) An area for cutting full sheets of plywood.
(4) Space around the workbench and any installed machinery such as saws or planers.

A cramped boatshop can be satisfactory if there is room to spread outside for larger jobs, such as setting up a steam machine, or even simply turning a plank end for end.

Plans

Plans can be obtained from several sources: designers, class associations, or design agencies. Professional yacht designers, whose advertisements appear in the yachting magazines, will provide a brochure that gives details of their stock plans and the services they offer. Actually commissioning the design of a yacht is extremely expensive, but to purchase something off the peg with perhaps some minor modifications is relatively cheap, though still a considerable sum. The advantage gained by going to a designer is that he should

10

provide a complete service, so that if any problems crop up, or modifications are necessary, he can be turned to for guidance and advice.

The price of plans for a design which is popular with amateur builders will be much cheaper, and where a class association exists they often hold the plans. The designer will no longer be involved, but the association itself may well be able to give useful hints based on experience with previous craft. Another cheap source of plans, based on a larger number of sales, is to buy them through a design service, such as those offered by some magazines like the American publication *Wooden Boat*.

Although with plans obtained from these less expensive sources no back up service is provided, boatbuilders can still make modifications and check scantlings by referring to one of the books of 'Rules': systems that have been worked out to provide minimum safe scantlings for various types and sizes of craft.

The most well-known of these in Britain are *Lloyd's Rules for Yachts and Small Craft*, published in a loose-leaf folder to which different sections can be added. The complete set is prohibitively expensive, but unnecessary, as it includes sections on wood, steel and glass fibre construction, and machinery installation, not all of which will be needed for any one boatbuilding project. Herreshoff's Rules can be found in *Skene's Elements of Yacht Design,* and although not so detailed are equally complicated to extract information from.

For the construction of workboats a less widely known set of rules is published in Britain by the Sea Fish Industry Authority, called *Rules for the Construction of Fishing Vessels*. They produce separate volumes for timber, glass fibre, and steel construction. These rules are considerably easier to use than the others as a single reference figure is worked out for the boat, and with this scantlings can be read directly from all the tables. The results obtained from these rules are of course heavier than those provided by Lloyd's and Herreshoff's rules for yachts.

The amount of information provided in a set of plans can vary enormously. For a small dinghy it may only consist of one or two sheets, while pages and pages of details may be provided for a large craft. The basic sheets usually consist of the lines drawing, the construction plan, and a sail plan. In addition there is likely to be a general arrangement plan, deck plan, and some details, such as the ballast keel, or a plan showing alternative arrangements for keel or deck stepped masts.

11

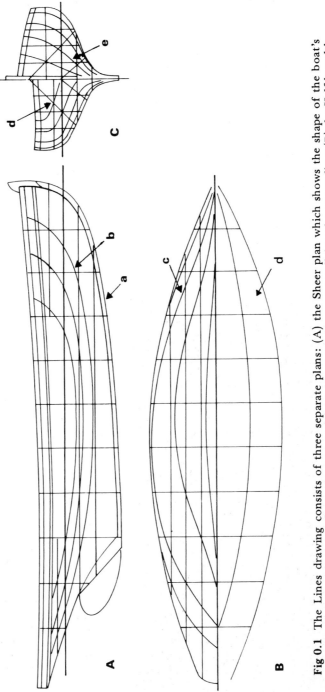

Fig 0.1 The Lines drawing consists of three separate plans: (A) the Sheer plan which shows the shape of the boat's profile (a), and the shape of the buttock lines (b), these are sections cut parallel to the centre line; (B) the Half breadth plan, the curves above the centre line are water lines (c), and those below are diagonals (d); (C) the Body plan which shows the shape of regularly spaced cross-sections through the hull called station lines (e). On this plan the forward stations are normally drawn to the right of the centre line, and the aft stations to the left. The position of diagonals (d) are also indicated on this plan.

The construction plan is used to build the boat, and the general arrangement — probably with many modifications — is referred to when fitting out.

The plan that is most difficult for the inexperienced to understand is the lines drawing, an example of which is shown in Fig. 0.1. This gives the actual shape of the hull. It is in three parts, each showing a series of cross-sections through the hull cut on different planes. The sheer plan shows the boat's profile, and the shape of slices taken parallel to the centre line; the half breadth plan shows the shape of the water line and slices taken above and below it; and the body plan shows the shape of the hull at intervals along its length, as if the boat had been put through a bread slicer. It is this last plan, the body plan, that is used by the builder to obtain the boat's shape, making full size patterns of each 'slice', or station. These patterns are called moulds, and when set up at the correct intervals form the jig around which the boat is built (Plate 0.8).

Plate 0.8
From a full size body plan, called the scrieve board, patterns of each station line are made. When these are set up at the correct intervals they form a jig on which to construct the hull. *Naja*, shown here, is built upside down, and the 'patterns' remain permanently in the hull as each is either a frame or a bulkhead.

In order to make the moulds the builder produces a full size body plan called the scrieve board, but to ensure that the lines on the scrieve board are fair, and that together they will produce a fair hull, the entire lines plan has to be reproduced full size in the process called lofting.

Lofting the plans is the first stage of constructing any boat, but in many cases it is not the builder who does it. After all, if a boat has been lofted once, it should not be necessary for each builder to repeat the work if he can obtain a copy of the scrieve board. Plans for older boats sometimes include a full size paper scrieve board, and even with new boats some of today's designers do their own lofting and provide the information. When obtaining plans it is worth enquiring if this is the case, as it does save considerable work.

Part 1
Techniques

1. Lifting Shapes from Plans

Every part of a wooden hull is curved. To transfer the correct curve from plans to timber is a basic problem. Sometimes the curve can be found only on a scale drawing. It may be on full size paper plans, or it may be full size but on a solid surface: the scrieve board or loft floor. In each case a different technique is called for.

From Scale Drawings

Simple curves that have not been lofted can be marked onto the timber by taking measurements from a base line. Fig. 1.1 illustrates

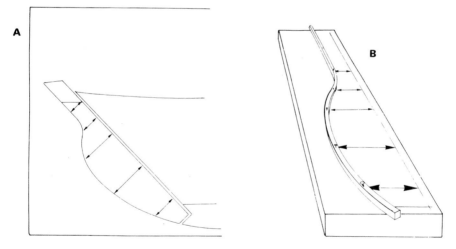

Fig. 1.1 A shape can be copied from scale drawings by taking perpendicular measurements from a base line (A), and marking these onto the timber (B), and connecting the points with a fairing batten.

a rudder outline being transferred by this method. As the forward edge of the rudder is straight, this edge can be used as the base line. On the plan perpendiculars are raised at regular intervals along it and the distance to the curved edge measured at each. A base line is drawn on the timber and the correctly scaled perpendicular

17

measurements marked from it. A flexible batten tacked at each of these points will then produce the required shape. The batten is tacked on the 'waste' side, the side that after cutting will be lost, so that the tack holes do not start checks in the timber. The curve is also checked for fairness before being marked and the tacks moved slightly if irregularities are found (see Section 6, Fairing.)

From Full Size Paper Outlines

Many designers loft their own drawings and include with the plans some full scale outlines. On chine dinghies these may be profiles of all the important parts, including expansions of the planking shapes. On larger craft it may only be the transom, although sometimes a complete paper scrieve board may be available, showing the shapes of the moulds at every station.

Paper plans of this kind have to be used carefully as distortions can easily occur. If a series of boats are envisaged it is wise to make plywood templates from the plans. Although bulky, these are quicker to mark from on subsequent occasions. The paper plans store neatly, but become increasingly difficult to use with every handling.

The shape is transferred by taping the outline to the plywood, or other timber stock, and then pricking through the paper at regular intervals along each line. The plan is then removed and the marks found and joined, using a fairing batten as described above. If the awl is held at an angle to the paper when pricking, errors occur, so it should always be held vertically.

Small shapes can be transferred by using carbon paper between the plan and timber, and drawing round the outline.

If a template is not being made, but a second mirror image has to be produced (as with planking), the first is marked and cut out, then that used to mark the second. Sometimes this is not possible, for example where small moulds are being produced from a single piece of plywood, but only one half is shown on the scrieve board. In this case the centre line is marked on the ply and the centre line of the paper scrieve board aligned on it. One half is pricked, then the paper is turned over and the centre line realigned. By pricking back through the first holes, the second half is also marked.

From A Solid Scrieve Board

When making the moulds or frames the requisite shapes must be obtained from the loft floor. Their lofted shapes have been drawn out on the full size body plan, the scrieve board, but they have to be redrawn onto the timber that will make up the moulds.

The traditional way to do this is to use a large number of tacks. These can be used complete, but are more effective and accurate if each one has half its head filed away. These are then placed *on their sides* on the scrieve board, their heads aligned along the line to be copied. The mould stock is then carefully placed over them, and pressed down firmly (Fig. 1.2). The tack heads press into the timber, and when it is lifted up they are picked up by it, or at least leave indentations. These marks are then faired with a batten in the usual way.

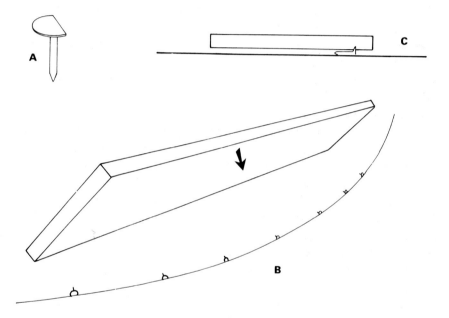

Fig 1.2 The traditional method of picking up station lines from the scrieve board. Modified tacks (A) are placed along the line (B), so that when the mould stock timber is carefully pressed onto them indentations are made in it (C). These marks are then joined to reproduce the line.

Problems can arise when using a grainy wood for the moulds, as the indentations left by the tacks can be hard to find. This can be overcome by giving the timber stock a single coat of paint so that the marks show up more clearly.

This method, although tedious, is well tried and tested. There are other ways that may be more suitable in some circumstances. One is simply to transfer the shape to long lengths of tracing paper, and then prick through this onto the mould stock as described for paper outlines.

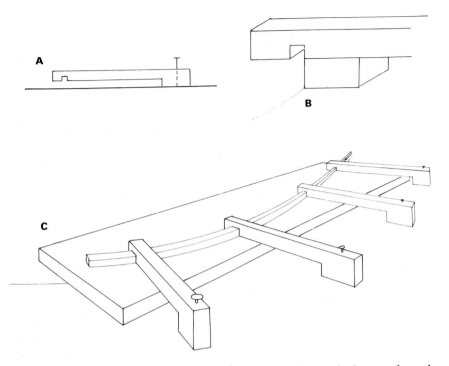

Fig 1.3   Another method of copying station lines: tailor-made 'batten clamps'
(A) are accurately positioned over the line with a scrap of timber (B).
When all are fastened in position the mould stock and batten are slid
beneath them (C) and the line marked.

Another method is to make about a dozen batten clamps (Fig. 1.3).
These are weighted or tacked to the loft floor at one end, while the
other end has a slot to accept a batten. They are shaped so that the
mould stock can be slid underneath. These are first positioned and
fastened down so that the batten will follow the curve to be copied.
The mould stock is slid under them, and with the batten inserted,
the line drawn.

Deck Camber

Deck camber is the shape of the deck athwartships, a gentle curve
from the crown down to the sheer. This curve is not shown clearly
on any of the plans, but usually expressed as a numerical form in a
note. '4 in crop in 8 ft beam' would mean that over an 8 ft beam (2.4 m)
the crown of the deck would be 4 in (100 mm) above the sheer. The
beam measurement used is usually slightly greater than the maximum
beam of the boat. The deck camber can be expressed in this way as
the curve is always a part of the circumference of a large circle.

A deck beam pattern is made by cutting the appropriate concave curve from a piece of stable timber. The pattern is then used for marking out the beams and also, by laying it square across the boat, to bevel the gunwale and sheer strake, and to fair the beams and carlings prior to laying the deck.

There are three methods for marking out this curve. The first seems more suited to the workshop, and the second to the drawing board or loft floor, but they both produce an equally good pattern. For an example in both these cases a 4 in crop in 8 ft beam will be used. The third method is for mathematically-minded boatbuilders with small boats — or perhaps for anyone with a calculator and a lot of space.

Workshop Method

On the pattern material a straight line is marked near one edge, and two nails tacked on the line 8 ft (2.4 m) apart. From their midpoint a perpendicular is drawn and a third nail is tacked 4 in (100 mm) from the first line. On a second piece of wood an isosceles triangle is drawn with a base of 8 ft (2.4 m) but height of only half the crop, i.e. 2 in (50 mm). Ignoring the base line, this timber is cut and planed to the other two lines. This second piece of timber is placed on the first with its two planed faces pushed up against two of the nails and, with a pencil held at its apex, is slid past them. This process is then repeated against the other two nails as in Fig. 1.4, producing the full deck camber. By cutting to this line, ensuring that there are several inches of timber at its midpoint for strength, the deck beam pattern is made.

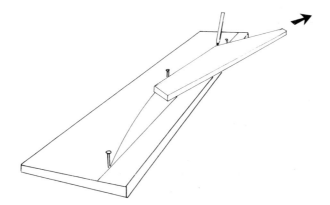

Fig 1.4 Marking out the deck camber for the deckbeam pattern by the 'workshop method'.

Draughtsman's Method
As with the previous method the base line and central perpendicular are drawn, with the beam's extremities 8 ft apart (2.4 m) marked on the first and the crop of 4 in (100 mm) marked on the second. This time a quarter circle with a radius equal to the crop and its centre at the midpoint of the base line is drawn. (Fig. 1.5.) With a protractor,

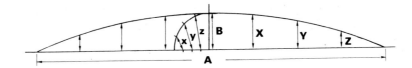

Fig 1.5 Constructing the deck camber by the 'draughtsman's method'. (A) is the beam and (B) the crop. Distances (x), (y), and (z), are marked at (X), (Y), and (Z).

the arc is then divided into four equal parts of 22½ degrees each. The base line from its midpoint to where the arc cuts it is also marked off in quarters, in this case 1 in each (25 mm). The points on the base line are then joined to their corresponding points on the arc, and the lengths of these lines measured. These lengths are then used to construct the camber: perpendiculars are raised at intervals a quarter of the way along each half of the base line and the corresponding lengths marked on them. These points joined with a fairing batten produce the deck camber.

Mathematician's Method
The deck camber is part of a true circle, the radius of which can be found with this formula:

$$\text{Radius} = \frac{x^2 + y^2}{2y}$$

where x = ½ beam, and y = crop

This method could be used in model making, drawing the deck beam pattern with a pair of trammel heads set to the calculated radius, but it is impractical with most craft, because their radii are so large (about 24 ft or 7.3 m in the above example). A length of string could be used to draw the required arc, but varying tension would cause different amounts of stretching and an unreliable curve. Light wire would produce better results.

Changing Camber

On some boats the deck camber changes along the length of the boat, in which case several patterns would have to be made. At each station the height the crown of the deck is above the sheer is measured on the sheer plan, while the beam at the corresponding station is taken from the body plan, giving a series of crop to beam ratios throughout the length of the boat.

Where the deck camber is not part of a true circle, as may be the case on the deckhouse or coachroof, the shape will be shown on the plans and will have to be lifted by one of the methods described earlier.

2. Three Dimensional Shapes

The shapes lifted from the plans in the last section are all two dimensional. In some cases, such as moulds, that is all that is required, but in others, it is just the first step; further shaping in the third dimension being necessary. Working on a large piece of timber, paring away until it looks and feels right, is similar to carving. The problem is that it must not only 'look and feel right', it must be faithful to the plans as well.

This is successfully achieved by marking and cutting several times. After thicknessing the timber to the maximum required the first step is to cut out the profile. The series of marking and cutting steps that follow gradually get closer to the requisite shape until it is near enough to dispense with the marking, and fair up free hand. Most parts are symmetrical, so where possible a centre line is marked and measurements are taken from that. To illustrate this technique three examples follow: rounding a spar, shaping a spoon oar, and shaping the members of the centre line structure. Two more cases then describe the special techniques used to make a ballast keel pattern, and to bevel frames.

Rounding a Spar

The first stage is to reduce the timber to a square section with dimensions equal to the diameter of the round required. Marks are scribed down each side as guides to plane off the corners to produce octagonal stock. The corners are repeatedly removed, each stroke of the plane reaching the full length of the spar, to avoid longitudinal dips and humps. Finally it can be sanded to a smooth round section. This process is illustrated in Fig. 1.6, which also shows a spar gauge. This simple tool saves accurate measurements being taken when marking, as it automatically scribes lines in the correct position. It can equally well be used on rectangular stock if an oval is required, or even on tapering stock, as when making an oar with a heavy inboard end and light neck.

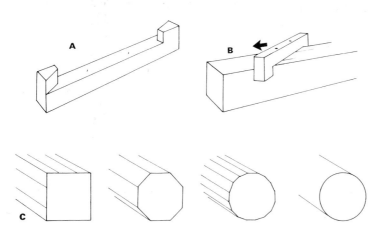

Fig 1.6 Rounding a spar: the spar gauge (A) is used to mark each side of the timber (B). Planing to the scribed lines produces octagonal stock, from which the spar can be rounded freehand. (C) shows cross-sections at successive stages, until finally it is sanded smooth.

A spar gauge can be made any size, but distances between cheeks and nail tips must be in the ratio 7:10:7. For example a gauge with a maximum capacity of 6 in would have the nails located 2½ in apart and 1¾ in from each end, (60 mm apart and 42 mm from the ends). The tool is slid along the timber at an angle, its guiding cheeks firmly pressed against each side, while the nail tips accurately scribe the required lines.

Plate 1.1
The blade of a spoon oar.

A Spoon Oar

Shaping a spoon oar (Plate 1.1) is achieved by first marking and cutting both profiles, then marking and shaping in the series of

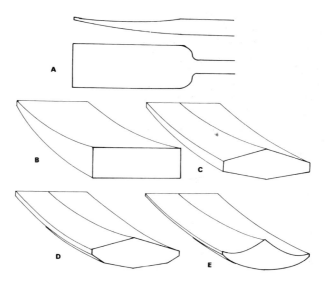

Fig 1.7 Shaping a spoon oar: templates (A) are used to mark the profile in both directions, but the cross-section after cutting out the profiles is still rectangular (B). Intermediary shaping stages are shown (C) and (D) after which it can be faired freehand to produce the finished shape (E).

stages illustrated in Fig. 1.7. To ensure an identical pair of oars the profiles should be marked from templates. Subsequent shaping to the back is done with a hand plane and spokeshave, but a small round-bottomed compass plane is needed for the concave faces.

The Backbone

In the last example, remaining faithful to the drawing is important for aesthetic reasons, but not much is actually at stake, except the boatbuilder's reputation, which would not be improved by producing an odd pair of oars. Where parts have to mate with others, accuracy is of greater importance; the centre line structure — stem, keel, stern knee and post — are key parts, the foundation for the whole boat.

The method is similar. Thicknessed timber is cut to the profile shape, but each piece may be several inches thick and awkward and heavy, so templates, lifted from the loft floor are made in plywood, Plate 1.2. If the backbone is to be made from a number of solid pieces, these templates can be given to the timber yard supplying the stock. The yard's heavier gear can cut the parts roughly to shape. If a single centre line structure is laminated in the boatshop, the templates are used to make the jig and then clean up and profile the laminated timber.

Plate 1.2
Templates for the stem, keel, stern post and stern knee.

In either case the second step is to bevel the forward side of the stem and lower part of the keel so that they will eventually fair in with the planking, and to cut the rebates where the planks land and are fastened. Centre lines are marked inside and out, and the rebate and station lines are marked on both port and starboard sides. These could be included on the original templates and marked onto the stem, keel, etc., by drilling a series of holes and marking through. The bevels and rebates are all relative to the rebate line, but are changing throughout the length of the boat. The exact bevel and rebate can be found for each station by reference to the body plan. Similarly they can be found for the stem by reference to the water lines on the half breadth plan. If plywood cut-outs (Plate 1.3) are made of these shapes they can be used as guides, but care must be taken to use them not only at the correct station, but at the correct angle: vertically for the stations, horizontally for the water lines, and not simply square from the keel or stem. If the water lines and station lines are carried across on both the inside and outside faces of the timber, this is not a problem.

These small cut-outs are used by carving a slot, about ½ in wide (12 mm) at the appropriate station. These slots are gradually worked

27

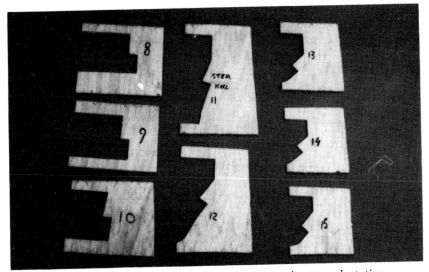

Plate 1.3 Cut-outs of the stem and keel cross-section at each station.

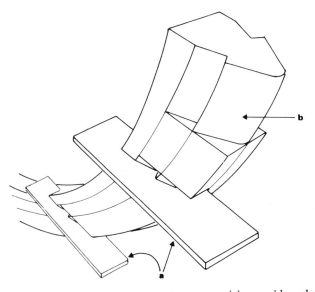

Fig 1.8 Shaping the stem: using plywood patterns (a) as guides, slots are cut on each water line (or station line). The slots then act as guides for shaping the entire length, as shown at (b).

back until the pattern fits into them exactly (Fig. 1.8). With a slot at each station or water line as a guide, the entire length can be cut with confidence, and the changing angles and bevels accommodated easily. It may still be wise, especially toward the top of the stem, to leave some trimming of the rebate until the planks are actually being

28

offered up, especially with a heavily raking stem, as in this area the angles are difficult to gauge.

A Ballast Keel Pattern

A lead or iron ballast keel is cast by pouring the molten metal into a mould of packed sand. The foundry make this mould by ramming the sand around a wooden pattern, usually supplied by the boat-builder. This pattern or plug must be strongly made to take the pressure that is exerted on it by the sand. It also needs strong fittings to lift it out of the completed mould and, for that to be possible, the sides must taper toward the bottom. The designer will have allowed for that, but if it does appear to be an awkward shape consultation with the foundry is advisable before making the pattern.

If the keel is of a simple shape, straight tapering sides without any curved flare, the pattern can be made like the boat itself: moulds set up at every station and plywood planks attached. A thick solid base may be necessary from which to shape the bottom.

If the keel is of a more complicated form, with sides that twist or flair, a 'bread and butter' method is better. The pattern is made up of several 'slices', each accurately cut to the required shape at that level, as illustrated in Fig. 1.9.

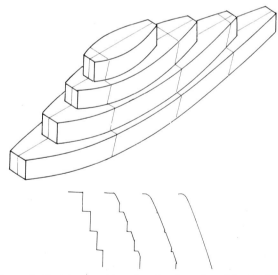

Fig 1.9 Shaping a ballast keel pattern by the 'bread and butter' method: each slice is accurately cut to shape, then they are fastened together using the station and centre lines to ensure correct alignment. Fairing is straightforward, planing the steps until they just disappear, as the cross-sections at the bottom show.

To obtain these shapes a series of additional water lines are drawn across the keel on the loft floor sheer plan. How far apart these are spaced depends on the thickness of timber to be used, but 1½ in or 2 in (37 mm or 50 mm) is reasonable. These extra water lines are not necessarily parallel with the true water lines; it is easier if they are parallel with the top of the keel. By referring from the sheer plan to the half breadth plan a series of offsets can be obtained for every station on each slice. From these the shapes can be marked out and cut. When fastening all these square edge pieces together, the station lines (and centre lines) must exactly match. If the slices are not parallel with the true water lines, the stations will cross them at an angle. This can easily be obtained from the plans and marked on the sides of each lamination with a bevel gauge, thus ensuring they are accurately positioned.

Although the keel at this stage looks very ungainly, a series of steps from top to bottom, it is easy to fair in. The steps are simply planed away, the accurate inside corner of each being a continuous guide.

The positions of the keel bolts are normally marked on the completed pattern by the addition of 'prints'. On the top, these are short dowels of the same diameter as the bolts will be. On the underside, pieces of wood of the same shapes as the holes required to accept the bolt heads are screwed in the correct position: these are effectively 'positives' of the 'negative' holes required. The marks they leave in the sand are used by the foundry to locate the core boxes that will make the actual bolt holes. The 'prints', seen in Plate 1.4, also have to be tapered.

Bevelling Frames

During construction, the shape of a boat is established by moulds or frames. Moulds, which are removed after construction, need not be bevelled; sawn or laminated frames, which form an integral part of the hull, have to be bevelled to accept the planks which are fastened to them. These bevels are planed from the frames at the workbench prior to setting up. There are many methods of obtaining the bevels, all of which involve measuring perpendicular distances from one station to the next on the scrieve board (Fig. 1.10A) and then relating these measurements to the frame spacing. The method described here involves making a 'universal' bevel board, but once made, the process is simple and quick.

The bevel board consists of a piece of plywood on which a base

Plate 1.4 A ballast keel plug made by the 'bread and butter' method.

line is drawn. At one side, and perpendicular to the base line a batten
is fastened, marked with accurate measurements from the base line;
a section of broken rule would be ideal. From the graduated side of
the batten a distance is measured along the base line equal to the
frame spacing (centre to centre). This point is the pivot for a rotating
arm. The arm is raised from the board by inserting a wooden washer
of the same thickness as the graduated batten, when bolting the two
together, and is shaped so that its lower edge would pass through the
pivot point, as illustrated in Fig. 1.10B.

The universal bevel board is used in conjunction with the scrieve
board or body plan on the loft floor. The station line representing
the frame to be bevelled is marked off at appropriate spacings.
Measuring at right angles to the station, the distance between it and
the next is then noted for the first point. If the arm of the universal
bevel board is then moved until its lower edge crosses the graduated
batten at this distance from the base line, its angle to the base line
is the required bevel. In practice, a piece of wood (parallel sided
and with the same width as the frame siding) is slid under the arm
and held firmly against the batten while the bevel is marked. A
separate piece of wood is used for noting the changing bevels of
each frame: the frame number is written at the top, and beneath it
the bevels for each point on that station are accurately marked.
Working down each section in turn, a board with a permanent record

31

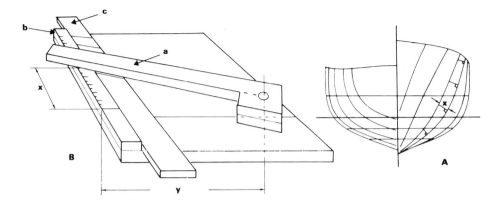

Fig 1.10 Measuring frame bevels: (A) on the scrieve board each station in turn is marked off at regular intervals and, at each of these points, the perpendicular distance between it and the next is measured. In this example (x) is the perpendicular distance from station 4 to station 3 at the turn of the bilge. (B) The universal bevel board is constructed such that (y) is the distance between frames. The pivoting arm (a) is swung to cut the scale (b) at the distance (x) as already measured on the scrieve board. The bevel for that point is then marked onto a piece of wood (c) slipped beneath the pivoting arm.

of the bevels for every frame of the boat can be rapidly drawn.

By squaring across at each bevel, and measuring the distance between the square and bevel line, a measurement for the amount of timber to be planed off at each point can be found, as shown in Fig. 1.11. Marking these measurements, and joining them in a fair line, gives the bevelled shape of the frame.

When using these bevels, care has to be taken that they are applied in the correct direction. Careful consideration of each frame will establish which way to apply the bevels: in general if the station represents the face of the frame nearest the point of widest beam, the bevels are acute; if it represents the face nearest the ends of the boat, the bevels are obtuse, as shown in Fig. 1.11D. Station lines that cross each other on the body plan must be considered in two parts — but in such cases the bevel is usually minimal.

Acute bevels are planed from frames that have already been sawn square-edged to the moulded line (Fig. 1.11B) while obtuse bevels have to be marked as additional to the moulded line; this second line is then sawn to, finally bevelling back to the original line. These stages are illustrated in Fig. 1.11C.

Frames are cut with a band saw, and if it has a tilting table, the bevels can be cut roughly at the same time. Accurate finishing is achieved with planes and spokeshaves.

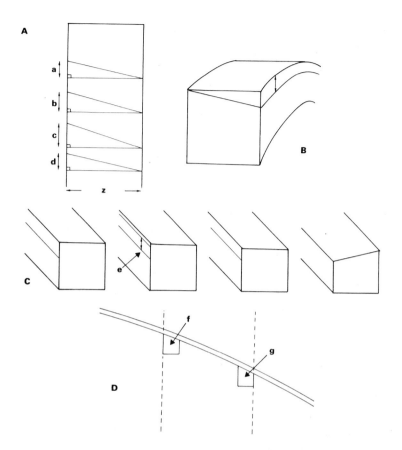

Fig 1.11 Cutting frame bevels: (A), if the piece of wood used to record the bevels in the 'Universal bevel board' is the width of the frames themselves (z), the depth of timber to be removed can easily be measured as shown at (a), (b), (c), (d). (B), if the bevel is acute the frame is planed to the station line and the measurements marked and cut from it as shown. (C), if the bevel is obtuse the measurements are added to the station line (e), the frame planed square across first, and then bevelled back to the line. (D) a plan view of two frames and the hull planking showing the difference between acute and obtuse bevels. The dotted lines represent two station lines, giving frame (f) an acute bevel and frame (g) an obtuse one.

3. Marking Shapes from the Hull

During the first stages of hull construction the shapes required are obtained from the plans, but as work progresses each additional part has to fit what is already there. Once the keel is laid and the frames set up, each new member is made to fit that individual hull; reference is made to the plans for positions and scantlings, but bevels, dimensions and shapes are for the most part taken from the boat itself.

In sections 1 and 2, methods to mark and make shapes from the plans were described. In this section and the next, the ways to mark and then fit parts to the curves and awkward corners of complete and part complete hulls are examined.

Scribing and spiling are the methods used to mark one part so that it will fit against the shapes of another. These techniques are basic to boatbuilding, and the boatbuilder uses them in numerous situations.

Both methods consist of marking a set distance from the curved face, and this can be done with a pair of compasses or dividers. Alternatively several rectangular pieces of plywood, each accurately proportioned in a series of sizes from perhaps ¾ in (19 mm) to 4 in (100 mm) or more, do the job more easily and accurately. Such a set of purpose-made 'dummy sticks' (Plate 1.5) are a useful item in any toolbox, but anything with parallel sides of an appropriate dimension can be used: match box, tobacco tin, or just a scrap of wood.

Scribing

A simple example to illustrate the method is a piece of furniture that rocks because the leg lengths are uneven: it is set on a flat level floor, and wedged under the short legs until it sits level and firm. By marking with a pencil and dummy stick around each leg, (Fig. 1.12) and cutting to these lines, the chair, sawing horse or whatever will stand firmly on the ground.

34

Plate 1.5 Dummy sticks.

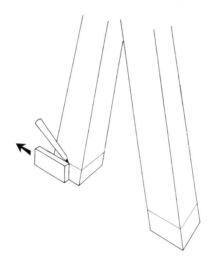

Fig 1.12 Simple scribing to obtain equal length legs on a sawing horse: with the horse level and standing on a flat surface all four legs are marked and then cut to the scribed lines.

Items to be fastened to the deck can be marked in a similar way. A deck pad for a cleat or winch is positioned and wedged until its top is level. The bottom edge is then scribed to the shape of the deck. In this case, because the deck is curved, a caution must be observed; throughout the marking the dummy stick is held horizontally, one corner only touching the deck, with the pencil held at the corner opposite. In this way a line is scribed a standard distance,

35

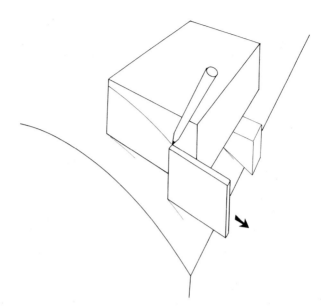

Fig 1.13   Scribing a pad to fit a curved cabin roof. The pad is wedged in the correct position, then the deck shape scribed onto it, maintaining the dummy stick at a constant angle.

measured vertically from the deck (Fig. 1.13). When cut, the pad will be lowered that distance to sit neatly in its place.

Holding the dummy stick at a constant angle is an important element of scribing, and it should be remembered that when cut, the scribed object will move in the direction that it was scribed. A pre-built locker being fitted into the hull could be scribed in two directions (Fig. 1.14): it could be set up at the correct height and scribed horizontally to ease back against the hull, or set up above the correct position and scribed vertically to ease down into the bilge. In either case its ultimate position is controlled by the size of dummy stick used — it will ease back, or down, the dimension scribed off.

On occasion the dummy may be neither vertical nor horizontal. Hanging knees can be marked by first planing the back of one arm, and with this clamped to the underside of the deck beam, scribing the more complex shape of the other arm. The dummy stick is in this case held at the same angle as the beam, so that when the shape is cut, the knee slides back along the beam to fit against the hull (Plate 1.6).

With a very gentle curve, maintaining the correct angle is unnecessary. Fitting one bulkhead to another that should be straight, but is in fact slightly bowed, can most easily be done by scribing half the

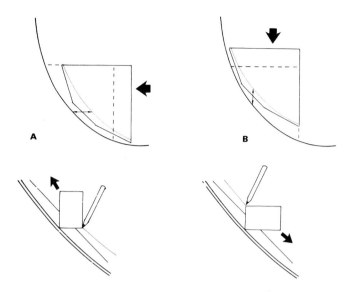

Fig 1.14 Scribing a pre-built locker into the hull. Its final position is shown by the dotted lines, but it can be scribed in either of the two directions: positioned at the correct height and marked horizontally (A); or clamped above the final position and scribed vertically (B).

Plate 1.6 Knees that have been fitted by clamping one arm to the deckbeam, then scribing the complicated hull shape on the other.

pencil width. Holding the bulkhead as nearly in position as possible a pencil is simply held flat against the bowed bulkhead, its point pressed against the other, and slid up and down, marking the shape to be cut. This does not take account of the changing angles, but the error is so slight as to be discounted. Fitting is never simpler than that, but things can get much more complicated. When scribing is inadequate the boatbuilder turns to spiling.

Spiling

A case where spiling is necessary is for example a half bulkhead that has to fit under side decks, around the gunwale, and perhaps around a stringer too. The shape is complex, with overhangs and cut-outs. Scribing is impossible. Instead, a spile board is made up: this is something that approximates the shape required and fits in the correct position (Plate 1.7). It is most easily made in situ, out of offcuts of plywood. Diagonals or other strengthening should be included, to ensure that it does not distort when being removed. Removal should be borne in mind while making it or, although it fits beautifully, it will not come out.

Plate 1.7   Fitting a bulkhead: a frame-work spile board is clamped in position in the hull so that the required shape can be marked onto it.

The shape required is marked onto the spile board, once again using a dummy stick. This time it is held hard against the hull at all times, (Fig. 1.15) so that the shape is marked parallel to that required. This is easier than scribing, as the angle of the dummy stick is no longer a problem. It is simply held flat against the hull, while the pencil is held against either of its corners.

With the shape marked on the spile board it is removed and laid onto the plywood from which the bulkhead is to be cut. The shape is then dummied back; the same size dummy stick is placed with one edge just touching the spiled line and the other edge is marked on

38

Plate 1.8 The spile board is then removed and the shape transferred to ply.

Plate 1.9 When cut out, the bulkhead should fit neatly into place.

the plywood. The dummy stick is moved along the line, and again its edge marked. Slowly the complete line is transferred to the ply, and this line is the true shape required.

Several points should be watched when spiling in this fashion. The edge of the bulkhead will eventually be bevelled to allow for the

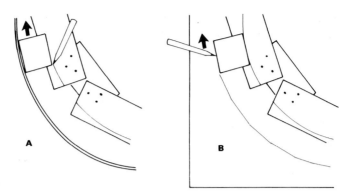

Fig 1.15 Spiling. On the spile board a line is marked parallel to the hull (A). The spile board is then transferred to a sheet of ply, and by dummying back from the spiled line (B) the correct shape is marked.

shape of the hull, so one face is larger than the other. The shape of this larger face is always spiled, to allow for bevelling when fitting. However tatty the spile board is, the parts being marked on should all lie in the same plane; structural pieces holding it all together should, if possible, be on the back.

When spiling, several different sized dummy sticks can be used, but the line drawn by each should be labelled so that the same one is used to dummy back. Spile boards can sometimes get very complicated, with messages and instructions all over the place; it is best not to delay, but mark out the shape immediately before all that graffiti becomes meaningless.

Once a bulkhead such as this has been cut out, actually getting it into position can be a problem. Fitting bulkheads before the deck has been laid, or at least before the cabin roof is put on, helps, but even then stringers and carlings may conspire to make it impossible to position. The only way out is to cut a corner off the bulkhead; just above the stringer is often the least noticeable place.

Floors, and knees that are awkwardly shaped, cannot be scribed but must be spiled as above. The spile board for these only needs to be a piece of plywood roughly cut to shape and clamped in position. If a floor is being fitted over a keel bolt already in position, the bolt is also marked on the spile board and transferred to the floor. This line is used as a guide when drilling (see Section 7, Boring). The hole is bored oversize to allow the floor to be slid into position for fitting.

Once the shape has been spiled and cut, the next stage is often to offer it up and scribe a more accurate line. Spiling and scribing are similar and can be confused, their differences can be understood by comparing Figures 1.14 and 1.15.

The 'Joggle Stick'

With simple shapes, particularly those with straight edges, such as worktops or shelves, a slightly different technique can be used. Although it appears to be very different, the principle is the same: a measured distance is marked from hull to spile board, then transferred from that back onto the timber stock. In this case the spile board need not approximate the shape; any reasonably-sized piece of scrap plywood is adequate, and it need not even fit in the space to be spiled. It must be in the same plane as the shelf, and clamped as close as possible. Lines are then drawn that point directly toward each corner, with the distance to each measured and marked. When

Fig 1.16 A joggle stick.

the spile board is transferred to the timber stock, the direction and distance of each corner is indicated; these can be marked, and when joined with straight lines, produce the shape required.

A metal rule held on edge marks and measures the lines satisfactorily, but a purpose-made joggle stick (Fig. 1.16) is quicker. This is a piece of wood, tapering to a point at one end, with a straight edge one side and a series of numbered joggles on the other. To use it, the point is pushed into the corner (it does not matter at what angle) and where it crosses the spile board both the straight edge and joggled edge are marked. If two of the joggles are numbered, the stick can easily be relocated once the spile board has been removed and placed on the timber stock. The tip of the joggle stick is then at the position of the corner.

Fair curves can also be marked by touching the tip at a series of points around the curve, then joining these points with a fairing batten. However, bear in mind that the inside of a hull is not necessarily a fair curve.

Trimming Gauge

In some situations the shape required can be obtained directly from the boat: with plywood planking or decking it is often possible to place an oversize piece of plywood in position and mark on the underside the shape required. It can then be removed and cut to size. Better still is to roughly cut it to shape and then actually fasten it down. A trimming gauge can be used to mark the shape on the top of the plywood. This has the advantage that any bevel is accurately accounted for by the gauge, and in many cases it can be cut and planed to this line without removing again.

A trimming gauge, shown in use in Plate 1.10, is simply a wooden straight edge with a bite taken out of it. The lower part of the straight edge is held hard against, and slid along, the deck beam or carling beneath, while a pencil marks where the top half of the straight edge meets the ply.

Plate 1.10   A trimming gauge in use.

Plate 1.11 A profile gauge takes the shape of any pattern it is pressed against.

Other Ways

Shapes can be copied without spiling if tools are used to reproduce them mechanically. A simple example of this is the profile gauge (Plate 1.11) which, when pressed against an awkward shape, reproduces and retains it. These have limited application, being restricted in size.

Another tool old-time boatbuilders in the North West of England used is not limited in size; it was used both to lift frame shapes from the loft floor and bulkhead outlines from the boat itself. Similar to a bicycle chain in design, it had wooden links joined with copper rivets. The chain was dumped in a bucket of water prior to use, and once the wood had taken up, became stiff enough to hold the shape it was arranged in, until marking had been completed. Accuracy would be determined by the size of links.

Shaping to Avoid Hard Spots

Once floors and knees have been fitted, their inside curve can be marked and cut. Although the plans will indicate the position of knees, their scantlings, fastenings and arm lengths, the actual shape is usually left to the boatbuilder. A fair curve which tapers the arms considerably toward their ends (which are rounded) is all that is required, but the tapering is important for more than merely aesthetic reasons. If the solid knees end abruptly, a 'hard spot' is formed at their ends, causing undesirable — and possibly damaging — stress when the hull is worked.

Hard spots arise when any member ends abruptly. This can be avoided either by continuing the part to terminate at another heavier member, or by tapering and then rounding or bevelling the ends. Doubling members designed to reinforce longitudinals (such as clamps which strengthen the gunwale around chain plates) should taper toward their ends. Backing plates to deck fittings normally avoid hard spots at their edges by spanning between beams, but where this is not possible, as with a moulded glass fibre deck, they should be well bevelled at every edge.

When fitting out any hull that is a monocoque structure, with the strength primarily in the skin, great care should be taken to avoid hard spots. This clearly applies to glass fibre hulls, but also to lightly-framed cold moulded ones.

4. Fitting

Scribing and spiling are only the first stage in persuading something to slot neatly into place. Little account has been taken in the above examples of bevels, but even once these are cut the 'first-time fit' is a rarity. Some tinkering is usually necessary, and if not tackled carefully can be a slow job. When dealing with floors with considerable width, ill-considered modifications can easily make the fit worse.

Bevels

Bevels are lifted from the boat with a bevel gauge. Bevels for bulkheads, floors, and knees, can be taken at the same time as spiling, measuring the angle between the spile board and hull. Points where the bevels are taken are marked on the spile board, then once the bulkhead has been cut out the bevel can be marked and planed off. Holding the bevel gauge against the square edge of the bulkheads shows how much must be removed. Slight bevels can be removed without marking, constantly checking with the gauge until it is right. Larger bevels, or those that vary, can be marked as shown in Fig. 1.17, by measuring the distance (a) and marking it at (b).

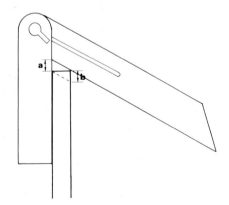

Fig 1.17 Bevelling bulkheads: distance (a) is measured and marked at (b).

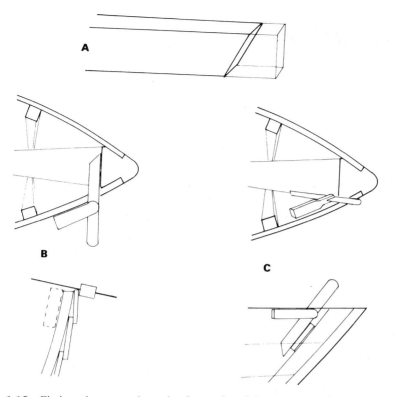

Fig 1.18 Fitting the gunwale at its forward end is a matter of marking and cutting bevels in two directions (A). When measuring the athwartship bevel the gauge must be angled to reflect the gunwales position, not the sheer strakes (B), and when measuring the vertical bevel a piece of plywood slipped under the blade allows an accurate measurement to be made (C).

When using a bevel gauge, the angle that it is held at must always be borne in mind, as this affects the angle being measured. For bulkheads and floors, it is simply held perpendicular to the surface of the spile board, but in other cases it can be more difficult.

Fitting the forward end of the gunwale is an example. It is a simple shape that does not need spiling: measuring the bevels in both directions is all that is required, but this must be done with care. The athwartship bevel is the angle between the sheer strake and the stem. Holding the bevel gauge firmly against the sheer strake will be correct for carvel or cold moulded planking, but with a clinker boat the angle of the sheer strake is different to that of the gunwale, as shown in Fig. 1.18B. The bevel gauge is therefore tipped slightly to take account of this when measuring this bevel. Measuring the vertical bevel, the angle of the stem, presents a different problem: the thickness of the handle of the bevel gauge prevents the blade being pushed hard up against the stem. This can be overcome by placing a scrap of plywood under the blade, away from the handle. This allows the angle to be measured without obstruction. (Fig. 1.18C)

The fit of a flat face such as this can be ensured by clamping the two parts as close as possible and running a saw down the join. The method, obtaining a 'saw-cut fit', is very effective, but should be used with great care, as it is easy to continue sawing beyond the parts being fitted, scoring and weakening the part behind.

Tricks for Fitting

Once the shape has been cut and bevelled, it should fit. An accurate spile is a good start, but errors creep in. The part, bulkhead or whatever, is offered into place and the problems found by close examination. This is straightforward for a bulkhead, as the points where it is touching can usually be seen directly. The whole perimeter must be examined though, or a lot of paring away can be done at one point, when another, unnoticed, is really causing the obstruction.

Difficulties arise when trying to fit floors or knees, or even thick bulkheads, where the bumps that are preventing a fit are completely out of sight. This is exacerbated if only one side can be examined, the other being hidden by a frame. Several tricks help to find the high spots causing the problems:

Feeling
The bumps cannot be seen, but they can be felt. An old hacksaw blade, or better still, a mechanic's feeler gauge, can be pushed under the floor, and the obstructions found.

Chalk
If the hull is marked with chalk, or even scribbled with pencil before the floor is offered into position, when it is removed the high points will be marked by the chalk. The marks are clearer if the floor is held firmly in place and moved minutely back and forward.

When irregular indentations have to be cut to allow for fitting over copper nails and roves, their position can be marked initially by rubbing them with chalk, and subsequently checks can be made that the holes are large enough in the same way. It is very easy, otherwise, to be convinced that it is the nail causing the problem, and keep enlarging the allowance made for it unnecessarily.

46

Rocking

This can be a useful method of fitting, particularly over large areas, perhaps a pad fitting against a plank that has considerable twist. It only appears to indicate which corners are too high, but with a little subtlety more information than this can be gleaned. The rocking is done with two hands, or fingers, each pressing alternately. The hands start at the outside edge, but gradually one is brought toward the middle. When it ceases to make the pad rock the high point must have been passed as both hands are now pressing on the same side of the pivot point. The process can be repeated, moving the other hand, and by this means a more precise idea of where the trouble spot is located can be obtained.

Just how much timber should be removed from a high spot once it has been located is a difficult decision: too little and the repeated offering up and examination seem to go on for ever; too much, and everywhere else needs trimming. How big the gap is, or, in other words how far it is from fitting, is a guide. The choice of tool to use depends on the awkwardness of the shape: planes if possible, otherwise spokeshaves and chisels; the clearance holes for nails and roves can be made with gouges, or the small sized dowel cutters used in an electric drill can be very neat and effective.

When it fits, the job is done, but one hundred percent perfection is not called for in every case, and time can be saved. Bulkheads which are not structural, and have their edges hidden, are an example: perhaps one side is in a locker, the other butts up against a frame; if it fits well enough to fasten to the frame, it is sufficient. Structural members are a different matter. Poor fitting in these cases could lead to unfair loads, all the stresses being taken at the tight spots, when they should be spread evenly.

Fitting Longitudinals

Internal longitudinals, such as the gunwale or stringers, are a special problem. Marking the shape of their forward ends is straightforward and achieved with a bevel gauge, as just described, but obtaining the length so that they fit perfectly from stem to transom is another matter. It could be done with a spile board clamped inside the hull, but this is not very satisfactory, and ideally the spile board should be clamped to every timber; even then it would follow their shape, whereas the heavier gunwale may pull the timbers to its own fairer curve.

A better procedure (illustrated in Plates 1.12 to 1.15) is to fit the

47

Plate 1.12
Fitting a gunwale: the forward end is fitted and fastened first while the after end is allowed to run out over the transom.

Plate 1.13
A batten (a) is touched at the point on the transom the gunwale will reach.

Plate 1.14
Then, with the batten's forward end unmoved, its after end is transferred to the gunwale and the required length marked.

the forward end first, then, leaving the gunwale oversize, start to fasten it in position. Its after end is allowed to lie out over the transom while fastening, working from forward and continuing as far aft as possible. On a small dinghy this may be only half the length, but on larger craft it may be two thirds or more. When fastening can continue no further, a batten is positioned along the top of the timbers, its after end just touching the transom at the point that the top outboard corner of the gunwale will reach it.

Plate 1.15
From this point the bevels are marked and cut. (RNLI Boarding Boat).

Where the other end of the batten reaches on the already-fastened part of the gunwale is marked. With the batten continuing to be held at that marked point, the after part is now held along the top outboard edge of the gunwale, and where its aft end reaches is marked. This has established the length the gunwale should be cut to. The after end is of course also bevelled in both directions, so these bevels have to be taken from the boat and marked onto the gunwale before cutting, but if they are marked with reference to that one point which is correctly measured for length, when the gunwale is cut it will fit. This method requires care, but produces accurate results.

The same system is effective for fitting stringers, the main difficulty being holding them in position while fastening progresses. Because of the planking, clamps cannot be used. Shores are the answer, stretching from the opposite gunwale, or even outside the boat.

Fitting Deck Beams

The problems with deck beams arise from the complexity of the angles involved: the beam itself is plumb-sided while rising toward the crown; the gunwale is rising with the sheer, closing toward the bow or stern, and spreading with the topside flare.

There are many joints of varying complexity to make the gunwale/deck beam junction, but when deciding which to use, the three jobs that the beams do should be borne in mind. Two are obvious: they support the deck, and they brace athwartships, strengthening the hull when it is sandwiched between another vessel and the quay. The third is not so clear: they tie the hull together, preventing the opposite gunwales from spreading. This tends to happen every time the boat is lifted by waves at the bow and stern; she tries to sag, and in doing so, tries to stretch the beams. The beam gunwale joint must not only support the beam but lock it home as well. With some joints, this is

49

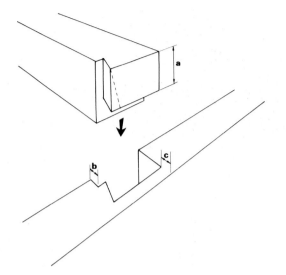

Fig 1.19 The half dovetail joint at a beam end. Dimension (a) is normally ⅔ of the beam, while (b) and (c) are ¼ of the gunwale. The dovetail is cut on the side of the beam facing the ends of the boat as this gives a full dovetail effect due to the angle between the beam and gunwale. The dotted line indicates the modification necessary when the gunwale has a lot of flare.

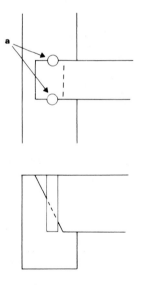

Fig 1.20 Plan and section of a simpler deckbeam joint, in which dowels (a) provide a dovetail effect.

only achieved with the fastenings, but with the two illustrated in Figures 1.19 and 1.20, there is a mechanical key as well.

Plates 1.16 — 1.25
Fitting deckbeams: cutting and fitting the dovetail is divided into three stages, the homelet in the gunwale, the half dovetail at beam ends and the dovetail housing. Each stage is done for both ends of the beam before proceeding to the next.

Plate 1.16
The homelet. The beam is positioned accurately and wedged plumb, its position across the gunwale is then marked.

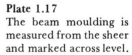

Plate 1.17
The beam moulding is measured from the sheer and marked across level.

Plates 1.16 to 1.25 demonstrate cutting and fitting the half-dovetail joint. A similar, but simpler, method would be used to cut the dowelled joint. Whatever joint is used, the main problem is measuring the correct length, i.e. obtaining a reference point at each end from which to mark the bevels. In the photographs this is done by turning the beam over and marking the distance directly onto the top of the beam. This is the most accurate method, but is not always possible. The alternative is to use a spirit-level to plumb the relevant point from the top of the gunwale to the top of the beam.

Plate 1.18
The homelet can then be cut, its depth one quarter of the gunwale moulding.

Plate 1.19
The dovetail. With the homelet cut in both gunwales the beam length is accurately marked. To compensate for the gunwale's flare the beam is turned over and one corner of the homelet marked on its top at both ends.

If half-dovetails are used, problems can be experienced when there is considerable flare at the bows of the boat. The dovetails in each end of the beam will fit beautifully individually, but due to the flare, both cannot be fitted at once. One of the dovetails is modified as shown by the dotted line in Fig. 1.19. With the other fitted first, the tapered dovetail can both enter its housing from the awkward angle, and fit snugly when right home. Dovetails are slow to cut, and of course no one will ever see them once the deck is on, but they are there for strength, not show.

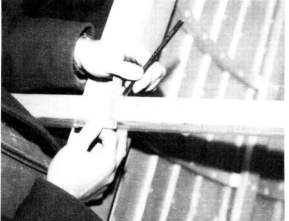

Plate 1.20
When the beam is turned back over, the point is marked on the wrong side; it is therefore squared across.

Plate 1.21
This position is the back of the homelet. To obtain the full length required the dovetail length is measured and marked in addition.

Fitting Carlings

The same joint is used for the carlings as that used on the deck beams. Hatch carlings present little problem, as they are straight and can be marked and cut in the same manner as the beams. Main carlings around the cabin and cockpit are more difficult as they normally curve. Temporary supports are built to hold the carlings in position until the side deck beams lock them there. One way to do this is to use plywood 'web' supports between the gunwales and temporary cross beams shown in Plates 1.26 and 1.27. A slot is cut to accommodate the carling in these plywood webs. To mark

53

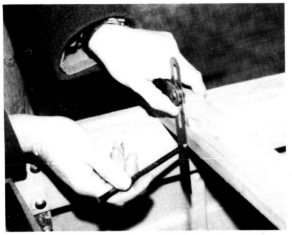

Plate 1.22
The bevels, both fore and aft, and vertical, are measured and marked at these points.

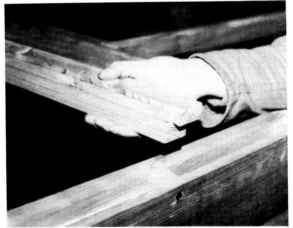

Plate 1.23
The dovetail can now be easily marked and cut.

accurately the position of these slots, the plywood is fastened in position and the beam crop pattern placed against them, across the hull. A line is then drawn on the plywood marking the beam height. From the plans, the distance from the carling to the outside of the planking is found and marked on the plywood. If the cabin side slopes inward, the carling will too, so the slot should be cut at the correct angle (also found on the plans).

The carlings can be sprung into position. The joint at one end is cut and fitted first, then, with that in position, the other is marked and fitted. As the carling cannot be turned over, the joints are marked using the alternative method already described for fitting beams.

54

Plate 1.24
Dovetail housing. With the beam slotted into the homelet the dovetail shape is marked.

Plate 1.25
Once cut, the beam fits snugly home.

55

Plate 1.26 Fitting carlings: notches are cut into web supports fastened to temporary cross beams.

Plate 1.27 These support and position the carlings until the side deckbeams are fitted.

5. Planking

Making the curved form of a hull from flat boards of timber requires each to be shaped to fit tightly against its neighbour. Whatever the type of construction, this problem must be overcome, and with all (except strip planking) it is achieved by cutting each plank to the shape dictated by the last. The shapes of the planks change subtly as progress is made around the hull. On a dinghy or workboat of traditional design the shapes range from a banana (ends downward) at the garboard, to the reverse banana (ends upward) at the sheer, and include amongst the variations in between an 'S' shape at the turn of the bilge.

The traditional spiling techniques used to obtain these shapes are described, but as will be seen they are slow and tedious. Modern construction methods not only take advantage of greatly improved adhesives, but try to minimise the time spent on planking by short-cutting or even eliminating the spiling process.

Before any type of planking can commence, the entire hull shape must be created. This is the reason for lofting and making moulds. Some kind of former, jig or mould must be built, around which the planks can be bent and fitted. In some cases (carvel, strip, and hard chine) the jig is a permanent part of the boat, while in others (clinker and cold moulded) it is a temporary mould, removed after planking. With the 'Constant Camber' method, the mould is not of a complete hull, but only half. One situation where the hull is shaped without a jig is that of a small clinker or lapstrake dinghy being built by an old builder with a large store of experience; but he has the jig fixed permanently in his head. In a similar way, Scandinavian boatbuilders traditionally worked without a jig.

Clinker or Lapstrake

Moulds set up along the keel form the temporary jig around which the planks are shaped. The planks are not at any time fastened to the moulds, which are just guides for planking. Once the moulds

57

are removed, the planks themselves hold the shape of the hull, extra strength being added when the timbers are steam-bent into place.

Prior to commencing planking the run of all the planks is marked, by 'lining out'. The girth at each mould is measured and divided by the number of planks it will carry. These equal distances are then marked off. Light battens are tacked to each mould to check for fairness as shown in Plate 1.28. On clinker boats, this is most important as the very nature of the construction makes the run of the planks a feature. They must look sweet, and to achieve this, some adjustment may well be necessary. At the ends of the boat, particularly on yachts with a raking stem, there is a danger of a porpoise shaped drop in the top planks at their forward end, (Plate 1.29), variously called a 'sny' or 'the Yarmouth Hump'. To avoid this, the lower planks are brought higher up the stem than would seem necessary if considering them in isolation. Some adjustment to plank widths can also be made at the turn of the bilge, (and tuck if there is one) when the curves are tight. Narrower planks will follow the curve more easily. The garboard can also be made a distinctive shape and size, if it helps the run of the remaining planking.

Plate 1.28   Lining out: light battens tacked to the moulds ensure that the run of the planks will be fair. *(Osea Jol)*

Plate 1.29 The 'Yarmouth Hump' is apparent at the forward end of the nearest boat.

Once the projected position and size of all the planks are considered satisfactory, the batten positions are marked on each mould, and then the battens removed.

With the exception of the garboard, which is marked in the same manner as described for carvel planking below, all the planks are marked in the same way. A spile board is bent around the moulds overlapping the previous plank for its entire length and clamped to it. Care must be taken that the spile board is allowed to lie around the moulds naturally: it must not be forced against them. In order to achieve this, the spile board must approximate the shape of the plank. While one board will be adequate for several planks, their gradually changing shape will require that it be modified, or another made with more or less curve as necessary. Spile boards are normally about the same width as the planking, but of thinner timber.

With the spile board lying naturally around the moulds and clamped to the plank below, a pencil is run along the top of that plank, marking its shape onto the spile board, as in Plate 1.30.

The position of the moulds is also marked, and the angle of the transom and stem. The stem is spiled off using an appropriate dummy stick. The spile board is removed from the boat and placed onto the planking stock. After it has been ensured that the plank will be cut from sound timber, and with the grain following the curve of the plank as closely as possible, the information on the spile board is transferred to the timber. The transom and mould positions can be

Plate 1.30 Clinker planking: with the spile board clamped to the last plank, the shape required is marked onto it.

marked by continuing them above and below the spile board. When it is removed, the missing section of the line is filled in, marking their correct position and angle. The shape of the top edge of the last plank can be marked either by using a dummy stick to transfer it onto the timber stock (as for carvel planking, see Fig. 1.23B) or by tacking nails through the spile board at intervals to prick the shape onto the timber below, fairing the line afterwards with a batten. That line represents the bottom edge of the new plank. The top edge is marked from this; measurements taken at each mould from the top of the last plank to the position marked for the top of this one are transferred, with the addition of the overlap required. These points are again faired with a batten. In this way the plank shape is marked, and it can be cut out with a hand-held circular saw, or band saw, and planed to the lines.

Before the plank can be fitted, the 'gerald' or 'chase' has to be cut at each end. These are the rebates that allow each plank to run into the one below for the last eight or twelve inches, so that at the stem and transom the planks are flush. Figure 1.21 shows the cross section through two planks as they approach the stem, and a detail of the rebate that is required. Because of the changing angles, this is not an easy joint to cut; it is achieved with a rebate plane, chisels, and care. It also improves with practice.

Once the geralds are cut, the plank can be offered up, and its fit inspected. The geralds are the most tricky part, but it must fit all along its length at the 'brow'. This is the bevel at the top outside edge of each plank (or bottom inside on the reverse curves of the tuck)

60

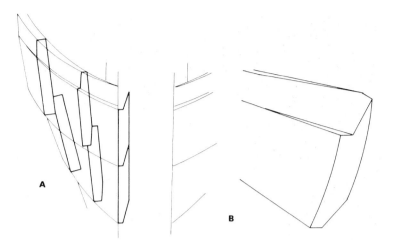

Fig 1.21   With clinker (lapstrake) construction, plank ends are rebated so that
           they are flush at stem and transom. (A) shows the cross-section
           through two planks over their last 12 inches, while (B) illustrates the
           actual shape required at each plank end.

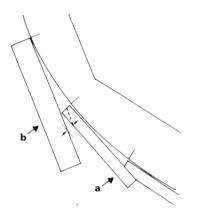

Fig 1.22   Measuring the brow: the plank (a) is clamped in position and at every
           mould a straight edge (b) is held against it, with one end touching the
           next plank mark. The dotted line indicates the bevel required, and it
           is measured between the arrows.

and is most easily cut before the plank is fastened in position. The
bevel necessary is measured at each mould with a straight edge
(Fig. 1.22). With the plank back on the bench, the brow can be
planed off with a rebate plane, although some slight adjustment may
be needed later, when the next plank is being fitted to it.

    With all this done, plank shaped, browed off, and the geralds cut,
the plank is ready for fastening: bronze screws into the stem and
transom, and copper nails clench it to the plank below. Two nails are
normally fastened between the projected position of each timber.

61

Carvel

Clinker planks are fastened to each other, only subsequently being fastened to the strengthening timbers. The edges of carvel planks only butt up to each other, and they have to be fastened to the frames which hold them to the hull shape. The 'jig' for carvel planking is therefore a permanent part of the boat, providing both the shape when planking and the strength when complete. It can consist of grown or laminated frames, cut and bevelled prior to setting up; of steam-bent timbers, bent to the shape formed by ribbands sprung around moulds; or a combination of the two.

As with clinker planking 'lining out' is necessary, and carried out in the same manner, although precision is not so vital, as the run of the planks on a carvel hull is not so clearly seen. The process can be short cut, simply dividing the frames equally to give plank widths, and then checking each is fair only when measuring for that plank. This saves having to batten the run of all the planks at one time, but can lead to some unevenness in planking widths, as adjustments are made to each plank individually, with little account being taken of the effect on others.

Spiling the plank shapes differs from clinker planking: the spile board is tacked to the frames as close to the last plank as possible, but it must not be forced by pulling it up or down at the ends, but just allowed to take its natural shape around the frames. This is important, as if it is distorted, an incorrect spile is obtained. Once the spile board has been tacked in position, the shape of the plank below can be marked with a dummy stick, as with normal spiling (Fig. 1.23). In places the spile board may be very close to the lower plank, even touching it, while at other places it may be several inches away. Several different-sized dummy sticks can be used to spile the shape (label which dummy stick is used in each case) but if the spile board is too far from the lower plank the result will be inaccurate; it is better to modify the spile board or make another one that approximates the shape required more closely.

As with clinker planking, the position and angle of frames, stem and transom are recorded on the spile board, which can then be removed from the moulds, laid on the planking stock, and all the information transferred from it. The shape of the plank and stem are dummied back using the same dummy sticks, and the frame and transom positions and angles are marked with a straight edge. The top edge is marked in exactly the same way as the clinker planks: measurements taken from the frames on the boat are marked on

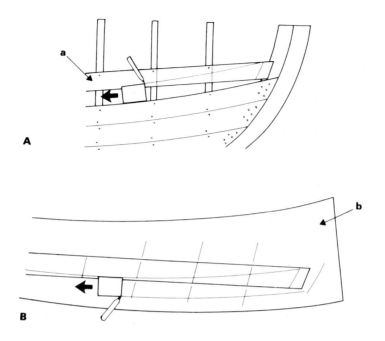

Fig 1.23 Spiling a carvel plank: (A) onto the spile board (a) are marked the shape of the plank below, the stem, and the position of frames; (B), these are then transferred to the planking stock (b). The plank widths at each frame are measured on the hull, then marked on the frame position lines; joining these points with a batten gives the shape of the plank's top edge.

the frame lines on the planking stock. Then the series of points is faired with a batten.

After this, the plank can be cut out, and with carvel planks no further shaping is required, except for the slight bevel on the lower edge to allow for the changing angle of each plank relative to its neighbour. The plank is offered up and adjustments made as necessary to obtain a good tight fit with the plank below. Unlike clinker, carvel planks can be 'edge-set' slightly, that is, forced down against the last plank by using clamps or wedges between the plank and ribband above. Once an acceptable fit is obtained, the caulking seam is planed off the outside edges of the plank and, with suitable luting, such as white lead and linseed oil, between the plank and frames, fastened to them with copper clenched nails. Again, at the stem and transom bronze screws are used.

Carvel planking is simpler than the clinker or lapstrake method as less precision is required; to some extent the planks can be persuaded into position, whereas the clinker planks, once cut to shape,

Plate 1.31   Carvel planking: progress can be made simultaneously from the garboard and the sheer, toward the bilge. *(Tara)*

must be allowed to lie as they want. On a large boat carvel can also be faster, as several gangs can work at once; commonly planking is simultaneously progressing from both the sheer and garboard (Plate 1.31) toward the bilge, where a 'shutter' plank is finally fitted by spiling both edges, to close the gap.

Strip Planking

The boatbuilder's attempts to reduce spiling time are, with this method, completely successful. Planking stock of approximately square cross sectional dimensions is bent to the shape required, not cut. By forcing each plank down to meet its neighbour, spiling is dispensed with. Even the ends need not be fitted if each plank is run past the apron; when planking is complete all are sawn off flush and the end grain covered with the stem (Fig. 1.24).

As each plank is edge-set into position (not only bent around the moulds, but sprung edgeways to fit against the previous plank), the run of the planking can be a problem. If no corrective measures are taken, the extra number of planks needed amidships leads to the

64

top strakes running out fore and aft at the sheer; no sheer strake exists, only a series of plank ends feathering to nothing. This is not really a problem unless the hull is to be varnished, in which case it can be unsightly, detracting from the lines of the boat. Tapering all the planks or adding feather-ended stealers below the water line amidships are ways to overcome this, but the most effective solution is to build upside down and plank from the sheer toward the bilge: planks neatly parallel to the sheer result, and any clumsiness in the run of the planking where stealers are necessary will be well out of sight. The garboard is usually fitted as for carvel planking, and its upper edge can be shaped to help the run of the other planks.

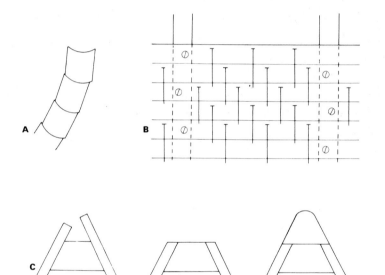

Fig 1.24 Strip planking: (A), this cross-section through planks shows how machining edges hollow and round saves bevelling; (B), a typical fastening system has ring nails driven edgeways through planks, and screws fastening to frames, (this diagram is schematic — nail spacings are established by trial); (C), fitting the plank ends can be avoided by running all past the apron, sawing them flush, and covering with a false stem.

Strip planking stock is machined with a half-round on both edges, thus speeding planking further as bevelling is also eliminated, each plank mating with the previous one perfectly at any angle. If the upper edge of each plank is the concave one, whether building right way up or upside down, glue is retained until the next plank can be positioned and fastenings driven. These are normally ring nails driven edgewise through the planking. The large number of edge

65

fastenings and the glued monocoque structure allow fewer frames to be used than with traditional planking methods. Timbers can be steam-bent into position after planking is complete, in which case each plank is clamped to the moulds until the glue has set. More usual practice is to build around pre-bevelled laminated frames, to which each plank is glued and screwed. This is far more satisfactory, as the planking can proceed without the obstruction of the clamps holding the previous plank.

Cold Moulded

Many different planking schemes are covered by this term which refers to hulls laminated from several layers of wood veneers. This method was made possible by the development of synthetic glues during World War II, but the early products needed high pressures and temperatures to cure. Planked hulls, pressurised by vacuum bag techniques, were placed in autoclaves to heat until the glue had set. Further developments in glue technology allow low pressures and room temperature to be used, so the construction method no longer requires the ovens, and is called cold moulding.

On large hulls, several diagonal layers can be laminated on a strip-planked foundation. This rapidly builds up the required planking thickness, and eliminates the need for a complete mould: frames are still set up but the strip planks fastened to them take the place of the many ribbands normally found on the cold moulding jig.

Hulls are normally built upside down on a jig constructed by springing closely-spaced ribbands around the lofted moulds (Plate 1.32). Boatbuilders are continually experimenting with different planking patterns, but most are based on skins of diagonal planks set at opposing angles. Three layers are the minimum, and many more are often used. Strong hulls are strengthened further if a single skin run fore and aft is included, but this is slower to laminate, as each plank has to be spiled, as for carvel planking. Despite this, it is preferable for the final layer to be run this way on a varnished hull, as its appearance is more pleasing than diagonal planking, though the workmanship must be of a high standard. An inner fore and aft laminate need not be quite so perfect, reliance being placed on the gap-filling properties of the glue.

On large hulls, several diagonal layers can be laminated on a strip-planked foundation. This rapidly builds up the required planking thickness, and eliminates the need for a complete mould: frames are still set up but the strip planks fastened to them take the place of the many ribbands normally found on the cold moulding jig.

Marking the individual laminates to butt up to each other neatly is achieved by straightforward scribing. One is fastened at forty-five degrees to the keel, and the next is temporarily stapled as close as possible. The shape of the first is scribed onto this (Plate 1.33).

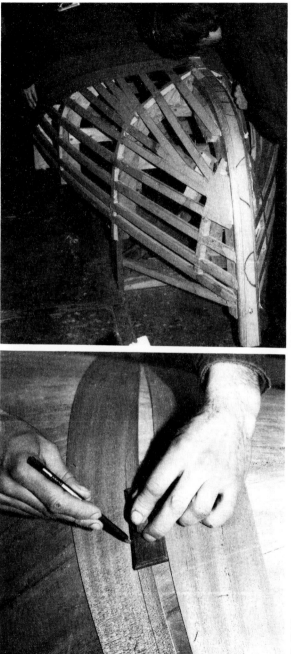

Plate 1.32
Cold moulding: first layer of veneers being fitted over the jig.

Plate 1.33
Scribing a veneer to fit against the first plank.

It is removed, cut (on a band saw or jig saw) and planed to the line, then refastened in position; the process is repeated for the next, and so on.

Care should be taken that the angle to the keel remains constant: there is a tendency for it to change progressively. One complete layer is marked and fastened dry, then removed for gluing and final fixing with staples. These can be fastened over canvas tape to help removal after curing. Tools used to remove staples tend to damage the surface, so the final layer is stapled through cardboard, enabling removal without disfigurement. Before each layer is started, the previous one is quickly faired to remove the bumps at planking edges.

Scribing planks for this construction method is very quick, but as there are multiple layers of planks, the number to be scribed is much increased. The method does produce a strong hull, reducing the number of strengthening frames needed, and in some cases timbers of any sort are entirely eliminated.

Plywood Hard Chine

On a hull of chined design, planking time is drastically reduced because there are so few planks. With a simple single chine hull, there are only two either side.

With a boat of this construction the planks are bent around permanent frames, or bulkheads. On small dinghies additional temporary moulds may be included which are removed after construction. On larger boats, not only are the frames joined with chine logs, but intermediate stringers are also run fore and aft to support the planks between the chines (Plate 1.34).

Planks are made of plywood sheets, scarfed together into lengths of an appropriate size. Factory scarfed sheets can be bought, but these are in straight lengths 4 ft (1.2 m) wide. If the sheets are scarfed in the boatshop, more economical use can be made of the timber by scarfing them at an angle allowing the curved planks to be cut with minimum wastage.

The same method is used for fitting plywood planks as carvel: a spile board is wrapped around the hull and the shape of the rebate dummied onto it. This shape is then transferred to the plywood stock. The upper edge of the plank can be marked directly onto the ply when it is in position. With the lower edge cut the oversize sheet of ply is offered up, and when fitted the position of the upper edge marked. If the plank edges are simply overlapped, it can even be roughly cut to shape, then planed back to size, after being fastened in position. Marking can be done with a trimming gauge as described in Section 3.

Plate 1.34 Hard chine: the wide planks will be supported by transverse bulkheads and longitudinal chine logs and stringers. *(Naja)*

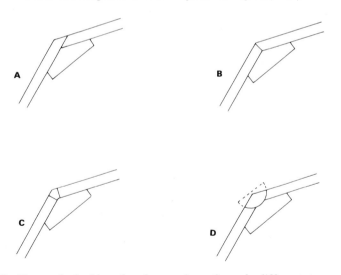

Fig 1.25 Plywood planking showing sections through different types of joint at the chines:
(A) Overlap, simple to make but leaves exposed end grain.
(B) Planks bevelled to butt up to each other.
(C) Plank seam filled with synthetic filler.
(D) The seam is enlarged with an electric router, then D section baton is glued into it, planing flush afterwards.

69

Different systems of butting the plank edges at the chine are illustrated in Fig. 1.25. Overlapping the planks is the simplest but it does leave end grain exposed. A much better result is achieved by bevelling the planks to butt up neatly to each other, though this is inevitably slower as it needs much more careful work. A third system is to leave both planks short of the corner, and then fill the gap. This can either be done with a synthetic filler, or by routing a 'D' shaped groove, into which a strip of wood, machined with a matching section is fitted. The excess is planed off.

Planks are glued and fastened with screws or ring nails.

Constant Camber *

Construction by this method is in two stages; first, two curved sheets of plywood are made, each the full length of the boat, then from these the hull is constructed. Cold moulding techniques are used to construct the curved sheets, but the production is much faster than with cold moulded hulls because the sheets are made with a constant curve in both directions, like segments from a huge doughnut-like ring.

It is from this shape that the construction method derives the name 'Constant Camber' and it can only be used on hulls designed with this technique specifically in mind. It tends to be most suitable for craft with a canoe-like shape, such as the hulls of catamarans and tris. Because several hull shapes can be created by distorting similar sheets in different ways, one mould will make all that is required for the three hulls of a trimaran. By combining the Constant Camber sheets with ordinary ply, a more conventionally shaped hull can be produced.

The advantage of laminating sheets whose curve is continuous and unchanging is that the shape spiled for one plank is identical for the next. All the planks can therefore be produced at one time: a jig can be set up for mass production, or a bundle can be sawn to shape together, or a block can be planed to the required shape, and then the planks sawn from it as slices.

Further advantages are gained if vacuum bagging techniques are used (see Adhesives) as all the laminated layers can be glued at once, with no time lag while the glue sets between each lamination. Vacuum bagging also reduces the time spent pulling staples.

Once the sheets are made they are fastened around frames or bulkheads in a similar manner to plywood chine construction, but the number of frames needed is much reduced. The Constant Camber sheets have greater stiffness than plywood and the amount they can be distorted is very limited, so a few frames to act as guides are all that is needed. For multihulls, each sheet forms one half of the hull, and once joined they produce a very rigid structure that needs little in the way of internal stiffening, either longitudinal or athwartships.

* The Constant Camber technique was devised by the American multihull designer, Jim Brown.

6. Fairing

All curves on a boat need to be fair. Below the water line unfair shapes spoil the performance by creating unnecessary turbulence. Above the water line unfairness spoils the appearance.

'A fair eye' is an important asset for any boatbuilder, although unfair bumps are often found by touch not sight. The aid that is indispensable to all is the fairing batten.

Battens

Battens come in an infinite variety of shapes and sizes, and in any boatshop it is useful to have several of differing lengths. One longer than the boat will always be necessary, but for smaller jobs the excessive length is too clumsy. For very small jobs a metal rule can sometimes be used, and for tight curves an old band saw blade or strip of Formica will bend further without breaking; though to use these, two pairs of hands are needed as they cannot be tacked down.

The usual battens are timber, and cut from good clear stock without knots or wavy grain that might create hard spots. Cross sectional dimensions might be anything from ⅛ in by ½ in (3 mm x 12 mm) to ¼ in by 2 in (6 mm x 50 mm). These dimensions really depend on how flexible or stiff a batten is required for the curve in question. The batten should be accurately thicknessed to these dimensions, as a variable width will confuse the eye when trying to obtain a fair line.

The timber from which a batten is cut need not be straight, and even if it is, the wood may 'spring' when cut. It does not matter as long as the curve in the batten is itself fair. For this reason it is better to cut long battens from a single length of wood as a scarf joint may leave an unfair kink, or at least a hard spot that will not curve neatly with the rest.

If a sufficiently long batten cannot be found for a job, two can be used, overlapping as in Fig. 1.26. The line being faired is that between the two i.e. the top edge of one and the bottom of the other.

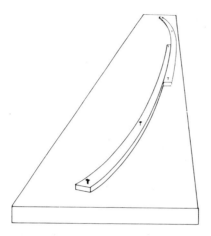

Fig 1.26 When necessary two battens can be used to fair a line.

A good batten is worth taking care of as during the boat's construction it will be put to repeated use. When stored it should be supported on a thicker piece of wood; if it is simply pushed up into the rafters out of the way, or across a series of nails tacked into the wall it will droop in a series of loops, and probably retain them when taken down for further use.

Fairing Lines

Battens are used to fair all curved lines — both those on the loft floor, and shapes marked for cutting: stem, rebate line, moulds, frames, planks, rudder, coamings etc. In most cases the batten is tacked to touch a series of accurately measured points, the shape it takes between them giving the desired curve. Before marking it though, the curve should be checked to ensure that it is in fact fair; moving one or two of the tacks as little as ⅛ in (3 mm) can make all the difference.

The ability to see unfairness in a line takes practice, the curve is in any case a changing one, tighter at one end than the other perhaps, or reversing itself into an 'S' shape. What is wanted is a gradual and even change to the curve, not sudden changes of direction, humps or corners, or even the opposite, straight sections in an otherwise gently curving batten. Looking along the batten, from one end and then the other, is the way to check for unfairness, but it is best not to get too low down as any unevenness in the face being marked on, perhaps where the plank sags between supporting trestles, will mislead the eye.

Once the shape has been cut and planed it is a good idea to check for fairness again, without the batten, simply looking along the cut edge. Dips and humps may have been planed into it accidentally, and especially when planking these can make fitting the next much more difficult. Bumps and hollows can sometimes be detected by feel, sliding one hand gently over the planed edge.

Fairing Shapes

When fairing solid shapes the difficulty is to be able to remove timber quickly without fear of removing too much. The shape can usually be checked with a pattern or fairing batten, but if the work is continually being interrupted to check progress, the job is slow and tedious. A way to avoid this is to use a rebate plane to cut channels across the grain first. These channels are cut accurately, and they form a guide for the bulk of the work: planing with the grain rapidly and confidently until the channels just disappear. Particular applications of this technique are described in the examples that follow.

Fairing Deck Beams and Carlings

A deck, teak or plywood, cannot be faired once it is laid. To avoid bumps and hollows the beams and carlings must be shaped and bevelled so that they all run fair and form a true foundation for the deck to follow.

The deck beam pattern provides a guide for shape athwartship, while a fairing batten laid over the beams acts as a guide for the bevels fore and aft. If the deck beam pattern is positioned on the gunwales and pressed firmly against each beam a line can be drawn on each side to act as a guide. With a rebate plane channels are planed in fore and aft members, such as the carlings, until the pattern sits neatly on the channels and the gunwales. The lines on the deck beam sides, and the channels in the carlings act as guides while the bulk of the fairing is done. At the finishing stages, continual checking is necessary with both beam crop pattern and battens (Fig. 1.27).

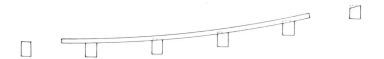

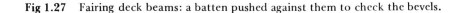

Fig 1.27   Fairing deck beams: a batten pushed against them to check the bevels.

Fairing Before Planking

Like the deck, a chined plywood hull cannot be faired after planking. Instead the 'skeleton' is faired, resulting in a fair hull once the planks are fastened to it.

The skeletal structure in this case consists of the frames and bulkheads with chine logs, and sometimes intermediary stringers, spanning between them. The guides for fairing in this case are the frames; their shapes and bevels were lifted from the loft floor and are considered true. The problem is to fair the corners off the chine logs throughout their length, (Fig. 1.28), to form an even support for the plank edges.

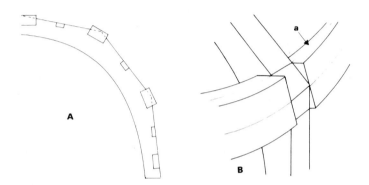

Fig 1.28　Fairing chine logs prior to planking: (A), the corners of each have to be removed throughout their length; (B), guides are provided at each frame by cutting channels with a rebate plane. By springing a batten around the frames just above and below the chine logs, guide lines can be marked on their edges, (a).

Two guides can be provided: first with a rebate plane channels are cut through the chine logs at each frame; secondly a batten sprung around the frames and butting up against the edge of the chine log can be used to mark a curved line on each edge of it. With these two guides most of the work can be done. When finishing, a straight edge laid across from chine to chine is a further check of their angles.

When stringers are let into the frames between the chines they are normally light enough to be pulled or pushed into shape by the plank itself. If they have a lot of edge set they may tend to bulge out stubbornly between frames in which case some fairing will be necessary. A straight edge between the chines acts as a guide but if a lot of timber has to be removed the stringers will appear odd if they are in a position that will be seen from inside: they will be full size at each frame but inexplicably thinner on one edge in between.

Fairing a Planked Hull

'Scrubbing off' a smooth skinned hull, whether carvel, strip, or cold moulded, is quickly described, but a long slow job to do.

The problem is that the beautifully fair shapes of the moulds or frames inside the boat become a very unfair series of short straight lines across each plank on the outside of the hull. The top and bottom edges of each plank have to be planed off to obtain a smooth hull, together with any other unfairness, possibly at scarfs or where some edge set has caused a plank to bulge slightly between frames. On a cold moulded hull all the staples have to be removed first, care being taken not to damage the wood; on a strip planked or carvel hull all fastenings to the frame are counterbored into the planks, and the holes plugged with dowels. The glued dowels are trimmed back before scrubbing off can begin.

Plate 1.35 A sanding board or sanding plane being used to fair up a cold moulded hull.

Fairing the hull is done with a smoothing plane, although as work progresses a sanding board is better, and can be seen in Plate 1.35. A hand slid across the hull often feels unfairness that cannot be seen simply by looking at the expanse of cleanly sanded hull. The only other guide that can be used is a short batten bent against the hull. As the batten is slid across it, high and low spots can be seen by watching from close to the hull, one cheek pressing against it. Alternatively, chalk rubbed on the batten before it is slid across the hull, indicates high spots. Another visual method of fairing is to give the hull one coat of paint. The sanding board then quickly finds the humps. At some point the job ceases to be fairing and becomes painting and finishing. Instead of looking for bumps and hollows, small blemishes and imperfections have to be remedied, by painting, filling, and sanding.

7. Boring

Boring deep holes through substantial pieces of timber is always a nerve-racking process, and in boatbuilding it crops up quite often: fastenings through deep-throated floors and knees; edge bolts for rudders; rudder stocks; edge bolts for cabin sides; keel bolts; and of course the propeller shaft. It is nerve-racking because while the hole is being bored no one can see just what is going on, and an error can cause a lot of damage. In practice it is not that difficult and, if care and time are taken, need never be a disaster. The points to remember are these:

(i) Start with a small pilot hole, it will do less damage if an error is made. If necessary re-drill at a better angle and plug the mistake. Follow the guide hole with successively large bits.

(ii) Do not rush; gentle pressure then back off and press again (a sharp bit helps). Repeatedly pull the bit right out to clear the shavings and dip it in grease before re-entry.

(iii) Drill from the side where accuracy is most important; if the bolts are to fasten metal fittings, mark the positions from them and drill from the marks, not toward them. Edge fastenings through a rudder should be drilled from the after edge, which is the narrower edge, where they can be easily located on the centre line; if the holes have wandered off centre by the time they reach the forward edge, there is more meat there in any case, so it is less likely to matter.

There are several methods of boring long holes, the three described here successively produce more accurate results, but also require more equipment.

Spoke Bit

This is a cheap and simple way to bore holes that are just beyond the range of a normal set of twist bits. A spoke bit is simply made from

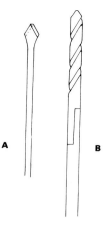

Fig 1.29 (A) a spoke bit: the end of a piece of wire or light rod is flattened, then opposite corners are filed off.

(B) an extended bit: a length of mild steel rod is brazed to an ordinary twist bit.

a piece of wire or thin rod, one end of which is flattened and the corners filed off: it looks similar to a bicycle spoke, and is illustrated in Fig. 1.29. Used in an electric drill it can be effective even when as long as 1 ft (300 mm) or more. Usually it is used to drill a pilot hole which is then enlarged to the size required by drilling from each end with a standard bit.

Greater lengths can be drilled in this manner if the hole passes through several pieces of wood which have not been finally assembled: with the parts positioned together the spoke bit is used to drill the hole through all, then they are taken apart and an ordinary bit used to drill each part in turn from each side. Difficulties arise in hard wood unless the parts are very accurately repositioned before driving the bolt — very slight misalignment can be enough to prevent a bolt driving cleanly through.

Extended Bit

Any small engineering shop will extend an ordinary twist bit by welding or brazing a length of mild steel bar to it. The bit and bar must be accurately aligned, and the joint must not swell the thickness of the bit or it will jam. If on larger bits ⅜ in (9 mm) bar is used they can be held in a standard chuck. Bits larger than ½ in (12 mm) will have to be turned by heavier industrial drills.

Bits extended in this way can happily be 3 ft (1 m) or more in length but even when drilling holes much shorter than that a guide is necessary.

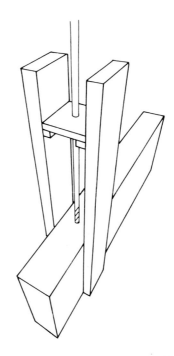

Fig 1.30 A boring jig which physically holds the bit in correct alignment.

Physically holding the bit in alignment with a jig that supports it is shown in Fig. 1.30, but unless drilling a pilot hole for the prop shaft, is usually unnecessary. Normally a visual guide to check that the correct angle is maintained is satisfactory. This can be achieved by clamping a straight edge to the work to be drilled, aligned at the correct angle. In some cases, it may need to be wedged if the part tapers, and in others it will have to be clamped independently. This would be the case when drilling through the stem or keel from inside the boat: the correct alignment could be found with a plumb bob, then the straight edge clamped to temporary supports. However it is clamped, the straight edge must be aligned correctly but offset from the hole by an inch or so.

With this as a visual guide it is easy to hold the drill so that the extended bit lies parallel to the guide (Fig. 1.31). Greater accuracy is achieved if someone else can watch the operation from a distance to one side. He can tell the operator when the straight edge and bit are aligned accurately, and if any deviation is occurring during the drilling process. This is the best way to work, with two pair of eyes: the operator, holding the drill at waist level can align it in one direction, while his assistant, standing to one side, can check the other.

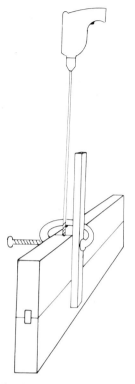

Fig 1.31   A visual guide for boring: the angle required is indicated by a straight
edge clamped at one side.

So long as excessive pressure is not exerted, and the drill is continually withdrawn to remove shavings and be re-lubricated with
grease, this method can produce reasonably accurate results. Very
twisted grain (or a dull bit with too much effort behind it) can still
lead the bit astray, and once it starts to wander, that is the line it
follows.

Where greater accuracy is required a boring bar is used.

Boring Bar

With this method great precision is obtained. Normally accuracy of
this nature is only required for the prop shaft, but on larger craft the
method may be used in many situations including the keel bolts
and rudder stock.

A boring bar (Plate 1.36), is comprised of a length of steel (over
twice the length of hole required) threaded for half its length. At its
midpoint is a hole that will accept different sized cutters, (Plate 1.37).

Plate 1.36
A boring bar is positioned accurately by the two bearings: the near one allows it to turn freely, but the far one is threaded, pulling the bar through the hole as it is turned.

Sometimes the hole passes right through and the cutters are double ended, sometimes two holes are used, one either side, and twin cutters fixed. The cutters are simply made from tool steel sharpened at the ends.

Before the bar can be used a hole through which it can pass must be drilled. The advantage of the boring bar is that any inaccuracy in this preliminary hole can be corrected; so long as it is within the diameter of the final full hole, it is sufficient.

This pilot hole can be drilled in the manner already described, with a jig to support the bit for greater accuracy. The hole is enlarged until the boring bar will pass through it; the system can then be set up. The bar is supported at one end by a single bearing that positions it accurately but allows it to turn freely. The other end is screwed into a threaded plate that is clamped firmly in position. The smallest cutters are then fastened in place and the bar turned. As it turns the bar is slowly pulled through the threaded plate, and the turning cutters work their way through the timber, enlarging the hole. The first cut is likely to be very heavy as the chippings block the hole, and the bar may have to be removed completely after the first cut to clear them.

Plate 1.37
A hole at the centre of the bar accepts different sizes of cutter, held in position by a grub screw.

Once the hole is enlarged, the positions of the bearing at one end, and threaded plate at the other can be corrected, and the great accuracy of this system is realised. The bar can be aligned exactly as the shaft will run, precision is guaranteed. With the bar in its correct position it may be necessary to cut again with smaller blades, but each time the bar is wound through, larger blades are used until the desired diameter is achieved.

Turning the bar is normally done manually, a handle being fitted at one end, (Plate 1.38) but, as the hole gets larger and cutting easier, an industrial size electric drill could be attached to speed things up. Winding the bar through a long hole is slow; if after cutting one way, the next size of cutters are inserted facing the other, cutting can be done while both winding the bar in and winding it out. Alternatively, if the threaded plate is made in two parts, so that it can be opened to release the bar without disturbing its position, (Plate 1.39) the bar can be shunted back quickly after each successive cut.

It is possible to avoid boring for the propeller shaft at all. The shaft log can be made in two parts, each with half the shafts cut from it before they are joined.

Plate 1.38
The bar being used to bore for the rudder stock on *Arethusa*.

Plate 1.39
If the threaded bearing can be opened without disturbing its position the bar can be quickly shunted back after each successive cut.

8. Boatbuilding Joints

Loose Tenon

When the mainframe is made up from its constituent parts (as opposed to being laminated in a single piece) these have to be joined in some manner. The plans usually show the shape of each part and the way they connect. Except for two part stems which are hook scarfed, these joints are normally shown as straightforward overlaps: forefoot to keel; stern post to keel with the stern knee or deadwood strengthening the joint. If these joints are made as drawn on the plans, only the through bolts prevent sideways movement. The addition of one or more tenons makes a joint that can stand lateral knocks and pressure far better.

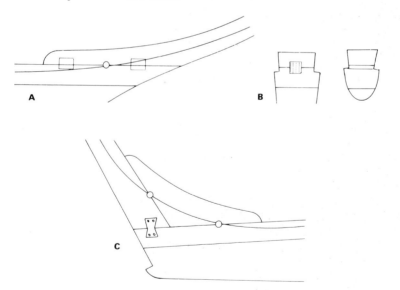

Fig 1.32 Main frame joints: (A), stem to keel showing the position of loose tenons and stopwater, with (B) cross-sections through each. (C), keel, stern post, and knee showing stopwaters and dovetailed bronze plate. Plates are located on each side and are in addition to a loose tenon which is not drawn.

An ordinary mortise and tenon could be used on the stern post, but it is often offset at a considerable angle, and the tenon tends to be short grained. Ordinary tenons on the forefoot would be quite impractical, having little strength across the grain, and the member would need to be cut from a wastefully large piece of timber. A better solution in both cases is to use a loose tenon: mortises are cut in both parts and a separate tenon inserted between them, as shown in Fig. 1.32A.

The loose tenon has two advantages. Firstly it can be set with the grain running directly between the two main members to gain the most strength; secondly it is far easier to obtain a good fit: both faces can be planed absolutely flat and the fit ensured before the mortises are cut and the tenon inserted. This is a major advantage as often the areas in contact are quite large. Working around an integral tenon, trying to find where the fit is unsatisfactory over this large area, much of which cannot be inspected, is slow and awkward.

These joints are not normally glued, but liberally luted with white lead or mastic, and held together with the main bolts. At the aftermost end of the keel it may be difficult to position a bolt that will successfully hold the keel up against the heel of the stern post. In this case bronze plates, roughly wine glass shaped are let into the timber on either side to form a dovetail in both directions linking these members. These two plates can be through bolted to each other, but screws are quite adequate as the stresses they are subject to are taken by their shape, not their fastenings (Fig. 1.32C).

Whenever the rebate line crosses a joint in the mainframe, stop-waters are inserted to make the joint watertight. Stopwaters are softwood dowels, treated with preservative, driven through the joint as illustrated in Figs. 1.32 and 1.38. If water does creep along the joint the softwood swells against the harwood members, effectively sealing the joint. They are normally located at the joints between stem and keel, keel and deadwood, and deadwood and sternpost.

Loose Tongue

This, a similar technique to that just described, is used for edge joining boards. Instead of lapping, or tongue and grooving, a loose tongue is fitted their full length. This can be seen in Fig. 1.31. Again, the main advantage is the accuracy of the fit that can be obtained. The two boards can be planed, butted together to inspect the joint and modified until a perfect match is made. Only then is the groove cut on the edges of both, and the tongue fitted and glued between them. The groove is most easily cut on a bench saw.

This joint can be used wherever wide expanses of flat timber are needed, and plywood is considered unsuitable. It can even be used to join thick sheets of plywood if one is not large enough, such as on the bulkheads of a large boat. Other examples of timber being joined in this way are a rudder, and a flat transom. With both of these, extra strength has to be added across the grain, the direction in which the wood is weakest, whether a single piece or jointed timber is used. On a transom this strength is provided internally by the stern post and fashion pieces, and in larger cases additional members are added parallel to the stern post. On a rudder reinforcing is internal and takes the form of bolts or drifts set at different angles passing right through the wood fore and aft.

Scarfs

Scarf joints are used to join timber end to end. When boards of a sufficient length are not available for a particular job, two pieces are scarfed together. Scarfs may also be used for reasons of economy: on a 20 ft boat (6 m) it may be possible to cut the full length of each plank in a single piece, but the curved shapes of such long planks will require wide boards; scarfing the planks (with due attention to the 'shift of butts' described below) reduces the curve in each half, allowing two planks to be cut from the same width of board.

The thought of cutting a scarf intimidates many people, without good reason. In many cases if it does not fit, it can be cut again, with little wastage, except of labour. If care is taken it will not be necessary.

For all the scarfs illustrated the method is straightforward. Accurately measure and mark the scarf on one side of both pieces of timber, square across the ends (and hook or table if there is one), then mark the scarf on the other side as well. Work out and clearly mark which is the waste side in both cases. Carefully make the cross cuts with a tenon saw, and remove the waste with chisels or a plane where possible. When finishing check with a metal rule that every face is absolutely flat. If all the faces are true, and accurately cut to carefully measured lines, it will fit.

The important points are:

(i)   measure and mark accurately
(ii) ensure all faces are true.

A scarf's strength is dependent on its length in relation to the thickness of wood being joined. This relationship, the scarf ratio, is used to describe every scarf, and in general the larger it is the stronger the joint. In a glued joint a 4:1 ratio is about sixty-five percent as strong as solid wood of the same section, and this strength increases rapidly as the length increases to about eighty-five percent at 8:1. Beyond this, efficiency is only gained slowly reaching ninety percent at 12:1 and ninety-five percent at 20:1.

Glued Scarfs

For joints that are to be glued either a feathered scarf or single-lipped scarf is used, (Fig. 1.33). Lips and hooks weaken a glued scarf joint,

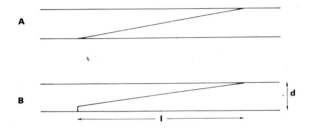

Fig 1.33   Glued scarfs: (A), a feathered scarf; (B), a single-lipped scarf. Lips are normally ⅓ to ¼ depth. The scarf ratio is their length to depth or (l):(d). Lloyd's Rules specify minimum ratios of 4:1 for planking and 6:1 for bolted scarfs. Plywood is normally feather scarfed with an 8:1 ratio.

but occasionally the single lip does have advantages. One is that it helps to locate the two members, making it less likely that they slide out of alignment when clamping, although dowels can be used for this. Secondly, if one face of the finished work is to be moulded in any way, rounded or chamfered, the single lip keeps the appearance looking tidy. This consideration would apply to toe-rails or rubbing strakes, whose upper or outside edge is rounded. A feathered scarf would tail away from the centre, while the lipped scarf would appear as a butt from one direction, and a scarf from the other.

When gluing feathered scarfs they should be fractionally over-lapped as this ensures that clamping pressure closes the joint; the faces of an underlapped joint are pulled apart as the clamps are tightened. (Fig. 1.34.)

Plywood sheets are joined with feathered scarfs. A ratio of at least 8:1 is necessary if the sheets are to be treated as a single piece and not have extra support fastened behind the joint. Both sheets can be cut together if they are stacked one on top of the other, and the

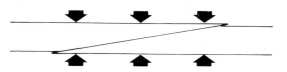

Fig 1.34 Clamping a glued feathered scarf: it should be fractionally overlapped to ensure that clamping pressure closes the joint, not opens it.

angle marked and planed from both at once. An electric plane can quickly remove most of the wood, finishing being done by hand. Support should always be given to the lower edge when planing a feathered scarf, otherwise it drops under planing pressure, producing an incorrect angle.

Planking Scarfs
On carvel or clinker (lapstrake) boats planks are joined with a single-lipped scarf. This is orientated correctly if the aft plank tucks inside the forward one, with the lip on the outside of the hull. Scarfs are always positioned on a timber, and look neat if the inside feather edge is actually hidden by it. With clinker construction, where the timbers are steamed into position after planking, their position has to be anticipated. When the timbers are being fastened a wedge is fitted between the timber and scarf to allow a nail to be fastened in the centre of the plank without tending to distort and split it.

Carvel planks are not always scarfed, but can be simply butted with a butt strap fastened behind for support. In this case the butt is sited between frames with the strap stretching between them, bevelled at its top, as in Fig. 1.35, to avoid trapping water. Straps overlap the planks above and below by at least ½ in (12 mm).

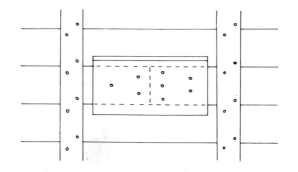

Fig 1.35 A butt strap: carvel planks can be butt jointed between frames. The supporting strap overlaps adjacent planks by ½ in (12 mm) and is bevelled to allow drainage.

Whatever joints are used it is necessary to ensure that there is adequate 'shift of butts'. If two adjacent strakes are scarfed in close proximity the hull is weakened. The specification laid down by Lloyd's Rules is a good guide to follow; this states that scarfs in adjacent strakes must be at least 4 ft apart (1.2 m) and that three clear planks must lie between two scarfs on the same timber as in Fig. 1.36. Before planking commences a schematic diagram should be drawn of the planks and frames and the position of scarfs marked on it. Other considerations when drawing this up are to avoid excessively short planks at the ends, particularly forward on a bluff bowed boat where considerable shape is bent into the planks, and to separate the position of scarfs on the gunwale and sheer strake.

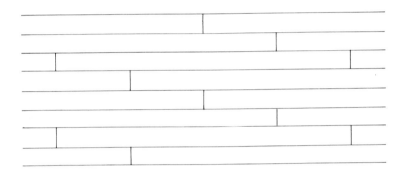

Fig 1.36   The 'shift of butts': a schematic diagram of part of the hull planking showing how scarfs or butt joints should be staggered. The minimum requirements set out in Lloyd's Rules are that 4 ft (1.2 m) should separate scarfs in adjacent planks, with three clear planks between joints on the same frame.

Lloyd's Rules also specify a ratio for planking scarfs of 4:1. This should be considered a minimum, traditionally clinker planks were scarfed at 8:1.

Normally scarfed planks are fastened to the hull in their two separate parts. The forward one is fitted into the stem rebate and fastened in position first; the second can then be tucked behind the first, and allowed to run off beyond the transom aft. The joint is luted with mastic or white lead, not glued, as this would make repair and replacement more difficult. An exception would be scarfed planks on small dinghies, which could be glued before fastening to the boat, and then treated as a single plank.

Bolted Scarfs

Where main structural members have to be made in two parts, whether to increase length or to allow straight grained timber to follow a curve (such as is often found in the stem), a bolted scarf joint is used. Bolted scarfs should at least have a lip at either end, and are better if hooked or tabled as well, as these physically lock the scarf and prevent it from sliding or twisting. Four are illustrated in Fig. 1.37.

When a table is inserted the grain should be aligned as in a loose

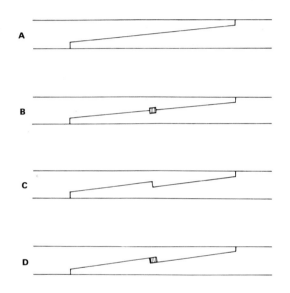

Fig 1.37 Bolted scarfs: (A), plain scarf; (B), tabled scarf; (C), hooked scarf; (D), tabled hooked scarf.

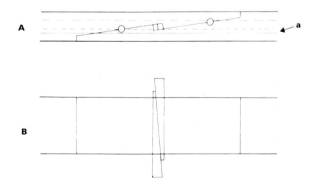

Fig 1.38 (A), a tabled hooked scarf in the keel showing the position of stop-waters in relation to rebate line (a). If the table is made from split wedges, driven from each side as shown in the plan view (B), then the whole joint is tightened.

tenon, at right angles to the scarf faces. A single piece can be used or split wedges (Fig. 1.38), driven from each side and then sawn off flush. Wedges used for tabling a hooked scarf tighten the whole joint.

One of these joints, normally a hooked scarf, is used on all main members; gunwales, stringers, stem, even the keel. When a scarf joint passes from the inside to the outside of the hull, one or two stopwaters are inserted to prevent the ingress of water, and are sited as shown in Fig. 1.38.

Lloyd's Rules specify 6:1 as the minimum ratio for bolted scarfs.

9. Fitting Out Joints

The curves that make a hull elegant and efficient externally, are internally awkward and impractical. Fitting out is a process of dividing the boat's volume into areas and surfaces that can be used. First the bulkheads are installed, then everything else is for the most part fastened to them. The joints of this second stage are easier, for although the design may be complex, with bunks, lockers, stowage shelves, folding tables and so on, the surfaces fastened to are flat, and the shapes straight sided, rhomboids or rectangles.

Bulkheads

The shapes and changing bevels where bulkheads meet the hull make this a difficult joint. Bulkheads are often structurally important parts in the design of a boat, holding the shape of the boat at points of stress such as the mast or chain plates. They can also act as web knees, commonly being the main support for the side decks. Some bulkheads may be built into the hull from an early stage, constructed integrally with frames, or replacing them altogether. On steel and ferrocement boats main bulkheads may be made from the same material as the hull; the reinforcing of ferrocement bulkheads would be linked with the hull armature and plastered simultaneously. Steel bulkheads would replace frames in a steel hull.

Bulkheads incorporated in this fashion will be stronger, but others inevitably have to be added after hull completion. Because of the changing shapes and bevels where a bulkhead meets the hull, the joint can be difficult. In many cases the problem is most easily overcome by the use of modern resins, with or without reinforcing, which conform to the required shape when wet, then set solid. Bulkheads are normally plywood; joining this to different hull materials requires different techniques.

Wooden Hulls

If bulkheads can be sited adjacent to timbers or frames, attachment is little problem. The bulkhead is screwed directly to them, with some mastic between. If the timber or frame is not plumb a shaped wedge is inserted between the two to correct for the error. On traditionally constructed boats interiors can be designed positioning the bulkheads at frames as they are closely spaced. This is not always possible, especially on a plywood or strip planked hull where the frames may be separated more widely. On a small cold moulded hull there may be no frames at all.

In these cases the traditional solution is a 'ground' fastened to the bulkhead. This is a cleat of solid timber around the edge of the bulkhead that is shaped and bevelled to fit the hull. It is screwed to both the hull and bulkhead, connecting the two, as in Fig. 1.39A.

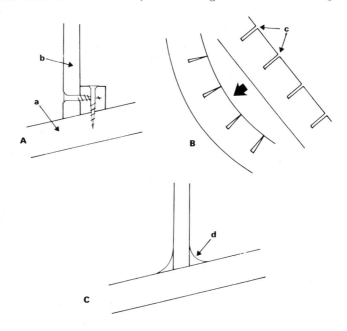

Fig 1.39 Wooden hull bulkhead attachments:
(A), fitted timber grounds are screwed to both hull (a) and bulkhead (b).
(B), amidship grounds, where little bevel is encountered, may be bent into position; saw cuts (c) allow timber heavy enough to accept fastenings to be bent to shape.
(C), epoxy paste fillets (d) are simple and quick.

After spending time getting a bulkhead to fit it is a daunting thought that the process has to be repeated for the ground, but fortunately this job is much quicker. The ground need not be made in one piece, but fitted as a series of shorter sections. Each can be shaped by using the bulkhead as a pattern, and final fitting can be done by simple scribing.

Bulkheads situated amidships meet the hull practically at right angles. In this situation little bevel is involved and it may be possible to bend a satisfactory ground into position. In order to allow heavy enough timber to be used to accept the fastenings, yet bend to shape, many saw cuts effectively reduce its thickness as illustrated in Fig. 1.39B. Gap filling glue should be worked into the cuts before it is fastened to seal them.

An alternative method of fastening is a fillet of epoxy paste (Fig. 1.39C). This process is simple and quick: the hull and bulkhead edge are coated with epoxy resin, then the bulkhead is clamped in position; epoxy paste is applied to both sides of the joint, it is shaped with a radiused spatula and the excess removed to produce a tidy joint. The strength of the joint depends on the size of fillet produced which, to equal that of the ply, must be quite large. A fillet radius of ⅞ in (22 mm) equals the strength of ¼ in ply (6 mm). Large bulkheads are expensive to install in this way, but the cost may be justified by the great saving in labour.

Fibreglass Hulls

Plywood bulkheads are normally glassed in to a fibreglass hull. With the bulkhead fitted and clamped temporarily in position fillets are moulded on each side of it. These are made from the same material as the hull itself, glass fibres in the form of 'chopped strand matt', impregnated with polyester resin.

The surfaces of the hull and bulkhead must be clean and free of grease before applying the resin, and light sanding of the hull helps to provide a key. The first strip of glass fibre matt is laid along the joint, which has been prepainted with resin. More resin is then stippled into it. Each layer of chopped strand matt is thoroughly saturated with resin before the next is applied to ensure complete impregnation. Rolling with a metal roller ensures no air bubbles or voids are left.

This joint can be made in several different patterns, illustrated in Fig. 1.40. To obtain optimum strength the design is quite important. The joint must be of the same thickness as the hull, that is contain the same number of layers of matt. In practice this means that if the bulkhead is supported from both sides, each fillet can have half the number of layers; if it can only be supported from one side, this must contain the full number. Secondly the fillet must not end abruptly, but taper away on both the hull and bulkhead. This is easily arranged by making each successive strip of matt wider than the last, so that the fillet is thickest in the corner and tapers on each side.

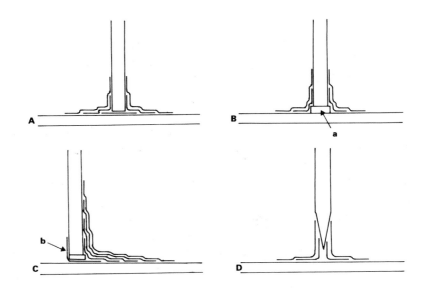

Fig 1.40 Fibreglass hulls: 'glassing in' plywood bulkheads. Each strip of glass matt should be wider than the last to taper the joint.
(A), a simple joint, but unsatisfactory as the bulkhead forms a hard spot, and can cause distortion as the resin contracts during curing.
(B), foam tape (a) edging the bulkhead avoids these problems.
(C), lay up when only one side of the bulkhead is accessible; strip (b) is applied to bulkhead just before installing.
(D), tapering or rebating the bulkhead edge makes a neater joint.

Each layer should be about 1¼ in (30 mm) more than the last on both the bulkhead and hull.

When designing the joint it should also be realised that the bulkhead must not butt up against the hull itself, but be connected to it by the curved fillets only. This is partly to avoid a hard spot in the hull, but also because while curing the resin contracts slightly; if the bulkhead is hard against the hull distortions can arise that strain the hull causing an unfair hump at the bulkhead position on the external surface. To avoid this the bulkhead can be held away from the hull with wedges while the fillets are being made up, but the more normal practice is to fix foam tape around the outside edge of the bulkhead before clamping it into position. The foam is then sealed into the joint when the fillets are made.

To ensure a neat joint masking tape is fixed at the limits of the fillet before applying the resin. An even better result is obtained if the bulkhead edge is tapered or rebated to accept the fillet without swelling its own thickness. This is particularly effective if the bulkhead is to be covered with another material, cloth or laminated plastic, as the joint is then completely hidden.

96

Steel Hulls
Bulkheads are bolted to the web frames on metal hulls. When frames do not occur in suitable places, plates are welded to the hull to facilitate attachment.

Ferrocement Hulls
Bolting to the frames is the method used on these hulls also. Attachment to web frames can be made at any point by drilling bolt holes through them, using tungsten carbide tipped masonry drills. When fastening, the loads must be spread by using large washers. Pipe frames are not attached to directly; instead the bulkheads are bolted to steel plates that protrude from the plaster. Obviously these plates must be welded to the armature before plastering. Careful planning is needed to ensure that sufficient plates are positioned in all the necessary places. Fig. 1.41 illustrates fastenings to both web and pipe frames.

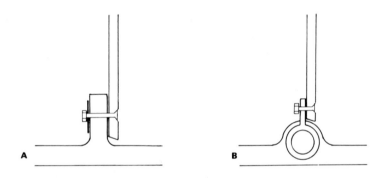

Fig 1.41   Ferrocement hulls: bulkheads are bolted in.
(A), with web frames large washers must be used to spread the loads.
(B), with pipe frames bulkheads are bolted to steel plates welded to frames before plastering.

Epoxy resins adhere to concrete if it is degreased, clean, and free of dust. Where bulkheads have to be attached in unplanned places they can be 'glassed in'. This is exactly the same process as described for fixing bulkheads in a fibreglass hull, except that epoxy resin replaces the polyester. The danger of hull distortion, described for light fibreglass hulls if bulkheads are butted hard against the hull, does not exist when glassing in to a ferrocement hull. However, with a heavily constructed full bulkhead there is still the problem of hard spots. This can be avoided in the same manner; edging it with foam tape before glassing in.

Soles and Thwarts

Bulkheads span the hull vertically, whereas cabin soles (the floor of the cabin), cockpit soles, and thwarts span it horizontally. Fixing these in position is a different problem; they are not structural members so a good fit and strong joint to the hull is not necessary, but what they do need is strong support. Soles are usually supported by cross beams called sole bearers. In most construction methods these can be attached directly to the timbers or frames: bolted in the case of steel or ferrocement; bolted or glassed in for fibreglass hulls; screwed to timber.

Dinghy thwarts are supported either side on a fore and aft member called a riser, or rising, which can be seen in Plate 1.40. This may be similar to a stringer, stretching much of the length of the boat, but not usually as far as the stem or transom. Sometimes it is quite short, only slightly longer than required by the thwarts. Stringers are usually through-fastened with clenched nails, but a riser can be simply screwed to the frames. This method can be usefully employed to support sole bearers, as it is sometimes easier to position and level the riser, fastening it to the timbers, then the bearers to it, than to fasten each timber individually to a frame.

Plate 1.40   Risers fastened to the timbers are the usual method of supporting thwarts.

The Hidden Cleat

Once the bulkheads and soles are fastened in position, the main joint used in fitting out is the hidden cleat. This is simply a piece of timber with a section suitably large to accept the necessary screws, ¾ in square (19 mm) being adequate, which is glued and screwed at the back of any plywood joints. It is positioned inside lockers and under shelves, if possible with the fastening screws driven from the cleat side so that neither cleat nor fastenings are visible. On some occasions the cleat has to be bevelled to allow the plywood to meet at irregular angles, but this bevel is planed easily and quickly as, unlike bulkhead grounds, the cleat is always straight.

Where the plywood may have to be removed for access to tanks etc., mastic is used instead of glue.

To ensure that the joint is tight the cleat should be fastened whenever possible in the order illustrated in Fig. 1.42. The cleat is fastened to the plywood edge first, possibly even setting it back fractionally; when the cleat is screwed to the plywood face the two are pulled together tightly. Fastening in the reverse order does not necessarily close the joint.

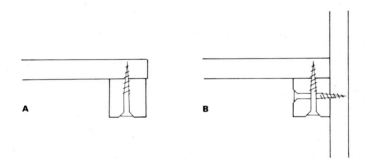

Fig 1.42   Hidden cleats: when possible the cleat is screwed to the plywood edge first (A), then to the plywood face (B), as this ensures a tight fit.

As an alternative to cleats, epoxy paste fillets can be used as described for fastening timber bulkheads.

Timber Mouldings

As a general principle end grain should not be left exposed. This is for two reasons; it absorbs moisture more easily, and has a less attractive appearance. The first is perhaps a more important consideration for exterior work, the second for interior joinery.

This principle applies to all timber, but you can never afford to neglect it with plywood. Unprotected plywood end grain looks unsightly, and once water enters it quickly leads to delamination. Even edges of plywood which will never be seen should be well protected with epoxy resin or several coats of primer. Edges that will be seen can be attractively covered with hardwood mouldings which can be cut easily on a bench saw.

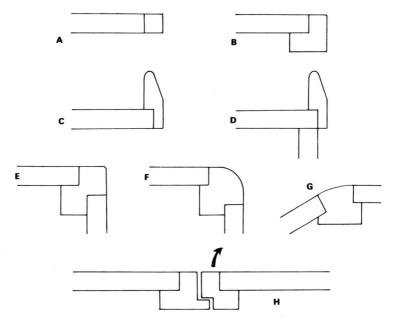

Fig 1.43   Examples of hardwood mouldings:
(A), simple trim to flush finish surfaces, glued and pinned in position.
(B), a similar but stronger pattern.
(C) and (D), a simple fiddle that can finish shelves or work surfaces.
(E), (F), (G), various bulkhead joints.
(H), one example of mouldings for locker doors.

These mouldings (of which some examples are illustrated in Fig. 1.43) can be designed to suit many situations, including joining plywood at right angles (or any other angle) and finishing work surfaces either flush or with stand up fiddles. Some mouldings, such as for fiddles, could be machined in quite long lengths and cut for use as required. In a few cases it is worth planning in great detail the shape of a moulding for a single situation. For example a cylindrical vertical grab rail may be rebated to accept a half bulkhead and galley front on one side from waist level down, and lower still accept a bunk front on the opposite side. If this is tailor-made from a single piece of wood it will look effective, but it needs careful forethought.

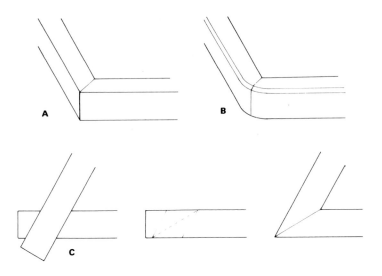

Fig 1.44 Mitres: end grain in hardwood mouldings can be avoided by using
mitre joints which look effective whether the corner is square (A),
or more sensibly rounded (B).
(C), marking and cutting a bastard mitre.

In some simple situations plywood can be edged with 'iron on'
strips of veneer. These can be bought in a variety of hardwoods and
have a hot melt glue on one face, which enables them to be literally
ironed into place. Although neither as smart nor as strong as a
moulded trim, they are a quick and effective way of finishing out-of-
the-way shelves, or the openings to lockers.

Where the mouldings themselves finish, end grain is effectively
overcome with a mitre joint. The forty-five degree mitre required
for most joints can be marked with a combination square. Whether
it is cut in a mitre board or free hand, it is important to cut with the
sides that will be seen (the 'face side', and 'face edge') toward you,
ensuring that the lines on these sides are accurately cut, to make a
good fit.

When the two mouldings meet at an unusual angle a bastard
mitre is necessary. This is marked by placing the two parts over each
other at the correct angle, and marking the position of each on the
other. Joining from corner to corner as illustrated in Fig. 1.44
marks the angle of mitre required.

When end grain cannot be mitred or butted to other wood it can
be disguised by bevelling or rounding. This is not acceptable with
plywood but is a common solution with solid timber.

Figure 1.45 shows both hidden cleats and hardwood mouldings being used in a simple piece of fitting out.

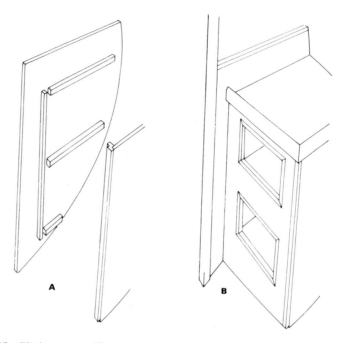

Fig 1.45   Fitting out, illustrating the use of hidden cleats and hardwood mouldings: (A), the cleats that will support plywood panels; (B), the finished effect, with mouldings covering all end grain.

10. Curved Grain

Whenever a part is curved the grain of the timber from which it is made should curve with it. If this rule is not observed the result is 'short grain': the grain crosses the part instead of following along it, (Fig. 1.46). This is a weak point because the timber's natural strength is lost. When stressed a split is likely, resulting in failure.

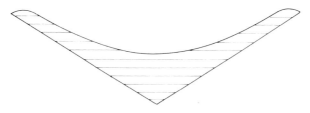

Fig 1.46 Short grain: even with the grain aligned diagonally the ends of this knee's arms would be weak as the grain crosses the curve instead of following it.

As nearly every constituent part of a hull is curved it is important for boatbuilders to be able to obtain timber with grain sweeping to the desired shape for every situation. Several techniques can be used to achieve this.

Using Straight Grained Timber

In some situations it is possible to glue together solid pieces of straight grained timber with satisfactory results. This is commonly the way knees are made for dinghies. Two pieces are joined at approximately the required angle with a simple half-lapped joint. From this the knee is then cut, as shown in Plate 1.41. Finishing the inside curve with a spokeshave is difficult as half the grain is orientated in each direction and plucking is inevitable. Heavy sanding is the easiest solution.

A similar technique is sometimes used on larger craft. Floors can be made from three pieces of solid straight grained timber: a plank on edge across the keel with arms or 'wings' glued and bolted to it

Plate 1.41 The stem knee for a dinghy made from two pieces of straight grained timber joined by a simple lap joint.

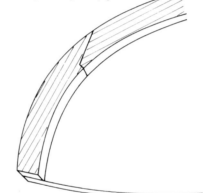

Fig 1.47 A correctly aligned scarf joint in transom fashion pieces.

on each side. The other common situation is the fashion pieces edging the transom. Their primary purpose is to provide solid timber to hold the plank fastenings and they can quite happily be made from several pieces of straight timber lapped or scarfed. Whatever joint is used it should be orientated as illustrated in Fig. 1.47 so that the plank fastenings will enter both pieces, pulling them together, not trying to enter the crack between the two parts, and separate them.

Using Plywood

Although it has drawbacks, plywood is undoubtedly the easiest way to obtain curved members from straight grain. The different angles of its laminations ensure strength in all directions, and most shapes

104

can be cut from it in safety. On dinghies, knees are commonly made from plywood where, for appearance sake, the grain of the face veneers is orientated diagonally across the knee. If a substantial knee is to be made from plywood it would be better to glue two ⅜ in (9 mm) layers together rather than using one ¾ in (19 mm) sheet. The face veneers of the two sheets could then be orientated to each other at the same angle required by the knee ensuring strength in exactly the directions required.

The problem with using plywood for knees is its inevitable end grain. On the inside curve it is unsightly and needs sealing to prevent water getting in and causing delamination. On the sides butting against the hull plywood is difficult to fasten into. This second problem is overcome if the knee is glued in position, being held by clamps while the glue sets. A better solution is to use through fastenings as follows: a thin piece of solid hardwood is bent and glued onto the inside curve, as shown in Fig. 1.48; this seals the grain on that edge, looks good if varnished, and also acts as a support for the roves of clenched copper nails. These will hold the knee more securely than screws.

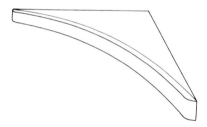

Fig 1.48　A plywood knee with hardwood laminate bent to the inside curve.

The other disadvantage of plywood is that in this situation it is inefficient. While half the laminations may be orientated correctly, the other half are not. Compared to an identically shaped knee made from solid curved grained timber, plywood would be weaker, a large percentage of its weight being short grained.

In practice this is not in fact the case, as a plywood knee should be designed differently from its solid wood counterpart. A plywood knee is usually a 'web', having a much smaller siding than an equivalent solid timber one, but a greatly increased moulded depth. In this way the weight to strength ratios of both types are similar, although their properties are different. A web has little give, while the solid type is comparatively flexible. The solid knee is also more neatly tucked away, but the web is easier and quicker to make.

Plywood, if used correctly, can replace many parts of a boat that traditionally would require curved grain. Some modern designs, even of medium sized yachts, use plywood for all the frames, either as bulkheads or very wide webs.

Naturally Curved Grain

Timber in which the grain follows a natural curve is found in two situations: crooks, and logs with 'hang'. Crooks are the very sharp curves found at the fork of a tree where branches separate, and are also obtained from its base where the roots spread. Trees that have grown crookedly can produce logs with a much gentler sweeping curve, most useful to the boatbuilder for planking stock and, when well shaped, deck beams. Unfortunately most other timber users only want straight stock, so the timber yards tend to reject curved logs, or saw them in a way that minimises the shape. Timber yards that specialise in supplying boatbuilders are worth searching out. They may be more expensive, but they keep the interesting logs and convert them to best advantage.

This consideration also applies to crooks which most yards split for firewood. The specialist retains them, cutting them through and

Plate 1.42
Larch planks with slight hang, useful to the boatbuilder.

Plate 1.43
An oak crook.

through in useful thicknesses, so that the boatbuilder can match his floor and knee patterns to see if the grain fits. A large stock of crooks are necessary to meet the knee requirements of a single boat. Plates 1.42 and 1.43 show larch planks sawn to take advantage of the natural hang, and an oak crook.

The shapes required for grown frames are more difficult to find as they are gentler than those found in crooks, but too tight to be cut from logs. The usual practice is to make the frames up in sections, each from timber that is roughly the shape required. These sections, called futtocks can be scarfed or joined with straps as shown in Fig. 1.49.

Another method to obtain useful timber for grown frames was devised several centuries ago: oaks were planted, interspersed with birches. The birches were pollarded every twelve years, forcing the oaks to grow above them before spreading their branches, producing the great sweeping curves needed for frames in the ships of that time.

107

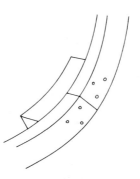

Fig 1.49   Grown frames: the futtocks can be butted and joined with a strap, which has the same section as the frame and is at least six times its moulding in length.

Unfortunately by the time the oaks had reached maturity, the ship builders had discovered steel.

Springing

Timber's natural elasticity makes it possible sometimes to bend wood into the shapes required. The techniques of laminating and steaming that allow much tighter curves than could normally be achieved are described next, but in many cases bending within the natural limits of the wood is sufficient. This is called springing and is used for most of the longitudinals: gunwales, stringers, main carlings, and shaped keels. Whenever timber is to be bent it is cut from straight grained stock, to avoid short grain which would fracture as the wood was stressed.

Springing is only really successful if the timber is bent in one direction, it being much more difficult if it has to be bent one way and 'edge-set' the other simultaneously. For this reason keels are straightforward, and stringers too, as their precise position is not critical: they can be allowed to rise toward the sheer at the ends of the boat to avoid edge setting. Gunwales are not so easy because they have to follow the sheer. In many cases springing is not possible, and they have to be steamed. To avoid this some builders make a horizontal sawcut down the gunwale for a short length from the bow if this is the area where edge set is most necessary. This can only be done on a decked boat as it may spoil the appearance of an open one.

The other method to obtain timber shaped in both directions, is to cut it from a log with hang in one, and spring it in the other. This is of course the process used in carvel or clinker planking.

108

Laminating

When tight curves are needed and timber cannot be found with suitably curving grain it can be manufactured. Straight grained timber is sawn into thin and flexible layers which can be bent and then glued together to produce solid crooks. Laminating produces excellent results, but is expensive. A lot of work, glue, and wastage occurs when converting solid timber. If the laminates are of a thickness equal to the saw cut it is after all fifty percent. Despite this it is often a sensible solution to the problem; a lot of time can be spent searching for crooks, and if the search does not prove fruitless, wastage is still high when cutting out the parts.

Laminated timber is used in many situations and is especially useful where curves are tight or complicated. Examples of its use are floors, knees, frames, stems (sometimes integrally laminated with the keel,) deck beams, and fancy shaped tillers.

Occasionally members can be laminated directly into the hull, but this is difficult especially where any bevels are involved, and is also very messy. Normally laminating is done on a jig, and the very rough and glue-encrusted results cleaned up and shaped when fitting. Sometimes the jig is the exact shape required, and the laminated timber only needs cleaning and bevelling. In other cases the jig is merely a rough approximation of the required shape and is intended only to produce the raw material, timber with curved grain, from which to cut the part. Floors and knees come into this second category, while stems and frames are normally laminated very accurately.

The thickest laminates possible should be used as this minimises wastage. Testing suitable thicknesses can be done by bending a single laminate around the jig. If it just bends without breaking it is suitable, as the whole bundle, lubricated with glue, will bend to a tighter curve than each laminate would individually.

When laminated timber is removed from the jig it has a tendency to spring open slightly as the timber tries to return to its original shape. This is more marked when it is made from very few laminates. A deck beam comprising only three layers will spring considerably, while a tight floor that needs twenty will not open at all. The jig should allow for spring and be made in a tighter curve than that required. How much allowance is necessary can only be found by trial and error. Excessive spring can be reduced by laminating the part from more and thinner laminates, or it can be trimmed to shape after removal.

Glues with gap filling qualities are required for laminating, resorcinol or epoxy resin being the ones most commonly used. Glues and gluing procedures are discussed in detail elsewhere in this book, but of particular relevance to laminating is the necessity to maintain clamping pressure for longer than would normally be required. Even after being unclamped the glue should be allowed to continue curing for several days before it is strained by being machined or tested.

The gluing is itself a slow process, painting both faces of the many laminates, and then getting all the clamps or bolts firmly tightened down. While the clamped item is curing there is also a delay of at least twenty-four hours (unless very warm temperatures can be sustained) before the jig can be used again. For this reason it is preferable if several pieces can be laminated on the jig at once. This can be achieved in two ways: either by laminating two on top of each other, piggy back, with paper or polythene sheet between to allow separation; or by using a correctly curved but overwide jig on which wide laminations can be glued; after curing these are sawn lengthwise into two or more pieces of the correct dimension. This is a better method as identical pieces are obtained whereas when one is laminated on top of another the two are curved to slightly different radii.

Before clamping the wet laminates to the jig, measures must be taken to ensure the jig is released when the glue has set. A sheet of waxed paper or polythene covering the jig is one way, but a better method is to wipe the jig with soft wax. Release is certain and spills of excess glue can easily be scraped off the jig. Generous application of wax is necessary on a new jig but on subsequent occasions a quick wipe with a waxed cloth is sufficient.

Designs of laminating jigs are varied, but in every case they must be strong as the forces involved are often surprisingly high. Examples for three specific items are described to suggest possible methods.

Deck Beams

A jig for deck beams can be made by screwing slats to two formers shaped from the beam crop pattern. A simple jig of this kind is illustrated in Plate 1.44. It could be improved by including a series of bolts on either side with another set of slats between them to clamp the laminates to the jig. Deck beam jigs can be much more sophisticated, boatyards often having a variable jig which can be set to the camber required for any boat.

Beams do tend to spring when removed from the jig, and this has to be allowed for when shaping the jig. Alternatively the true shape

Plate 1.44
A simple jig for laminating deck beams.

required is marked and planed from the laminated beams after they have sprung. If the shape is planed from the top of the beams, leaving the lower side following the sprung curve, the beams will taper towards their ends, a shape specified in some designs.

Knees

Although all the pairs of knees and floors throughout a boat are different, it is not necessary to make a jig for each. By carefully assessing the required angle for every one, and working out mean shapes, two or three jigs may be made to suffice. Once the curve has been established it can be cut from softwood and fastened to a sheet of ply. A jig of this nature is illustrated in Fig. 1.50, with the addition of hardwood backing pieces for clamping pads. These are necessary if many crooks are to be made from one jig. If the softwood shape is made from two or more pieces the pressures involved when clamping can tend to pull them apart. Lapping the hardwood pieces as shown ensures that the clamping pressure actually holds the jig together. Alternatively a brace could be fastened between the two arms.

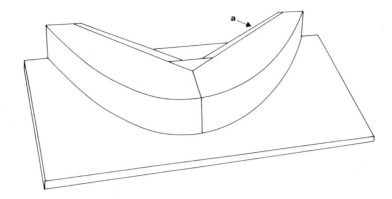

Fig 1.50   A jig for laminating floors and knees: shaped softwood is fastened to a plywood base. The hardwood backing pads (a) are lapped so that clamping pressure tends to tie the jig together.

Plate 1.45 Clamping a laminated knee.

The members laminated on these jigs (Plate 1.45) only make the arms or wings of the knee. Except for the shallowest of curves, a solid piece of timber has to be added to form the throat as can be clearly seen in Plate 1.6. The grain of this piece is normally aligned tangentially to the laminated curve, but if the angle is very acute, such as on the breasthook, it may be better to align it radially so that fastenings are not entering end grain.

112

Frames

A jig for laminating frames can be constructed in a similar fashion to that for knees: softwood moulds fastened to a plywood backing piece. The difference is that crooks only roughly follow the shape required, the precise shape being spiled and cut from the laminated material. Frames in contrast are laminated as accurately as possible to the shape lifted from the loft floor. For this reason the formers for a frame jig are not on the inside of the curve, as with knees, but on the outside, where the accuracy is needed. This type of jig is shown in Plate 1.46. Bevels have to be cut from the frames after they have been laminated, so it is much simpler if the bevels are acute i.e. inside the lofted lines. If the bevels are obtuse (in addition to the lofted line) a bevel allowance has to be added when making the jig.

Frames for chined hulls cannot be laminated to follow tightly into the corners of the chines, so solid pieces are inserted at these points, (Plate 1.47). This is done by making the jig to the chined shape required by the planks, corner pieces are then made up, their inside face cut with a gentle curve on a band or jig-saw, and positioned in the jig.

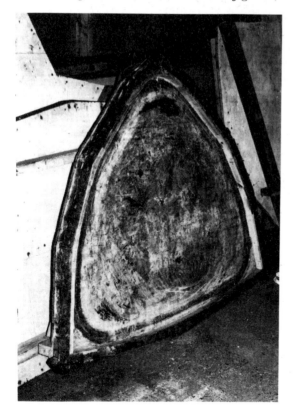

Plate 1.46
A laminating jig for *Naja's* 'ring' frames, on which the deck beams are made as an integral part.

113

Plate 1.47
Several of the ring frames showing how solid timber is incorporated into corners that are too tight to laminate.

When laminating is begun, glue is painted on the inside face of these pieces so that the laminates follow their curve and are glued and clamped to them.

Steam Bending

This is the traditional method for obtaining timber with the grain curving to the exact shape desired. Although it takes some organisation to set up, once that preparation is done it is far simpler, quicker, and cheaper than laminating, as no expensive glue is required, and wastage when preparing the timber is much reduced.

Steam bending is an adaptable and efficient method to achieve many shapes, including their bevels. On a strip or ply planked hull, with a few well spaced frames, laminating is practicable, but it would be a hard way to obtain the different curves and bevels found in each individual steam bent timber of a traditionally built hull as seen in Plate 1.48.

The Theory
To obtain these curves in the relatively substantial timber needed

114

Plate 1.48 Steam bent timbers, each with its own individual shape and bevel. *(Tirrick)*

for hull framing, advantage is taken of the fact that hot timber can be easily bent to shapes it would never accept cold, and that on cooling it retains its new shape.

115

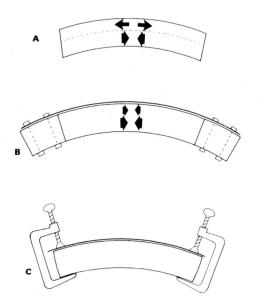

Fig 1.51   Steam bending theory:
(A), with unsupported bending the inside part of the timber is compressed while the outside part is stretched.
(B), far tighter curves can be achieved if the entire timber is bent in compression by using a flexible strap with end blocks attached.
(C), often end blocks are impractical, but an advantage can still be gained by simply clamping a strap to the timber to support the outside face.

Heating timber greatly increases its compressive qualities, but only slightly improves its ability to stretch. Figure 1.51 shows that when bending, the face inside the curve is compressed, while the outside face is stretched; the amount that the timber can be bent is dependent on how much the outside face can stretch without fracturing. If the timber can be bent with its whole thickness in compression, and none under tension, the bending limits at which failure occurs are greatly extended. Compression bending is achieved by wedging the timber tightly between blocks fastened to a flexible metal strap which supports the outside face during bending. The metal does not stretch and the full thickness of timber is compressed. On many occasions, as when the timber is let into a housing at one end, or the curve reverses itself into an S shape, a strap blocked at each end is not possible, but it may still be feasible to clamp the strap to the timber for part of its length. Although this is not so efficient an advantage is still gained and tighter curves can be achieved than would be possible with unsupported bending.

Selecting Timber

How small a bending radius can be achieved varies with different timber species, and with some a supporting strap makes little difference. (See Table 2, at the end of the section on Timber.)

The principal timbers traditionally used in Britain have been oak, elm, and ash, whose performance, particularly under full compression bending (a strap with end blocks) is quite remarkable. Elm, although classed as non-durable can be used in decked boats instead of oak. Ash, which is classed as perishable, is really only suitable for canoes where lightness is important and plenty of ventilation is guaranteed. Oak is most commonly chosen for steam bent timbers.

Timber that is to be used for steam bending should be fresh sawn (green and not seasoned) because the steaming process does actually dry out the timber. For this reason it can be soaked in water for several days prior to steaming. Timber should be carefully selected, have straight grain and be free of any faults. Failures that do occur usually start at an unnoticed pin knot or short grain. Ideally the timbers should be prepared so that, when fitted, the alignment of the annual growth rings is parallel to the hull planking as in Fig. 1.52. The wood will bend equally well if not correctly aligned but subsequently there is greater loosening of the fastenings should the timber be liable to repeated wetting and drying. This is because timber aligned incorrectly swells more in the direction of the fastenings and so compresses the wood beneath the nail heads and roves further, leaving the fastenings fractionally looser after drying out.

Steam Machines

The combination of crude plumbing, makeshift boilers, and seeping steam ensures that every steam machine appears to have been designed by Mr Heath Robinson personally. A heat source, a boiler, and a steam box connected to it are all that are needed.

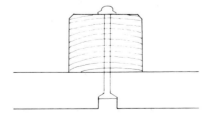

Fig 1.52 A timber with annual growth rings correctly aligned.

Plate 1.49   A steam machine, comprising an oil drum boiler, connected to a timber steam box.

In its simplest form the boiler and steambox are combined in a single length of drain pipe, but normally a small oil drum is the boiler and a wooden box the steam chest, (Plate 1.49.) Because oak stains when in contact with iron the steambox should be constructed without any ferrous fastenings. The steam is piped into it at one end and a roughly fitting lid closes the other to prevent the escape of too much steam. It must be long enough for the timbers, but need not have a large cross-section as only a few are in it at any one time.

Heat can be provided by gas burners or an open fire. Gas burners have the advantage that they can be used inside the workshop, and therefore the whole apparatus sited near to the hull. This saves wasting precious time running the hot timbers from the steambox to the boat. The gas burners should be large though, as vigorous boiling is required to keep a strong and continuous supply of steam. If a second tank is linked to the boiler a constant level of boiling water can be maintained without the danger of boiling dry or taking it off the boil when cold water is added in quantity. Commercial yards do sometimes use pressure steam generators such as those used by garages for cleaning and dewaxing.

When only a very localised area has to be bent by heating, simpler methods sometimes suffice. An electric kettle may be all that is needed, simply pointing the steam from its spout at the required point while clamping pressure is applied, or else pouring the boiling water over the part to be bent, after covering it with a cloth to retain some of the hot water at that place.

Steaming is not the only way to heat timber. Boiling is also possible, but it must be vigorous or the wood is heated too slowly: it 'cooks' and when cooled, is brittle.

Actually heating the timber directly by the flames is also possible; the charring can either be cleaned off afterwards or avoided by continually painting with linseed oil while the timber is heating. This is a rather drastic method but may be contemplated for bending a single piece without setting up the whole steam-generating apparatus.

Timbering Out

The traditional and most common use for steaming is to bend straight grained oak timbers into the shape required by the hull: timbering out.

Depending on the construction method, timbers are steamed to shape either before or after planking. Cases where they follow the planking are on a clinker or lapstrake hull and on strip planked hulls when additional timbers are bent between the laminated frames. They could also strengthen a completed cold moulded shell. Timbering precedes planking on a carvel hull, where they are bent to the sieve-like false hull formed by ribbands sprung around moulds. This is usually done inside the ribbands, but if the hull is being built upside down they are bent around the outside of them.

In order to avoid having to repeatedly get up steam all the timbers are normally bent in a single day, or with a larger hull in two sessions, returning on the second to replace broken ones and fill in gaps left once the moulds are removed.

For a successful operation good preparation and organisation of the team are essential, because speed is important. When each timber is removed from the steam box it is only pliable for two or three minutes at the most, in which time the job must be finished. The timbers should be lined up in the order to be used and labelled at their ends so that they can be easily identified in the steam box. If their heels are to enter housings cut in the hog or keel they must be cut to the correct shape to fit these. When timbers are to be bent into a planked hull their positions are marked, fastening holes pre-drilled and the copper nails inserted ready to be driven through the hot timber; the hull has then the appearance of a hedgehog or pin cushion (Plate 1.50). If they are being bent against ribbands plenty of clamps need to be positioned ready to hand.

Plate 1.50
On a clinker hull copper nails are inserted into pre-drilled holes on the entire hull before timbering out commences.

On any hull bigger than a dinghy four people make a good team, two inside the boat and two out. One tends the steam box, keeping the water boiling and logging the times each timber is placed in the box. How long they should be steamed is best discovered by trial; one is taken out at intervals until it is found to be ready, when it is noticeably more pliable, like stiff new rope rather than wood. For light stuff this may be after less then twenty minutes, while very heavy timbers may need up to two hours.

Once it is found to be ready it is passed quickly to the two in the boat; they first dip its heel in a pot of white lead putty then thrust it into the housing in the keel and gently but firmly bend it to the shape of the boat, carefully keeping to the line marked for it. It can be clamped at the sheer with a loose fitting pad which holds it in the correct fore and aft position while allowing it to slide down freely. Its head can even be hit with a mallet to force it into the turn of the bilge below. Timbers bent to a ribband hull are simply clamped to these until cool, but on a planked hull, as soon as the timber is in position, the copper nails are driven from the outside through the hot timber while a dolly, held firmly against it inside, ensures it is pulled firmly against the hull. If a nail bends or pierces the timber at an unacceptable angle it is left while the others are driven home, it being important to drive all the nails while the timber is hot. Mistakes are remedied later; the nail is pulled, the correct angle drilled through the now cold wood, and a new nail inserted.

In some cases it works slightly differently; on many boats the timbers do not enter the hog but reach right around the hull from sheer to sheer, as can be seen in Plate 1.51. The process is the same, but two teams can then be kept busy, each driving the nails in one timber on each side of the hull. If the timbers are breaking because the curves are too tight a backing strip is used. An old band-saw blade is quite adequate, for although it stains the timber it is only on the back, out of sight. This is clamped in position as soon as the timber is removed from the box, then slid out from behind it once the timber has been bent into shape, before fastening commences. The possibility of tighter curves more than makes up for the time lost.

Plate 1.51 Timbering out the RNLI Boarding boat: a hot timber is passed into the boat and gently but firmly pressed into place.

Plate 1.52
A dolly is held against
the timber inside . . .

Plate 1.53
while the nails are driven
from the outside.

Plate 1.54
Twisting the timber when positioning helps it to accommodate the greater bevels found at the ends of a boat.

Even tighter curves can be achieved by ripping the timber for most of its length before steaming. It is then effectively two pieces of wood each with half the moulding, which are held together, once bent to shape, by the through fastenings. This technique is often necessary at the stern to achieve the tight curves in the tuck.

The greater bevels encountered at the bow and stern are also difficult. The trick is to twist the timber, either by hand (Plate 1.54) or with the additional leverage afforded by a clamp, when positioning. It also helps to bend the timber in a fore and aft direction, pulling the head toward the end of the boat. This can be done once fastening has started, feeding the timber into position sideways, or it can be firmly bent by hand in the desired direction before being positioned at all.

There is a nice sense of achievement when timbering out is complete – marred only by the hundreds of gleaming nail points waiting for roves and clenching. If timbering out is a hard day's work, but very gratifying, clenching those nails is a hard week's work, and very boring.

Other Uses

Most members that require curved grain could be made by steam bending timber to a jig. Stems can be shaped in this way, as can curved cockpit coamings. A more unusual example is that of covering boards: Nathanael Herreshoff apparently bent oak to the shape required, then ripped it down the middle to get a matching pair.

Once the steam machine is set up, steam bending is a very neat way to solve many problems. The jigs described for laminating knees could be equally well used to steam bend the wood. All the knees for a boat could be bent in this way in a morning, instead of spending an hour laminating each, then waiting a day to re-use the jig.

11. Horning and Levelling

Obtaining square angles and level or plumb faces on a small scale is straightforward. The ordinary tools used, combination square and spirit-level, produce accurate results. If large members have to be levelled or squared accurately, different techniques are used. Simply extending the lines obtained, even by the largest tools, does not produce satisfactory results.

The Horning Rod

The technique used for ensuring angles are square is to compare the hypotenuse of two triangles: in the case of a rectangle, the diagonals.

These lengths are checked with a horning rod; a light stiff spline of wood with one end pointed. When gluing rectangular boxes, such as drawers, the point of the rod is pushed into one corner and held diagonally across the box and a tick marked on it where it crosses the opposite corner as shown in Fig. 1.53. The other diagonal is then measured in the same way. If the ticks do not coincide the rectangle is not true. Adjustments are made until the two diagonals are equal in length.

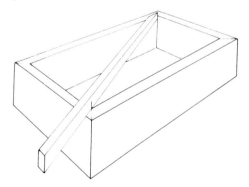

Fig 1.53   Using a horning rod to compare the length of diagonals. If they are equal the corners must be square.

125

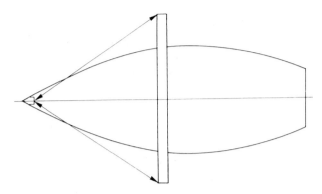

Fig 1.54   Marking square across the boat is necessary to position moulds, bulkheads, or deck beams: a straight edge is placed with its midpoint on the centre line, and is then horned by ensuring its ends are the same distance from the stem's centre line.

In a modified form this technique is used to ensure that members are square across the boat: moulds, bulkheads and deck beams are all positioned in this way.

A straight edge is needed (longer than the boat's beam) with its centre point accurately marked. This is positioned across the boat with its centre exactly on the boat's centre line. This can be achieved by either plumbing it to the original centre line on the keel, or by stretching a line from the stem to the transom.

The straight edge is then squared across the boat by comparing the distance its outside ends are from the centre of the stem, or any other point on the centre line (Fig. 1.54). This is again best done with a rod, although an extending metal rule could be used. Measuring the distance with a piece of string is unsatisfactory as this has to be pulled taut, and it may not stretch uniformly on each side.

It is important to horn to the ends of the straight edge, and not simply to the point it crosses the sheer. Although its midpoint is on the centre line, each side of the boat may not be identical. If the straight edge is horned to its ends, and then the position it crosses the shear marked on each side, the marks will be square across the boat even if there is a slight lack of symmetry in the hull.

Levelling the Hull

When a hull is moved after construction it must be set up level before fitting out. This means ensuring that the water line is on a level plane in order that surfaces positioned inside the hull will be either level or drain as they are supposed to when the completed boat is afloat. An older boat hauled out will have a clear water line to level, but a new moulding or just completed hull may not. They should at least have the position of the water line marked in some way at the stem and stern post, and these two marks are enough.

Levelling athwartship on a medium sized boat can be done with a straight edge and spirit-level set across internally. If the original water lines marked on the frames are visible, these should be used, but if no marks remain, simply levelling square across from sheer to sheer has to do.

Levelling fore and aft is done with a water level. This is a tool found on every construction site, and is simply made from an old piece of hose pipe. As illustrated in Fig. 1.55 it should have a section of transparent tube or glass at each end. After filling with water the pipe is held with one end at the bow of the boat, and the other at the stern. The water in the transparent tube at each end is naturally level. If it is arranged that the water is at the water line level at the bow, the boat's stern can be jacked up or down until it is also correct. For a water level to work well there must be no air trapped in the pipe. This is ensured when filling by coiling it slowly down into a bucket of water. Stoppering, or at least holding a thumb over each end retains the water while the pipe is set up in approximate positions. If when the stoppers are first removed the ends are not roughly level, much of the water is lost and the process has to be repeated.

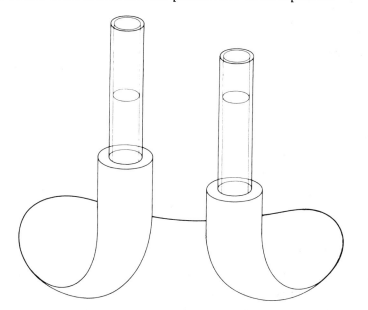

Fig 1.55 A water level is simply a length of garden hose with a piece of transparent tube inserted in each end: the visible level of water in these will always be the same.

Declevity Sticks

Although it is preferable to level a hull before fitting out, it is not absolutely necessary. It used to be common practice to build a hull with the keel level, even though it was designed to float with its heel trailing deeper than its forefoot. By using a declevity stick it could be fitted out without moving it. Similarly a hull in a cradle on a sloping railway can have work done without elaborate wedging.

The amount the boat is out of trim (how much it is down at bows or stern) must be known or measured by using the water level previously described. This angle is then marked and cut from a piece of ply, which is then called a declevity stick. Every time the spirit level is used fore and aft inside the hull, it is used in conjunction with the declevity stick, pointing in the right direction, ensuring that surfaces will be level once the hull is afloat, (Fig. 1.56).

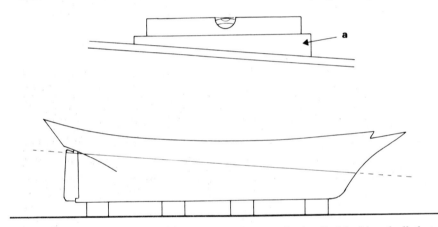

Fig 1.56   A declevity stick (a) enables surfaces to be levelled inside a hull that is not trimmed as it will float.

Declevity sticks are also used in a correctly trimmed hull to position parts that are not supposed to be level or plumb. Cabin sides may be required to lean inward; the angle can be taken from the plans, and a declevity stick made and used as an aid when positioning them. In this case, in practice, the declevity stick is used when positioning the carlings, as these are sloped at the correct angle and then the cabin sides, or coamings, fastened directly to them.

Scribing the Water Line

Marking the water line onto a hull is a straightforward process. The hull must be level athwartships, but need not be fore and aft.

128

Plate 1.55 Scribing the water line: a straight edge clamped at bow and stern with string stretched between them provides a guide. *(Tirrick)*

Plate 1.56 A flared boot top is marked by gradually moving the string up a wedge placed on top of the straight edge.

The water line position must be known at the stem and stern and at these points straight edges are fastened. They must be wider than the boat's maximum water line beam, and after levelling with a spirit-level are clamped firmly to temporary supports as illustrated in Plate 1.55.

129

A line is then stretched between the straight edges and slid along them until it just touches the boat amidships. With the line made fast at one end, two people proceed to mark the water line. One marks where the string just touches the hull, then holds the string at this position while his helper slides the free end of the line along the straight edge a few inches. This brings it again into contact with the hull. This point is marked, and again the string held and its end slid still closer to the centre line. In this way a series of marks are made that indicate the water line on one side of the hull from amidships to one end. Every time the string touches the hull it has to be held or taped at that point to prevent it rolling down toward the bilge. The same process is repeated from amidships to the other end, and then again on the opposite side of the hull. A batten is finally used to join all the marks to produce a clean water line. It is normal to scribe or scratch the water line onto a wooden hull in order to mark it permanently in a way that cannot be lost under future coats of paint.

If a boot top is required (a thin band painted a different colour at the water line) this can be marked in the same way. A parallel boot top is marked by placing a strip of wood the required width on top of each straight edge, then marking again. A flared boot top, which rises at the bow and stern looks fancier and can be marked just as easily: a wedge-shaped piece of ply is fixed on top of the straight edge along which the string is being slid in each case, which brings the line gradually higher as the ends are approached, as shown in Plate 1.56.

Part 2
Materials

1. Timber

The hundreds of species of timber that grow around the world have between them a wide variety of properties. Apart from their appearances, most of which are attractive and some extremely decorative; they differ in strength, density, and durability, as well as many other ways. The range of characteristics available means that between them they provide materials suitable for many purposes and environments.

In practice any woodworker is limited in the choice of timbers to those readily available in his area, whether they are grown locally or imported in bulk, perhaps from the other side of the world. Each species has its own particular characteristics; its behaviour as it dries, suitability for different environments, likelihood of splitting, and ease of gluing or painting. These characteristics can vary enormously, even within one species, the growing tree having been affected by environmental variables such as rainfall, soil richness, proximity of other trees and so on. With so many possible variables, when it actually comes to selecting timber a book has limited value compared to locally learnt experience. If a boatbuilder has little experience of his own he should try to borrow someone else's! This should be borne in mind when referring to Tables 2A and 2B at the end of this section which list the accepted boatbuilding timbers from around the world, and provide details of their properties and traditional usage. Some of these timbers are almost universally available; others are limited in their supply.

Timbers are generally divided into hardwoods and softwoods: hardwoods come from the broad-leaved, (and generally slower growing) trees found in a wide variety of climates; softwoods come from the needle-leaved coniferous trees which grow most extensively (and rapidly) in the temperate regions. Although hardwoods do tend to be harder, heavier, and darker in colour than softwoods, in individual cases the terms can be misleading. An extreme example is balsa, a 'hardwood' that is lighter and whiter than most softwoods, while conversely the 'softwood' yew, is fairly heavy and hard.

133

In the past the most important property required of a boat-building timber was durability, as the conditions aboard a boat often encourage fungal decay. In a few situations other considerations outweighed durability; for example the perishable timber spruce is used for spars because of its great strength and lightness. Today modern preservatives can considerably enhance a timber's natural resistance to decay, or alternatively, by effectively sealing all timber members (as is done with WEST System constructions) the conditions necessary for decay can be eliminated. These methods allow timber that would otherwise be considered quite unsuitable to be used for boatbuilding. As good quality timber becomes scarcer, and inevitably more expensive, boatbuilders will undoubtedly turn more and more to the quicker growing and more perishable species of timber, relying on modern technology to provide that which nature does not. Where possible the use of naturally durable species must be preferable though, as neither epoxy finishes nor chemical preservatives (if applied by brush or spray), penetrate deeply, so that the timber is again susceptible to fungal attack once it has been damaged.

A sensible boatbuilder also notes the traditional species used in different situations as their selection has often been based on generations of experience. Obvious examples are the use of oak for steam bending, and teak for deck planking where its natural oiliness makes paint or varnish unnecessary, the untreated wood providing an excellent non-slip surface which is kept smart by regular scrubbing. On the other hand the modern use of teak for interior trim is apparently based entirely on its prestige value. Many other timbers are equally attractive, and in the less harsh conditions below its qualities of durability are wasted and its oiliness makes it difficult to maintain except with specially formulated varnishes.

Log Conversion

A log can be cut in several ways to reduce it from a round butt to useful boards. Fig. 2.1 illustrates several cutting patterns that are used, the chief concern of the sawmill operator being to minimise wastage and cutting time. The more often the log has to be turned during cutting the slower the process, so variations of the plain sawn pattern are favoured by the mill operators. As faults are often found in a log near to the heart, systems that box the heart often produce timber of a better grade, and therefore of more value to the timber yard.

134

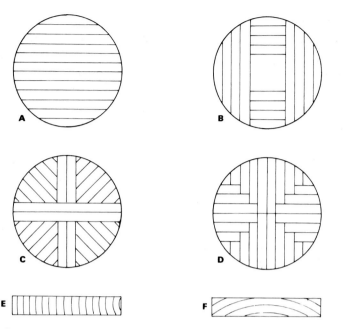

Fig 2.1   Some sawing patterns for converting logs to boards: (A), plain sawn through and through or slab sawn; (B), plain sawn, boxing the heart; (C), quarter sawn, (D), another pattern of quarter sawing that produces square edged stock, but is slower because more turning is required; (E) quarter sawn boards have radial grain; (F) plain sawn boards have tangential grain.

Unfortunately plain sawn timber produces boards that have tangential grain although boards with radial grain (see Fig. 2.1) are actually superior as there is less likely to be distortion of the wood during drying, as is explained when dealing with seasoning. Boards with radial grain are obtained by various patterns of quarter sawing, but as can be seen, these are slow and wasteful methods of conversion, and so are more expensive.

Timber that is plain sawn through and through (sometimes called slab sawn or flitch sawn) produces some boards of both radial grain and tangential grain. Planking timber is usually converted in this way as any natural shape or hang in the log can be taken advantage of, and maintained in every plank. Sawing through and through is straightforward for the timber mill, and can produce adequate boards for most boatbuilding requirements even where grain alignment is important. To illustrate this, deck planking can be taken as an example.

Deck planking, particularly if made of softwood such as larch or pitch pine, should always have radial grain as this is less likely to leak due to shrinkage in warm weather, and also looks and wears better. To obtain deck planking 2 in x ¾ in (50 mm x 19 mm) from through and through sawn timber the mill should be instructed to saw the log in 2⅛ in (53 mm) boards with perhaps four boards of ⅞ in (21 mm) through the heart; the extra ⅛ in (3 mm) being for thicknessing. The thick boards can then be ripped by the boatbuilder into ¾ in (19 mm) planks, and the thin boards into 2 in (50 mm) planks, so that all will end up of the required dimension, and appear quarter sawn when laid, as shown in Fig. 2.2.

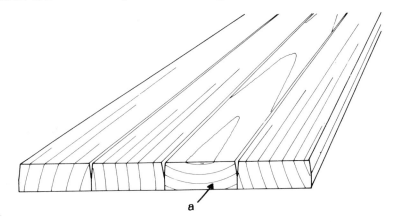
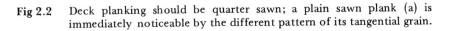

a

Fig 2.2   Deck planking should be quarter sawn; a plain sawn plank (a) is immediately noticeable by the different pattern of its tangential grain.

Seasoning

When a tree is felled over half the weight of the trunk is water. Often before the trunk can be moved, and certainly before it is usable timber, most of this moisture must be lost in a drying process that is called seasoning. Seasoning is a slow process but obviously the smaller the pieces of wood, the quicker the moisture can evaporate. As a rough guide it is reckoned that a year should be allowed for every inch of thickness (25 mm), although softwood does dry more quickly.

The moisture is contained in the timber in two ways: 'free' moisture which is in the open pores; and 'bound' moisture which is actually in the cell walls. The free moisture is lost first, and when it is gone and only the bound moisture remains the timber is said to be at fibre saturation point. At this stage the moisture content is about thirty percent, and it is after this, as the cell walls start to dry out, that the timber begins to shrink.

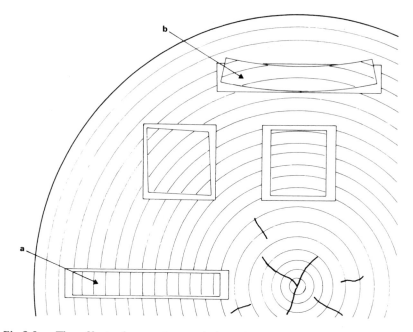

Fig 2.3   The effect of seasoning on timber: shrinkage is greatest parallel to the grain so the quarter sawn plank (a) shrinks and distorts less than the plain sawn one (b).

Timber does not shrink uniformly; shrinkage is greatest parallel to the annual growth rings, about twice as much as radially to them. In the direction of the grain (longitudinally) it is very slight, only perhaps $\frac{1}{12}$ of the radial or $\frac{1}{24}$ of the tangential effect. Unequal shrinking rates cause distortion to timber and the likely effect on different cross-sections is shown in Fig. 2.3. Of particular interest is the effect on plain sawn and quarter sawn boards with tangential and radial grain respectively. As can be seen the plain sawn board not only contracts more, but is more likely to cup. This greater distortion of plain sawn boards is one reason that quarter sawn timber is considered superior. Even so, understanding the likely distortion of plain sawn timber allows it to be used sensibly, as is also demonstrated in Fig. 2.2: the plain sawn plank will cup down to the beam, not lift along its edges.

Boards that become twisted or bowed during drying can be difficult to use, but these defects can be avoided by correctly storing the timber while it seasons. Drying timber is said to be 'in stick', because the piled boards are separated from each other by sticks about ¾ in (19 mm) thick, to allow air to pass freely between them. These sticks should be positioned every 18 in (450 mm) to prevent sagging,

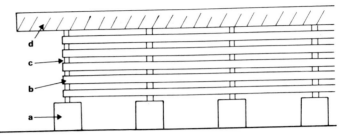

Fig 2.4   Drying timber 'in stick': (a) sleepers lift timber off the ground and provide a levelled base; (b) timber boards drying; (c) sticks separating boards to allow flow of air across each are carefully aligned one above the other; (d) overhanging cover keeps off the rain.

and should be carefully aligned one above the other so that the weight of the top board is transferred directly down the pile without distorting the lower ones. The bottom plank should be supported on sleepers laid on a solid level base. A pile of timber stored in this way is shown in Fig. 2.4. In this case in the open air. A storage shed should have a good roof, but slatted, or even open sides. This allows the air to circulate freely but keeps the rain off the timber, allowing steady drying. Boards dry fastest through the end grain, which can be the cause of splits and shakes at the ends of planks. Nailing slats across the ends of planks is a poor solution as the nails can actually start splits; as the timber dries it shrinks but the slats maintain their length, so forcing open checks. Painting the plank ends with primer or a bituminous paint slows the moisture movement through the end grain and reduces the likelihood of checks starting there.

Timber air-dried in Britain will have a moisture content (in summer) of fifteen to eighteen percent. This is adequate for traditional boatbuilding, but needs to be lowered still further when using some modern glues. If the timber is brought into a warm workshop after air drying, it will continue to lose further moisture. Alternatively kiln-dried timber can be obtained that has very low moisture contents. Kiln drying is a method of seasoning timber in a controlled environment at an accelerated rate: drying that would normally take months or even years is achieved in a matter of weeks. Although the timber can be severely damaged if insufficient care is taken, experienced timber yards can kiln-dry timber very successfully, and much imported timber is seasoned in this way.

Kiln drying can produce timbers with very low moisture contents, but it should be realised that timber is always absorbing or shedding water in an attempt to reach an equilibrium with the humidity of the surrounding atmosphere. Storing timber in an environment similar to that in which it will be used is a sensible way of ensuring the minimum of cracking or warping once a finished item is in service. This is the reason why air-dried timber is suitable for most boat-building requirements. If kiln-dried timber has been obtained for a specific reason, such as gluing, it should be realised that it will regain a moisture content of around fifteen percent if stored in the open air. It should be stored in a warm workshop, and used with the minimum of delay, if advantage is to be taken of its low moisture content. Storing it in solid piles (not in stick) slows the take up of moisture.

If the boatbuilder is seasoning much of his own timber, or using a glue such as WEST epoxy that requires low moisture levels, it is necessary to be able to check the actual moisture content of stock. The simplest way to do this is with an electrical meter that measures the resistance between two probes pushed into the timber. The meter is calibrated with a scale that shows the moisture content for different species, and is so quick and easy to use that measurements can be taken at several points on the timber, checking that the moisture level is sufficiently low throughout.

Meters are expensive and may not be justified when the precise moisture levels are only required on rare occasions. An alternative is to measure the moisture in a sample by weighing it both before and after drying in an oven. This method has several drawbacks, one difficulty being that the sample should be taken from the centre of a pile of timber, and even then may not give a true indication of the state of the rest of the timber. The timber can be stacked so that samples can be slid out easily for testing purposes. Inaccuracies may also creep in when taking the measurements, but the method does at least give a rough guide. The procedure is to weigh the sample, then to dry it in an oven until a constant weight is reached, which may take eighteen hours at 221 degrees Fahrenheit (105 degrees Centigrade), and then to weigh the sample again. The moisture content is found by the following formula:

$$\text{Percentage moisture content} = \frac{(\text{wet weight - dry weight}) \times 100}{\text{dry weight}}$$

Decay in Timber

Timber decays due to tiny fungi growing in the wood and using it as a source of food. The action of chemicals, insects, and weathering, can also cause timber to deteriorate, but rot is the result of fungal attack.

139

Different fungi attack timber in different ways, some needing living trees, while others can grow only once the tree is felled.

Many species have been identified in different parts of the world that prefer particular timbers or conditions, but these can all be divided into a few groups, based on the appearance of the decay. Table 1 identifies these groups by their common name, and gives the Latin names for some of the species of fungi that belong in each group.

Of the six groups it is the first, Brown or Wet rot that is most likely to affect the timber in boats, although White rot can also cause trouble in very warm conditions. Soft rot attacks submerged timber, but it can be prevented by ordinary antifouling paints and is also so slow acting that marine borers are more likely to cause damage to exposed timber than the rot itself. Dry rot, although the cause of extensive damage to timber in many buildings, is unlikely to affect boats. Despite its name it needs very humid conditions, with stagnant air, which can be avoided aboard a boat by the provision of minimal ventilation. Boatbuilders do not usually have to worry about Blue Stain either, as it mostly attacks the sap of softwoods, which would not be used in any case.

Blue Stain is in fact the only type of rot that has little effect on the strength of timber, all the others causing the wood to be drastically weakened from the very early stages of attack. Rotting timber also becomes porous and considerably less dense although this is not readily apparent as it is usually very wet. Only when it has dried out does its surprising lightness become evident.

Rot prevention in boats is based on two principles: avoiding the introduction of any rotten timber into the boat, or even timber susceptible to rot; and keeping the timber dry. For timber to decay it must be wet, generally above the fibre saturation point. Some species of fungi can grow with slightly drier wood, and once the attack has commenced the chemical action involved actually produces water, so that the moisture content is raised in the immediate vicinity of the rot. In practice a moisture content below twenty or twenty-two percent can be considered safe and any infection will not grow. It does not die though, and if the timber becomes wet again, the attack is renewed. Rot also progresses faster in warm conditions, and is slowed or even stopped in cold weather; but once again the check is only temporary, and the fungus is not killed.

Table 1 Fungi causing decay in timber

Common name	Latin names	Appearance & development	Comments
Brown rot (Wet rot)	Coniophora cerebella Poria vailantii (Paxillus panuides Poria xantha)	Yellow or brown streaks, becoming darker. Shrinkage causes cracking along the grain with some slight cracking across the grain. Eventually becomes crumbly.	Attacks softwoods or hardwoods, but softwoods are more susceptible. Poria vailantii. Looks like dry rot, but needs very wet situations and cannot spread to areas of dry timber.
White rot	Phelinus megaloporus (Poria medulla-panis)	White and stringy, eventually leaving only a lint-like residue which is easily crushed, but does not crumble.	Hardwoods are more susceptible. Requires very warm, as well as damp, conditions for active growth.
Soft rot	Chaetomium globosum	Surfaces of buried or submerged timber become soft and very dark, almost black.	Timber protected by conventional antifouling paints. Progress is so slow that exposed timber is liable to damage from marine borers before soft rot causes problems.
Dry rot	Merulius lacrymans	Softening and darkening of timber quickly forming cracks both along and across the grain producing a square or cuboid pattern; this pattern differentiates dry rot from brown rot. Finally dry rot leaves a dry powdery residue. This rot forms thick strands which can conduct moisture from saturated timber to enable the attack to continue on dry wood.	Although the cause of much damage to buildings ashore this is a rare problem aboard boats, as it needs very humid conditions which are avoided by minimal ventilation.
Blue stain (Sap stain)	Ceratostomella spp Endocondiophora spp	Bluish grey, sometimes almost black or very dark brown.	Mostly attacks softwoods. Affects hardness and permeability but has little effect on bending or compressive strength. Principal disadvantage is appearance, but as attack is usually confined to sapwood, which is not used in boatbuilding, this is of little concern to boatbuilders.
Mould	Pencillum spp Aspergillus spp Trichoderma spp	Mould growing on surface.	No detrimental effects; easily removed by brushing or surfacing.

141

Provisions for avoiding rot by keeping the moisture content down are:

(i) Use fully seasoned timber; either kiln-dried, or air-dried to a moisture content of seventeen percent or below.

(ii) Ensure good ventilation throughout. Avoid any spaces where air is trapped, as 'dead air' will inevitably cause trouble.

(iii) Avoid water traps: ensure that every little corner is either bevelled or filled with pitch to allow condensation to drain to the bilge.

(iv) Shelter from rain. It is fresh water that does the damage, so rain water leaking through the deck, or pools collecting in the cockpit can cause problems. A boat should be covered when layed up, whether ashore or afloat.

(v) Maintain paintwork as this prevents water penetrating into dry wood. Some systems are better than others: Epoxy coatings provide an exceptionally effective moisture barrier; polyurethanes are more effective than conventional yacht enamels.

Considerations when selecting timber are:

(i) Avoid all rot. If a large member such as the keel has some limited rot, perhaps in a knot, this should be cut out and a graving piece let in.

(ii) Avoid sapwood. The sapwood of all species is less durable than the heartwood.

(iii) Avoid the central area of the heart. In many timbers the central area of the heartwood is of poorer quality, softer, lighter in colour, and more susceptible to both shakes and rot.

(iv) Use naturally durable timbers.

(v) Use preservatives to protect susceptible points of all timber members and to enhance properties of timbers with little natural durability.

Preservative Treatment

If fungicides can be persuaded to penetrate wood and remain there, the natural durability of the timber will be improved. The fungicides may be those naturally occurring in the tar oils, such as creosote, or else poisons which enter the wood in solution and are left there once the solvent has dried. Application methods can be divided into four broad categories: sap replacement, diffusion, pressure treatment, and surface application. The first two methods are used for treating freshly felled trees for use as telegraph poles or suchlike, and it is only the second two that are of interest to the boatbuilder.

Application Methods

Pressure treatment involves a considerable amount of expensive equipment but is a service offered by large timber yards. Timber to be treated is placed in a large cylinder, which is then flooded with preservative and pressurised to force deep penetration. By altering the pressures before and after filling the chamber with preservative the treatment can either be 'full cell' or 'empty cell'. Full cell leaves preservative in the pores of the timber, which may lead to subsequent leaching, but empty cell systems remove the preservative again, leaving only a coating on the cell walls. This is more satisfactory, especially as less preservative is used.

A crude pressure treatment system that can be used with tar oils is called the 'open tank hot and cold process'. It involves placing the timber in a tank of boiling creosote, causing the air to be expelled from the timber as it heats. The heat source is then removed so that the cooling timber draws preservative into its pores. This is an effective method, often used to treat one end of fence posts, simply standing them in a barrel of creosote with an open fire beneath. Although not directly applicable to boatbuilding, it is useful in a boatyard when constructing jetties or other marine structures.

Surface application consists of brushing, spraying, dipping, or soaking. Brush or spray application is clearly the only possibility when treating a finished boat, but it should be understood that preservative is not applied in the same manner as paint. In order to get good penetration the timber should be flood coated with preservative, covering the surface with as much as it will hold. Once partially dry further coats can be added. When spraying, a coarse jet is most effective, as fine sprays tend to be wasteful. Respirators should be worn as all preservatives are to some extent toxic. For this reason they should always be handled carefully and kept away from foodstuffs.

Small items can be dipped or soaked before assembly, dipping being the equivalent of one brushed-on coat. Soaking or steeping is more effective the longer the timber can be left immersed, although the rate of penetration is fastest when first covered and slows with time.

143

Wood Preservatives

Wood preservatives are divided into three categories: tar oils, water borne, and solvent borne. Tar oils have been used as a wood preservative for many years and their efficiency is well established. They are relatively cheap and easy to apply, but have a strong smell, tend to bleed out of the timber, and cannot be overcoated with paint. For these reasons they are unsuitable for use on yachts, although they are often used on workboats. The volatile nature of tar oils means that evaporation causes the gradual loss of protection, so surface application has to be repeated after a few years. Pressure treated timber is effective for longer as the reservoirs within the timber replace tar lost by surface evaporation.

Workboats can be tarred regularly as part of their maintenance programme, and the concoctions used are often private recipes. Creosote is a coal tar, but wood tars (sometimes called Stockholm tar) are also extremely good fungicides, and mixing with paraffin (kerosene) or other fuel oils helps improve penetration. For good results tar oils should be applied hot, or at least on warm days, and to dry timber.

Water borne preservatives have the major drawback that seasoned timber swells when treated, and then has to be dried again. They are used by timber yards for pressure treatments, the timber being subsequently kiln-dried. Timber treated in this way is clean and odourless, and can be painted. The fungicides used are usually copper and chromium salts, sometimes with the addition of arsenic; other chemicals that are fire retardants or insecticides can also be added, treating the timber in several ways at one time. Commercial examples of this type of preservative are: Celcure A (from Rentokil Ltd) and Tanalith C (from Hicksons Timber Co).

Solvent borne preservatives are best for surface application as the very volatile organic solvents used (often white spirit or naphtha) effectively penetrate the timber, then rapidly evaporate off, leaving the active fungicides behind. They have the advantage that natural penetration is good, no distortion or swelling of the timber is caused, and they do not leak out when washed by rain or bilge water; they can also be painted over. During application and for a couple of days afterwards until the solvent has evaporated, there is an increased fire hazard, but this is no problem in a sensibly organised workshop. A wide variety of fungicides are used, sometimes with insecticides added. The active ingredient in many is either pentachlorophenol or a metalic naphthenate, and commercial examples of these types are: Cuprinol Clear (from Cuprinol Ltd) and Solignum Colourless (from Solignum Ltd).

144

Selecting Treatment

When deciding how to protect timber from rot, consideration should be given to the likelihood of attack and the timber's natural durability and permeability. In Table 2, column 4 gives each species' durability and column 5 classifies its heartwoods' permeability, or resistance to treatment. Applying a surface treatment to a timber whose permeability is so poor that penetration is negligible is a pointless exercise.

In traditional boatbuilding where most timber is bought in boards plain sawn through and through there is little point in having the timber pressure treated; most of the protected timber would be lost as members are cut and planed to shape. Instead the completed hull is given a surface coat of a solvent-borne preservative before fitting out commences. In addition, all joints, where rot is most likely to start, are luted or bedded with a white lead/linseed oil mixture; this acts as both a sealant and fungicide. Particularly susceptible items such as softwood stopwaters are soaked in a solvent-borne preservative to ensure effective penetration.

With modern construction methods where laminates or strip planks are often ordered from the timber supplier machined to size, it would be tempting to have these pressure treated by the empty cell method and redried before delivery. Although this timber would be very effectively protected from fungal attack it is not recommended practice as the fungicide may adversely affect the glue joints. In general laminated timber should be treated after gluing, not before, and if treated timber has to be glued the adhesive manufacturer's advice should be sought.

The use of creosote is confined to workboats and marine constructions such as piers etc. As already said, workboats can be protected by surface application, but pilings and other structures that cannot be repainted should be protected by the open tank hot and cold system. For these applications creosotes conforming to BS 3051 are suitable; those conforming to BS 144, while giving better protection have to be applied by pressure treatment.

Marine Borers

Unprotected timber in brine or saltwater may be attacked by marine borers. Two types of animal are a potential threat: shipworm, and gribble.

Shipworm, or *Teredo*, is a mollusc, that burrows into the wood in its first few weeks of life, when it is minute. It enlarges the burrow as it grows, maintaining contact with the saltwater only through its original tiny penetration hole. *Teredo* attack is therefore not visible externally although the wood may in fact be almost entirely eaten away. Examples of shipworm have been found over 20 in (500 mm) long.

Gribble, or *Limnoria*, is a crustacean and only attacks the surface of the timber, never burrowing deeper than ½ in (12 mm) although as the weakened timber gradually gets worn away by mechanical damage, so the attack progresses further. *Limnoria* are only about ⅛ in (3 mm) long and during the summer they leave their burrows and migrate to fresh timber.

Marine borers are a major hazard in warm waters, but in more temperate regions their occurrence is less predictable. Along British coasts shipworm is confined to parts of England and Wales, although gribble is found in colder waters. Neither can tolerate fresh water or prolonged drying out, so that a haul out for two weeks is one way to prevent further damage if a boat is found to be affected.

Some timbers, such as greenheart, teak, afrormosia, and makore (and to lesser extent iroko and danta) are more resistant to marine borer attack than others, and it helps to treat less resistant timbers with a preservative that will not leak out. No timber should be considered immune though, and the use of unprotected resistant timbers can only be considered for harbour constructions, where they may be expected to have a life of about twenty years.

Conventional antifouling paints provide protection for boats, although in tropical waters these should be of a strong variety and well maintained. If the antifouling is chafed away the hull becomes susceptible to attack. More permanent (and worry free) protection can be provided by sheathing the hull. Methods of doing this are described when dealing with sheathing systems.

Plywood

Timber is a remarkable material that is in most places readily available, worked easily with hand tools, and has surprising strength (Mahogany for example, can be three times as strong in tension, and twice as strong in compression, as a piece of mild steel of the same weight). Yet despite these attractive characteristics, it does have drawbacks as an engineering material. Apart from the problems associated with moisture and durability already dealt with, timber is an extremely inconsistent material, whose strength can be spoilt by the occurrence of defects such as knots, checks, thunder shakes, or awkward grain. In addition its strength across the grain is far less than that along the grain.

146

Plywood, by gluing together several laminates of timber, overcomes these problems. Man-made boards are very stable, have equal strength in all directions, and a uniformity that the boatbuilder can rely upon, reducing wastage due to the defects in the material to nil. So successful is plywood that boatbuilders use it extensively: it is the principal material for fitting out. Most boats are decked with it, even if only as a subdeck on which to lay teak planks. It is the planking on chine hulls, and sometimes even clinker ones. It can be used for structural members, frames, floors, knees, and even on occasion keels and stems, as with the Warram catamarans.

Boatbuilders have actually used plywood for every conceivable part of small boats, but in order to use it successfully its own drawbacks must be recognised. Its main weakness is end grain: whenever a plywood board is cut or drilled, end grain is exposed, and if moisture penetrates problems will inevitably arise. Winter frosts in particular cause moisture to freeze and swell, delaminating even the best quality plywoods. A second problem can arise when plywood is subjected to repeated wetting and drying; tiny shakes can appear across the entire surface due to the swelling and shrinkage of the outer veneer. Both these problems are overcome if the timber is given sufficient protection. Every time plywood is cut the end grain should be sealed with resin, glue or mastic. Well maintained paint or varnish can protect the surface veneers, although more permanent protection is afforded by sheathing which should definitely be considered for situations subjected to harsh treatment, in particular decks and hulls.

Marine grade plywood should always be used for structural and exterior work. In principle it should be used for all boatwork, although in some fitting out situations 'exterior' grade may be acceptable. Plywood for boat use must be bonded with adhesives that are 'weather and boil proof' (WBP), but it is not the glue that makes marine plywood superior, as many other grades are made with similar adhesives; it is the timber. Marine plywood manufacturers should use durable timber for both face and core veneers. Durable timbers commonly used are: agba, idigbo, makore, and utile; other timbers classified as moderately durable also used are African mahogany, luan (or Red meranti), and sapele. In addition the manufacture should be closely supervised to ensure that the face veneers are entirely free of defects, and joints in core veneers are neither lapped nor leave a gap greater than 0.02 in (0.5 mm). Plywood thicker than ⅜ in (9.5 mm) should have five or more veneers, three veneers being acceptable for the thinner boards.

In Britain the specification for marine plywood is BS 1088, and this should be stamped on each sheet. Genuine marine plywood will in addition have the 'kite' mark of the British Standards Institute, the manufacturer's name, and the nominal thickness of the board. Cheap marine plywoods, or those described as 'equivalent to BS 1088', must be treated with suspicion. Due to the durable nature of the timber used in the core laminates, marine plywood tends to be considerably heavier than other grades. In North America specifications are set by the American Plywood Association.

Special plywoods can be obtained for particular structural or decorative uses. Some plywoods are made with the veneers closely angled, giving greater strength in one direction than the other. These are particularly useful for dinghy centre boards and rudders. Plywood can also be teak-faced on one or both sides, and can even have the teak cut by black inserts to mimic the appearance of a teak laid deck.

Plywood can be stored in vertical racks, or in piles on a flat base. Racks, holding the different thicknesses of ply like toast in a toast rack, use little space and make access to the different sizes simple. The boards can become warped though, if the racks are wide and the timber is allowed to sag. Flat piles prevent any distortion, and in addition slow the uptake of moisture so helping to keep the boards at the low moisture levels they have after manufacture. Piles should be carefully kept straight, each board neatly covering the one below, as this avoids the unsightly strips of different coloured timber down the edges of boards removed from an uneven pile. These colour changes are due to the gradual darkening of exposed mahogany: the main part of the board is covered and remains its original colour while the exposed edge in a poorly stacked pile can darken quite considerably in a few months.

When cutting across the surface grain of plywood there is a tendency for the timber to splinter at the edges. Cutting with a hand saw at a very shallow angle reduces the problem, and if cutting from the 'face side', the one which will be seen, any splintering will only occur on the back and unseen side. If both sides are to be visible, or an electric jig-saw is used which causes splintering on the saw side of the plywood, the surface should be scored heavily with a Stanley knife before cutting. The knife cuts the grain fibres so that splintering does not occur and a neat finish can be obtained.

Table of Principal Boatbuilding Timbers

Table 2 on the following pages lists the principal boatbuilding timbers, divided into hardwoods and softwoods. Other timbers not included have sometimes proved satisfactory for particular local conditions. In colder climates, less durable timbers may perhaps be used as fungal attack is slowed. In Australia and New Zealand some locally grown timbers have proved good for boatbuilding, although unobtainable in other parts of the world; in particular spotted gum for timbers and kauri pine for planking, although this softwood is now in short supply.

Each column contains the following information:

Column 1:   Names and origin. Timber names can be confusing, and even misleading. Several names are often applied to one species, and infrequently one name used for several species. A prime example of this is 'Cedar', which can be a hard or softwood with a variety of characteristics. Another example is Douglas Fir, a label often applied to timbers inferior to *Pseudotsuga menziesii*, which is actually an excellent boatbuilding timber. Latin names for each species are given in italics as these cannot be confused: each name is specific to an individual timber. Where 'spp' follows the generic name it indicates that several species fall in that category.

Column 2:   Description. Colour, grain, and other characteristics such as stability and likelihood of resin pockets are given.

Column 3:   Comments. The usual situations that the timber is used in, and its ease of working.

Column 4:   Durability. This grading gives a comparison of natural durability, and is based on 'graveyard' tests, where 2 x 2 in (50 x 50 mm) stakes were found to withstand fungal attack for the following periods:

very durable	more than 25 years
durable	15 to 25 years
moderately durable	10 to 15 years
non-durable	5 to 10 years
perishable	less than 5 years

Column 5: Permeability. This grading indicates the degree of resistance of the heartwood to preservatives. In most species the sapwood is more permeable. Actual penetration of preservative depends on application technique and the figures given here should be taken as the likely maxima with pressure treatment for several hours.

very resistant	little penetration
resistant	up to ¼ in (6 mm)
moderately resistant	up to ¾ in (19 mm)
permeable	penetrates without difficulty

Column 6: Density, given in lbs/cu ft and kgs/m^3

Column 7: Bending characteristics. These give the average radii of curvature that can be expected (in inches and millimetres) under the following conditions:

(a) Laminates ⅛ in thick (3.2 mm) at 12 percent moisture content.
(b) Unsupported steam bending of 1 in (25 mm) samples.
(c) Compression steam bending of 1 in (25 mm) samples.

(Columns 4, 5 and 6 from *Timbers — their properties and uses*, Column 7 from the *Wood Bending Handbook*.)

Table 2A Principal boatbuilding hardwoods

1	2	3	4	5	6	7		
Names and origin	Description	Comments	Natural durability	Resistance to preservatives	Density lbs/cu ft (kg/m³)	Bending Characteristics inches (mm)		
						a	b	c
Afrormosia *Pericopsis elat* West Africa	Yellow brown. Fine grain. Very stable.	Alternative to teak. Exterior and interior joinery, decks and planking. Tendency to split. Stains when in contact with ferrous metals.	very durable	very resistant	43 (690)	6.5 (165)	29 (740)	14 (360)
Afzelia *Afzelia spp* Tropical Africa	Light or dark reddish brown. Irregular grain. Very stable.	Keels, stems, superstructure. Difficult to work.	very durable	very resistant	51 (820)	9.5 (241)	34 (860)	18 (460)
Agba *Gossweilerodendron balsamiferum* Tropical Africa	Light or pink brown with resin pockets. Fine grain. Stable.	Planking, decking superstructure.	durable	resistant	35 (560)	4.4 (112)	16 (410)	20 (510)
Ash *Fraxinus excelsior* Europe	White, sometimes pinkish. Medium grain.	Canoe framing, boathooks, tillers. Needs plenty of ventilation to avoid rotting.	perishable	moderately resistant	43 (690)	4.8 (122)	12 (300)	2.5 (64)
Cedar, Spanish (Honduras, or South America) *Cedrela spp* Tropical America	Pink to red brown. Open grain. Stable.	Interior joinery and planking for light craft.	durable	very resistant	30 (480)	-	-	-

Table 2A Principal boatbuilding hardwoods (continued - 2)

1	2	3	4	5	6	7		
Names and origin	Description	Comments	Natural durability	Resistance to preservatives	Density lbs/cu ft (kg/m³)	Bending Characteristics inches (mm)		
						a	b	c
Danta *Nesogordonia papave▼fera* West Africa	Reddish brown. Fine texture. Stable.	Keels, stems, framing and bent timbers. Moderate dulling of tools. Tends to split.	moderately durable	moderately resistant	46 (740)	5.3 (135)	30 (760)	14 (360)
Elm, Rock *Ulmus thomasii* North America	Pale brown. Fine straight grain.	Despite being non-durable used for deadwoods, keels, stringers. Moderately hard to work	non-durable	resistant	44 (705)	3.9 (99)	14 (360)	1.5 (38)
Elm, Wych *Ulmus glabra* North Europe	Dull brown. Medium grain.	As for Rock elm.	non-durable	resistant	42 (670)	4.6 (117)	12.5 (320)	1.7 (43)
Greenheart *Ocotea rodiaei* South America (Guyana)	Olive green. Fine straight grain.	Extremely heavy and tough. Engine beds, harbour construction. Difficult to work.	Very durable	very resistant	64 (1020)	7.3 (185)	36 (910)	18 (460)
Guarea *Guarea spp* West Africa	Pink or orange brown. Fine, straight grain. Moderately stable.	Planking, decking, joinery. Easily worked.	durable	very resistant	34 (545)	7.9 (201)	36 (910)	14 (360)

Table 2A Principal boatbuilding hardwoods (continued - 3)

1	2	3	4	5	6	7		
Names and origin	Description	Comments	Natural durability	Resistance to preservatives	Density lbs/cu ft (kg/m³)	Bending Characteristics inches (mm)		
						a	b	c
Idigbo *Terminalia ivorensis* West Africa	Yellow brown. Medium grain. Stable.	Stains yellow on contact with water. Interior joinery.	durable	very resistant	34 (545)	7.5 (191)	44 (1120)	32 (810)
Iroko (Mvule) *Chlorophora excelsa* East & West Africa	Yellow or brown, age darkens. Interlocked medium grain.	Keels, stems, planking, joinery. Alternative to teak. Tends to split and blunt tools.	very durable	very resistant	40 (640)	8.3 (211)	18 (460)	15 (380)
Jarrah *Eucalyptus marginata* Australia	Dark red. Medium grain.	Keels, deadwood, and harbour work. Contains sap pockets. May split. Difficult to work, dulls tools.	very durable	very resistant	50 (800)	6.8 (173)	39 (990)	17.5 (440)
Karri *Eucalyptus diversicolour* South West Australia	Red brown. Medium grain.	As for Jarrah, both are eucalyptus.	durable	very resistant	55 (880)	-	12.5 (320)	8 (200)
Luan (Merranti, Seraya, Philippine mahogany) *Shorea spp* Malaysia, Indonesia, Philippines	From dark red to light red, or even yellow. Coarse grain.	Should be used with care as light coloured timber readily absorbs moisture. Dark red varieties can be used for planking and joinery.	moderately resistant durable		33 (530)	6.5 (165)	36 (910)	30 (760)

153

Table 2A Principal boatbuilding hardwoods (continued - 4)

1	2	3	4	5	6	7		
Names and origin	Description	Comments	Natural durability	Resistance to preservatives	Density lbs/cu ft (kg/m³)	Bending Characteristics inches (mm)		
						a	b	c
Mahogany, African *Khaya spp* Tropical Africa	Reddish brown. Coarse interlocked grain.	Planking, laminating, joinery. Easy to work, but may be subject to 'thunder shakes' i.e. fractures across the grain. Poor durability in fresh water.	moderately durable	moderately resistant	44 (705)	6.8 (173)	32 (810)	36 (910)
Mahogany, Honduras or South American *Swietenia macrophylla* Central and South America	Light reddish to yellow brown. Slight interlocked grain. Stable.	Planking, laminating, internal and external joinery. Easy to work. Most expensive mahogany.	durable	very resistant	34 (540)	-	28 (710)	12 (300)
Makore *Tieghemella heckelii* West Africa	Pink to dark red brown. Grain fine even and straight.	Planking, laminating, works well, but tends to blunt tools.	very durable	very resistant	39 (625)	6.2 (157)	18 (460)	12 (300)
Oak, European *Quercus robur* and *Quercus petraea* Europe	Light brown. Grain usually straight, and fairly coarse.	Keel, stems, frames, bent timbers. Reasonably easy to work. Stains if in contact with ferrous metals in damp conditions. (Japanese oak is less durable.)	durable	very resistant	43 (700)	5.8 (142)	13 (330)	2 (51)

Table 2A Principal boatbuilding hardwoods (continued - 5)

1	2	3	4	5	6	7		
						Bending Characteristics inches (mm)		
						a	b	c
Names and origin	Description	Comments	Natural durability	Resistance to preservatives	Density lbs/cu ft (kg/m^3)			
Oak, White *Quercus alba* (and others) North America	Similar to European oak, more variable in colour.	Similar to European oak, (Red oak, *Quercus rubra* and *Quercus falcata*, are less durable).	durable	very resistant	40 (640)	5.4 (137)	13 (330)	0.5 (13)
Sapele *Entandrophragma cylindricum* Tropical Africa	Pinkish to red. Fine inter-locked grain.	Used as a mahogany. Good for cold moulding.	moderately very durable	resistant	39 (625)	6.3 (160)	37 (940)	30 (760)
Teak *Tectona grandis* Burma, Thailand, Indonesia	Golden brown. Straight medium grain. Oily, very stable.	All boat work; now principally decks and joinery.	very durable	very resistant	40 (640)	6.3 (160)	35 (890)	18 (460)
Utile *Entandrophragma utile* West Africa	Red or purplish brown. Fine striped grain.	High quality joinery. Moderately easy to work. Slight dulling effect on tools.	durable	very resistant	41 (660)	8.3 (211)	40 (1020)	36 (910)

Table 2B Principal boatbuilding softwoods

1	2	3	4	5	6	7		
Names and origin	Description	Comments	Natural durability	Resistance to preservatives	Density lbs/cu ft (kg/m³)	Bending Characteristics inches (mm)		
						a	b	c
Cedar, Northern White (Eastern arbor vitae, swamp cedar, post cedar) *Thuja occidentalis* North East America	Light pale brown. Fine texture.	Cold moulding hulls. Works easily, but lacks strength.	durable	very resistant	21 (340)	-	-	-
Cedar, Port Orford (Oregon cedar or Lawson's cypress) *Chamaecyparis lawsoniana* West Coast of North America	Pale pink brown. Coarse grain. Resistant to acids.	Light planking and decking. Easy to work, but tends to split.	durable	moderately resistant	31 (500)	7.4 (188)	18 (460)	34 (860)
Cedar, Southern White (Atlantic cedar, swamp cedar, false cypress) *Chamaecyparis thyoides* Atlantic Coast of North America	Pinkish colour. Fine grain.	As for Northern white cedar.	durable	-	23 (370)	-	-	-

Table 2B Principal boatbuilding softwoods (continued - 2)

1	2	3	4	5	6	7		
						Bending Characteristics inches (mm)		
Names and origin	Description	Comments	Natural durability	Resistance to preservatives	Density lbs/cu ft (kg/m^3)	a	b	c
Cedar, Western red (Giant arbor vitae) *Thuja plicata* North West America	Red or orange brown. Medium grain.	As for Port Orford cedar, but may stain when in contact with ferrous metals in moist conditions.	durable	resistant	24 (390)	8.0 (203)	37 (940)	35 (890)
Cedar, yellow (Alaska cedar, sitka cypress, Alaska cypress, nootka false cypress) *Chamaecyparis nootkatensis* North West America	Pale yellow, with fine even grain. Stable. Resistant to acids.	Planking, oars and paddles. Easy to work.	durable	resistant	31 (500)	-	-	-
Cypress, Southern (Louisiana cypress, bald cypress, swamp cypress) *Taxodium distichum* South & East Coasts of North America	Varies from pale yellow to dark red brown. Coarse straight grain. Oily.	Extensively used in boat-building. Works easily.	durable	moderately resistant	32 (510)	-	-	-

157

Table 2B Principal boatbuilding softwoods (continued - 3)

1	2	3	4	5	6	7 Bending Characteristics inches (mm)		
Names and origin	Description	Comments	Natural durability	Resistance to preservatives	Density lbs/cu ft (kg/m³)	a	b	c
Douglas fir, (Oregon pine, Columbian pine, red fir, yellow fir) *Pseudotsuga menziesii* West Coast of North America. Europe	Yellow to redish brown. Straight coarse grain.	Good strength to weight ratio, long lengths available. Good for planking, beams, spars, stringers. Name sometimes used for inferior timbers.	moderately durable	very resistant	33 (530)	5.9 (150)	33 (840)	18 (460)
Larch, European *Larix decidua* Europe	Light brown, to orange. Medium grain. Dead knots tend to fall out.	Planking, decking, stringers, beams. Larch from colder or mountainous regions is superior, i.e. Scottish larch. Japanese larch (*Larix leptolepis*) is faster growing and less suitable.	moderately durable	resistant	37 (590)	6.0 (152)	18 (460)	13 (330)
Larch, Tamarack (Hackmatack, Mountain larch, Alaska larch) *Larix occidentalis* and *Larix laricina* North America	Similar to European larch.	Natural crooks. Less widely used than European larch.	moderately durable	resistant	36 (580)	-	-	-

Table 2B Principal boatbuilding softwoods (continued - 4)

1	2	3	4	5	6	7		
						Bending Characteristics inches (mm)		
						a	b	c
Names and origin	Description	Comments	Natural durability	Resistance to preservatives	Density lbs/cu ft (kg/m³)			
Pine, pitch (Long leaf yellow pine, or long leaf pine) *Pinus palustris* and *Pinus elliottii* Central America and Southern USA	Yellow to red brown. Coarse texture, resinous.	Planking, stringers, sole bearers. Moderately easy to work. Bleeds resin.	moderately durable	resistant	43 (690)	-	28 (710)	14 (360)
Spruce, sitka *Picea sitchensis* West Coast of North America	Pale pinkish to white. Straight coarse grain.	Very good strength to weight ratios make it suitable for spars and oars despite its poor durability. Other spruces have similar qualities but cannot be obtained in clear lengths.	non-durable	resistant	27 (435)	5.4 (137)	32 (810)	36 (910)

2. Metals and Corrosion

In the construction of a boat metals are used in a multitude of situations: most fastenings, and moving parts; many fittings, and devices designed to give a mechanical advantage. The hostile marine environment is a difficult one for metals and if selected and sited unwisely they can deteriorate with frightening rapidity. However, if the type of metal is chosen with care and correct precautions are taken, they will give a long and safe working life.

Boatbuilders need a good understanding of the interaction of metals between each other and with the marine environment, for after all, metals are frequently performing vital functions: fastenings hold the hull together, skin fittings keep the water out. The subject is vast, involving many industries and continuous research, and probably has books enough written on it to fill several libraries. Even if the field is restricted to those metals commonly used on small boats, it is still a remarkably complex subject, but the more of it the boatbuilder can grasp, the better boatman he is.

The Marine Environment

There is not one marine environment that metals are subject to, but several, depending on their location in the boat, and even the location of the boat itself. Below the water line with the boat moored in a quiet backwater is one, but that changes once the boat gets under way and water is passing continually. The topsides, or area of the hull between 'wind and waves' is another, as is the deck itself which is for the most part dry but subject to frequent showers of rain or spray, and the occasional wave. Aloft is different again, as is the hull interior, and even there the metal may be sited clear of the bilges or liable to a frequent oily ducking.

The different conditions in each of these environments make them more or less suitable to different metals. Two factors in these environments will affect corrosion as they vary: the likelihood of immersion in seawater; and the presence of oxygen.

Salt Water

The corrosive effect of salt water is due to its excellent conductivity. The sodium chloride salt in sea water makes it many times more conductive than the relatively fresh water found in rivers and lakes, which is itself more conductive than unpolluted rain water. Because sea water conducts electricity, when metals are immersed in it electric cells can be set up. These take many forms, and vary from the interaction between steel and aluminium hulls tied alongside each other, to the tiny circuits between different molecules within one metal. This minutely localised effect occurs within brass in sea water, causing the zinc to be eaten out of it leaving only a brittle copper residue. Brass is quite suitable for interior joinery, but should not be used anywhere where it is immersed in, or splashed by, sea water

It should be realised that salt water is actually unavoidable anywhere on a boat as salt carried in the air can be deposited everywhere, including inside the accommodation and at the mast head. Salt attracts moisture to itself forming droplets of a saline solution that are far more concentrated, and corrosive, than sea water itself.

Oxygen

The corrosive nature of sea water (and the need to avoid the use of brass) is widely understood, but the part oxygen plays in the corrosive process is less well recognised. At this stage no account is being taken of differing metals in contact, examined next, but simply the effect of a corrosive environment on metals exposed in isolation.

Oxygen is required for any corrosion to take place, reacting with the metal to form an oxidised layer at its surface. This layer of oxidised metal has different properties with different metals, and radically affects their susceptibility to corrosion in different environments.

With some metals this oxidised layer is very tough, and adheres well to the metal below, and is what actually protects the metal from further corrosion. With others the oxidised metal is a poor substance, that easily washes or flakes off, and gives no protection to the metal below, even allowing corrosion to continue eating into the metal despite a thick surface layer of oxide, as can be seen in the rusting of untreated iron or steel.

Metals used in the marine environment that form a tough oxidised layer are: stainless steel, aluminium alloys, the copper/nickel alloys, (and nickel/copper alloys such as Monel,) chromium plate and manganese bronze. All these metals actually use oxygen to protect themselves, but they also need oxygen to maintain that protection.

161

If used in an environment deficient in oxygen, pitting corrosion may occur, or if shielded from oxygen in a localised area by barnacles, other fouling, contact with damp wood, or contact with rubber, crevice corrosion may start in that area. Once pitting has started, a cell is set up and the corrosion can progress rapidly. Some stainless steels are less susceptible to pitting and this is discussed when dealing with them, but in general it is better not to use these metals below the water line as, quite apart from fouling starting problems, in a quiet mooring oxygen levels can become unacceptably low. Flowing water, which is well aerated, is ideal for these metals and they can be used successfully for fittings that are subject to both wind and water.

Metals that do not form a strong oxidised layer are more suited to the reverse conditions. Where oxygen is scarce their corrosion is slowed, so they are ideal for use below the water line and in shielded situations, such as bolts passing through damp wood. Similarly the oxygen rich situations, such as fast flowing water, are harmful to them as corrosion is accelerated and what little protective skin is formed is immediately washed away. (This velocity effect of water is only a problem at higher speeds, but is a cause of corrosion on propellers and inside pumps and pipes, particularly at bends or other obstructions.) Metals that react with oxygen in this way, and are therefore more suited to underwater fittings, are copper and its zinc free alloys, the true bronzes.

Galvanic Corrosion

When two unlike metals are in contact, and in sea water, galvanic action occurs: a cell is set up (similar to an ordinary torch battery) a current passes between the two metals, and unfortunately corrosion occurs at one of them. For this to happen the metals need not be in direct contact, but simply in electrical contact, linked by a wire, another metal, or even damp wood. They need not actually be in the sea, either: a drop of salt water caught in the crack between a fitting and its fastening is quite sufficient. Guarding against galvanic action is difficult as it crops up in the unlikeliest of situations: an aluminium alloy hull electrically linked to a steel pontoon by wire hawsers or a metal gang plank sets up the action on a large scale.

Most forms of corrosion are galvanic action working in a particular way. (Electrolytic action is an exception and is examined separately.) Dezincification of brass, and pitting or crevice corrosion are all galvanic action working within one alloy. The cell in brass is formed by the molecules of zinc and copper, the cell in pitting corrosion is formed by the difference between the metal of the oxidised layer and that of the unoxidised metal in the pit.

The voltage that will pass between two metals in a galvanic cell can be measured, and by measuring it for all the relevant metals a table can be drawn up that shows the potential difference between any two. Many factors affect the exact position of metals on this table, including temperature and motion of the salt water, and its exact composition. Table 3 shows one version of the Galvanic Series.

Table 3 The Galvanic Series

Approximate PD relative to silver/ silver chloride half cell	NOBLE OR CATHODIC END
− 0.05	Stainless steel type 316 (passive)
− 0.07	Monel
− 0.08	Stainless steel type 304 (passive)
− 0.18	Stainless steel type 316 (active, in pits or crevices)
− 0.2	Nickel (passive)
	Silver solder
	Nickel/aluminium bronze (NAB)
− 0.25	Cupronickel alloys
− 0.3	Gun metal
	Silicon bronze
	Manganese bronze
	Aluminium brass
	50/50 solder
	Red brass
− 0.36	Copper
	Nickel (active, in pits or crevices)
	Brass (Muntz metal and cartridge brass)
− 0.4	Aluminium bronze
	Lead
− 0.48	Nickel cast iron
− 0.53	Stainless steel type 304 (active, in pits or crevices)
	Low alloy steels
− 0.6	Carbon steel
	Cast iron
	Cadmium
− 0.82	Aluminium alloys
− 1.1	Galvanized steel
	Zinc
− 1.6	Magnesium
	BASE OR ANODIC END

163

When two metals from the series are linked, corrosion will occur to the 'baser' metal, as this is the anode in the cell, while the 'noble' metal is the cathode, and unaffected.

The rate of corrosion at the anode is in part dependent on the potential difference between it and the cathode, so metals close in the galvanic series should be selected whenever possible. Other factors also affect the rate, the most important being the relative areas of the two. An anode with small surface area, relative to the cathode will be quickly corroded, but if the anode has the larger area the effect is slowed. This is particularly relevant when choosing fastenings for fittings below the water line; the fastening should always be more noble than the larger fitting. This factor is less relevant when dealing with deck fittings as often the corrosion is occurring in a localised area, perhaps a drop of water, and the surface area ratios are in practice one to one, as demonstrated in Fig. 2.5.

A second factor is that if the cathode is one of the alloys mentioned earlier that forms a tough oxide skin, corrosion of the anode is less than would be expected if consideration were simply given to their relative positions in the galvanic series; for example stainless steel bolts can be, and usually are used to fasten aluminium alloy fittings, despite the large potential difference between the two.

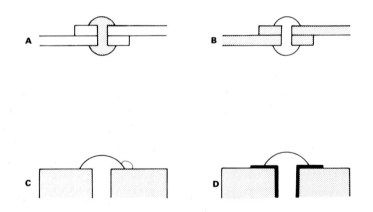

Fig 2.5   Fastenings below the water line: (A) if the rivet is a baser metal it will be quickly corroded due to the large area of surrounding noble metal; (B) but if the rivet is more noble, corrosion to the large area of plate is negligible. (C) Relative surface areas are not a consideration with deck fittings as the ratio is 1:1 in a droplet of water. (D) Metals with a large potential difference can be insulated with Neoprene sleeves and washers.

Corrosion Avoidance and Protection

Simple measures can be taken to avoid galvanic action, or at least ensure it is on a small and undamaging scale. Where serious corrosion is inevitable other procedures are needed to protect the important metal parts.

Avoiding the Use of Dissimilar Metals

The most obvious way to avoid galvanic action is not to have an electrical contact between dissimilar metals. Using fastenings made of the same material as the fitting is one way of achieving this, and another is to insulate two materials where they would otherwise come into contact. Neoprene or Tufnol can be used as insulators, but insulation has to be complete with gaskets, washers, and sleeves on bolts as also illustrated in Fig. 2.5. Mastic compounds can be used as insulators but the danger with these is that pressure will squeeze most of the mastic away, allowing contact at high spots. Silicone rubbers are good insulators, and if allowed to cure for several hours before pressure is applied, make excellent gaskets. A simple check that the insulation is effective can be made with a battery and bulb although a sensitive volt meter is better.

If a metal can be isolated successfully galvanic action in the normal sense cannot occur, although pitting or dezincification are still hazards that are only avoided by the correct selection of metal for that particular situation.

Correct Surface Area Ratios

Where dissimilar metals are inevitably in contact they should be as close together in the galvanic series as possible, and a potential difference of 0.2 volts should be considered the maximum when surface areas are equal. They should also be arranged so that the more important one, or the one with the smaller area is made from the more noble metal; in most cases this means fastenings are more noble than the fittings. Simply painting the noble metal can help to keep its surface area to a minimum. Painting the base metal, or anode, also protects it, but the danger is that if the paint is scratched the corrosive attack is concentrated on that one small unprotected area, with much more drastic results. Ensuring that the base metal is of ample thickness, so that some slow corrosion can occur, is another good provision.

Table 4 suggests which metals are acceptable for use as fastenings with different metal fittings, both on deck and under water.

Table 4 Fitting and fastening compatibility

Fitting	Fastening					
	Steel	Galvanized	Aluminium Alloy	Brass or Bronze	Monel	Stainless Steel
Iron or steel	✓			✓	✓	✓
Galvanized	✓	✓				✓
Aluminium alloy		✓	✓		✓	✓
Brass or bronze				✓	✓	✓
Copper/nickel alloys					✓	✓
Lead				✓	✓	✓
Monel					✓	(*)
Stainless steel					(*)	✓

(*) May cause pitting under head.

Sacrificial Anodes

In some circumstances it is impossible (or unacceptably expensive) to avoid corrosion by the simpler means described above. In these cases the metal threatened can be given cathodic protection. If instead of allowing it to be the base metal in a circuit, and therefore the anode, it is made part of the circuit's cathode, corrosion will not occur. This can be done by connecting it with another metal baser than itself, which then becomes the anode. As corrosion always occurs to the most base metal when several are connected, this method can be effective against all forms of galvanic action, including pitting and crevice corrosion, and dezincification.

For example, propellers are commonly made from manganese bronze which is liable to dezincify, but can be protected by the use of sacrificial anodes.

A base metal used to protect others in this way is called a 'sacrificial' anode because it is designed to corrode and waste away. Periodically it has to be replaced, so the anodes are usually mounted on studs either bolted or welded in position. For efficient protection the electrical connection between anode and parts being protected must be good. Welding or bolting directly to the part is most effective, but where a wire connection is necessary it should be of a heavy gauge wire to ensure low resistance.

Several types of anodes are available, made from zinc, magnesium, or aluminium, and in a variety of patterns. The actual placement,

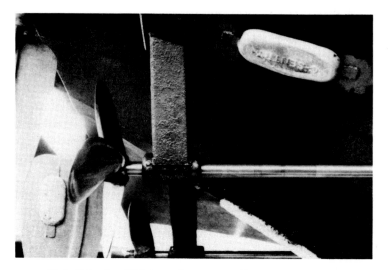

Plate 2.1. Sacrificial anodes on a small commercial vessel.

type, and number of anodes required in different situations have been discovered by trial over many years, and before fitting any it is wise to consult an expert. He can advise on the best system to ensure adequate, but not excessive, protection.

Sacrificial anodes (shown in Plate 2.1) should of course never be painted.

Impressed Current

Cathodic protection can also be given by imposing a current from an outside source. Electricity is fed into the water from an anode that does not corrode, preventing corrosion from occurring in the same manner as the sacrificial anode. The advantage is that the amount of protection can be regulated, either manually or in sophisticated systems automatically, to ensure sufficient protection. A sacrificial anode merely provides a fixed current which may in practice be inadequate or excessive.

Impressed current systems require such a large source of electrical supply that they are impractical for smaller boats, although most new ships are built with this system to reduce maintenance costs. Kits are produced by some engine manufacturers to protect the aluminium of their outdrive units.

Electrochemical Decay in Timber

In a wooden boat another hazard is encountered when a galvanic couple is set up. Although corrosion only occurs at the anode, and the cathode, or noble metal is unaffected, the timber in the immediate vicinity of the cathode becomes very alkaline. These conditions are detrimental to the timber, causing it with time to weaken, becoming soft and spongy. This is called 'electrochemical decay', and as it occurs in the immediate vicinity of the cathode, cathodic protection systems such as those just described, while protecting the metal arc liable to increase damage to a wooden hull.

Some timbers are more resistant to this form of attack and in general, softwoods resist it better than hardwoods, which is quite the reverse of fungal decay. Table 5 shows the relative resistance of several boatbuilding timbers.

Table 5   Natural resistance of some boatbuilding timbers to electrochemical decay

Very resistant:	European larch Spruce
Good resistance:	Pitch pine Teak
Moderate resistance:	Douglas fir Canadian rock elm
Poor resistance:	African mahogany English elm Honduras mahogany English oak Iroko

A particular form of this type of attack is 'nail sickness'. This is found in older wooden hulls where the copper fastenings are loosened due to the soft and spongy nature of the timber surrounding them. This is due to the hull timber becoming damp and allowing a couple to form between the copper nail and a nearby baser metal, often the ballast keel. A cell can even form around the nail itself, due to the differing concentrations of oxygen at the exposed nail head and the part embedded in damp wood. This problem is less likely to occur in a well maintained hull; a good coat of paint on the inside and outside of the hull reduces moisture penetration of the wood, and also prevents the nail heads becoming anodes and the ballast keel (or for that matter ballast keel bolts in the bilges) from becoming cathodes. An annual haul out also helps keep the timber dry.

Electrolytic Corrosion

An electric current passing between two metals in sea water will always cause corrosion, but if the current comes from an outside source and not from the potential difference between the two metals, it is called electrolytic action. This should not be confused with galvanic action as none of the normal rules applies: it can occur between any two pieces of metal, even if the same type; corrosion is as likely to occur to the noble metal as the base one; and corrosion can happen at a much faster rate.

Electrolytic corrosion occurs because of 'stray' current leaking from a badly installed electrical system or poor earthing arrangement. The underwater metal that finally earths the leak will be corroded, whatever metal it is, and if the leakage is due to a short circuit rather than a trickle caused by damp conditions, corrosion can be severe and rapid.

Prevention is a matter of good electrical installation, with an insulated return wire from each instrument and not the earth return system used on cars. The battery should be fitted with a master switch on the positive terminal to isolate it when the boat is not in use.

Marine Metals

Stainless Steel

Stainless steels divide into three types, depending on crystal structure: martensitic, ferritic, and austenitic. Only austenitic alloys are suitable for marine use, and these are sometimes referred to as 18/8 grades. A simple test for items of chandlery or bolts of doubtful origin is to see if they are magnetic. Only the austenitic types are not.

The identification system of the American Iron and Steel Institute (AISI) is a widely accepted way of referring to different alloys; the 300 series covers most of the austenitic grades. The two most widely used for marine purposes are 304 and 316, (sometimes called 18/8 and 18/10/3 respectively, referring to their composition). Type 316 is better than 304 as the addition of molybdenum improves its resistance to pitting. Both are still susceptible unless given cathodic protection, by either linking with large areas of a baser metal, or to sacrificial anodes.

169

Welding stainless steel can alter the crystal structure close to the weld, making it liable to weakening when in a corrosive environment, and possible failure when stressed later. This can be avoided in several ways: lightly made items can be annealed by heating to 1900 degrees Fahrenheit (1050 degrees Centigrade) and then quenching in cold water after manufacture; heavier items to be welded should be made from either low carbon alloys, identified as 304L and 316L, or 'stabilised' alloys numbered as 321 or 347.

Table 6 shows the composition of the most commonly used austenitic stainless steels, and the equivalent specification number for British Standards. AISI numbers are for wrought alloys; casting alloys are specified by the Alloy Casting Institute (ACI) whose equivalent numbers are also shown.

Table 6 Stainless steels for marine use

Identification			Composition			Comments
AISI (Wrought)	ACI (Cast equivalent)	British Standard	% Cr	% Ni	% Mo	All excellent for deck fittings but need cathodic protection underwater
304	CF 8	304S15	18-20	8-12		General purpose
304 L	CF 3	304S12	18-20	8-12		Low carbon for welding
316	CF 8M/12M	316S16	16-18	10-14	2-3	Better resistance to pitting
316 L	CF 3M	316S12	16-18	10-14	2-3	Low carbon for welding
321		321S12	18-20	11-15	3-4	Stabilised for welding
347	CF 8C	347S17	17-19	9-13		

(Cr = Chromium, Ni = Nickel, Mo = Molybdenum)

Iron and Steel
The crudest form of cast iron is pig iron, which contains up to four percent carbon and four percent of other elements. From this many different alloys can be made by refining it further, adding other elements, and altering the crystal structure. All cast irons have a carbon content greater than 1.7 percent, but when it has been reduced to less than that, it is classed as steel.

Carbon steel, or mild steel, is the cheapest steel and used in most construction work; it has the minimum of elements added. Low-alloy steels have small quantities of manganese, chromium, copper or nickel added. These give a higher strength and improved resistance to atmospheric corrosion, but do little to improve corrosion characteristics in sea water. Cor-Ten is an example of this type of steel. High strength steels, several times stronger than mild steel can be made by the additions of up to three percent of other elements. Table 7 gives the comparative densities and strengths of cast iron and two steels, together with that of stainless steel types 304 and 316, and aluminium alloy.

Table 7 Density and strength of iron, steel, stainless steel and aluminium alloys

	Density		Yield stress		Ultimate tensile strength	
	lbs/cu in	gms/cc	tons/sq in	N/mm^2	tons/sq in	N/mm^2
Cast iron	0.26	7.2	-	-	10-20	150-300
Mild steel	0.28	7.8	10-16	150-250	30	460
Cor-Ten	0.26	7.2	22	340	31	475
S.S. type 304	0.29	8.0	15	230	38	585
S.S. type 316	0.29	8.0	18	275	40	615
Aluminium alloys	0.10	2.8	8	123	18-20	280-300

Iron and steel are both economical, and strong. Unfortunately they rust, and because they are low in the galvanic series this corrosion is usually made worse when in contact with other metals. In order to be able to use these materials successfully the precautions already described have to be taken to avoid galvanic action and, in addition, the metal must be coated to prevent rusting. Before any type of coating is applied the surface must be clean and free of grease, and new metal must have the 'mill scale' removed. Mill scale is a flakey oxide which will both increase corrosion and prevent a good adhesion of any subsequent protective coating. It can be removed by shot blasting, or simply with a wire brush, but is easier if the metal has been allowed to weather first.

Protective coatings can be paint, or a layer of metal lower down the galvanic series. On large areas painting is often the only possibility, but it must be well maintained and scratches repainted quickly.

This is because the exposed metal at a scratch actually corrodes faster than if no paint had been applied. Coating with a baser metal gives cathodic protection when it is damaged, and is even 'self healing', as a deposit of the protective metal is gradually laid over the scratch. Zinc, cadmium, or aluminium can all be used to protect steel, and applied by electroplating, sherardizing, spraying, or hot dip galvanizing. Galvanizing with zinc is recognised as giving the best results as electroplating and sherardizing produce much thinner coatings, while a sprayed coat, although thick, may be porous.

Many small works around the country will hot dip galvanize fabricated items, and the specification for marine use is BS 729, (or ISO 1459-61). Galvanized protection lasts many years for deck fittings, but only about four or five in sea water. Painting can effectively lengthen this, but the paint should be well keyed by using a self-etch primer.

Nylon dipping is a recently devised form of protection, effective if the whole item can be coated and will not be subject to excessive chafe. An old form of protection, often used on fishing boat gear, was to heat the metal red hot, then plunge it into boiling pitch, so that the pitch entered the pores of the metal. This gives limited protection for a while, and is variously called Chinese or Swedish galvanizing.

Aluminium Alloys

Aluminium alloys are corrosion resistant in a similar manner to stainless steel: an oxide film forms on the surface preventing further corrosion. Unlike stainless steel, aluminium is low in the galvanic series and serious corrosion results from contact with other metals. Copper and the yellow metals (brass and bronze) should be avoided under all circumstances, and even steel in contact in wet conditions will affect it badly. Surprisingly, stainless steel can be used with aluminium alloys, because the two oxidised layers in contact react favourably; chromium plated fastenings can also be used for the same reason. Zinc or cadmium plated fasteners are also suitable but in this case it is because their position is close to that of aluminium in these cases it is because their position is close to that of aluminium sulated from the fitting by using sleeves and washers.

Unpainted aluminium alloys soon pit in sea air, but the pits are shallow and corrosion ceases after some months. They are unsightly, but not harmful. Paint lasts well on aluminium, as it does not tend to lift in the vicinity of a scratch, as on steel. Aluminium hulls should of course never be painted with antifouling paints containing copper or mercury salts, or even lead paints.

172

Anodising is a common protection given to aluminium alloys and is a way of thickening and toughening the natural oxide film. It prevents pitting and maintains a smart appearance, but does not protect from galvanic action.

One unusual effect found with aluminium alloys is called poultice corrosion. If the metal is in prolonged contact with a wet spongy material, such as timber or cloth, a sticky white oxide oozes from the area. Where contact with timber occurs both metal and wood should be painted with zinc chromate primer.

Only marine grade aluminium alloys should be used, as others, although considerably stronger, have poor corrosion resistance.

Wrought alloys, used for masts, hulls, fuel tanks, etc., are formulated differently from those used for casting deck fittings. Aluminium alloys are described by letters and numbers, the letters denoting a

Table 8 Aluminium alloys for marine use

Identification		Composition			Comments
BS	US Equiv	% Mg	% Si	% Mn	
LM5	514	5			Used for casting: Magnesium alloys are stronger but more difficult to cast than the silicon alloys
LM6	13		12		
LM10	520	10			
LM18	443		5		
LM25	356	1	7		
N3	3003			1	Low strength but good corrosion resistance. Used for fuel tanks.
N4	5052 (5050)	2			
N5	5154 (5454)	3.5			Used for hull plating and rivets.
N6	5056	5			Strong, but lower corrosion resistance. Used for rivets.
N8	5083	4.5		(*)	Used for hull plating.
H9	6083	(*)	(*)		Should not be welded.
H20	6061	1	(*)		Used for masts. Should not be welded.
H30	6082	(*)	1	(*)	Used for masts and rivets. Should not be welded.

(Mg = Magnesium, Si = Silicon, Mn = Manganese, (*) indicates less than 1 percent)

wide variety of things such as type, form, (bar, wire, bolt etc.,) and condition. LM indicates a casting alloy, while for wrought alloys the important letters are N and H: N indicates 'non-heat treatable', and can therefore be welded; H indicates 'heat treatable' and should not be welded as the strength may be drastically reduced near to the weld. Masts are commonly heat treated, to gain additional strength, so have to be riveted rather than welded.

Table 8 shows the composition of corrosion resistant alloys and their equivalent British and American numbers.

Copper and its Alloys

Copper has good natural corrosion resistance and being reasonably noble, is not itself corroded when in contact with most other metals. Copper is available in several types, but for most marine use the copper is described as 'deoxidised nonarsenical'. Other types are used for boiler making and electrical applications. Copper rivets are widely used in wooden boat construction (as nails clenched manually), and in copper pipework. Velocity effects can cause more rapid corrosion in pipes if too narrow a bore is used.

The main drawback with copper is that it is not very strong. This is overcome by alloying it with other metals, and in this way excellent materials are produced that are both strong and corrosion resistant for underwater use.

Copper alloys have been around a long time and unlike stainless steels and aluminium alloys are identified by name, not by number. This makes them easier to remember, but unfortunately can lead to confusion, particularly when the term 'bronze' is used.

Zinc is a cheap metal that can be added to copper in large quantities successfully increasing its strength properties. The alloy still has good resistance to atmospheric corrosion, but if immersed in sea water dezincifies, leaving a weak, brittle copper residue. Zinc rich copper alloys are called brasses: if the mixture of copper to zinc is 60:40 (Muntz metal) the strength is greater; if 70:30 (cartridge brass) the alloy is more ductile. Dezincification can be inhibited by the addition of small quantities of arsenic or tin, and these alloys are often given superior sounding names like naval brass, admiralty brass, or even naval bronze. Despite the use of inhibitors it is better to avoid the use underwater of any brass with more than fifteen percent zinc.

Bronze should really refer to alloys that are zinc free, but in practice does not. The most glaring example is manganese bronze. This is in fact a 60:40 brass with a little manganese added to make it very strong, but it still dezincifies readily. It is a good material for use on deck, but its reasonable price and good strength make it a frequent choice for propellers and shafts. Clearly because of dezincification it is not really suitable for this purpose, but by giving it cathodic protection in the form of sacrificial anodes (possibly by using zinc collars on the shaft) it can give a long service life.

True bronzes contain very little or no zinc and do not dezincify. They are strong and can be used underwater with confidence, but are more expensive. Gun metals are copper alloyed with five to ten percent tin, and a little zinc. Silicon bronze is widely available and used for fastenings in many situations. Aluminium bronze has a slight danger of dealuminification, but this is avoided if nickel is added, and is called nickel aluminium bronze, or NAB. Nickel/aluminium/manganese bronze should not be confused with ordinary manganese bronze as it contains no zinc. It is an excellent material for bolts and propellers.

Copper can be alloyed with nickel alone making a corrosion resistant material which is less susceptible to velocity effects, but it is expensive. Copper nickels with up to forty percent nickel have good antifouling properties, and it is an alloy of this sort used in the Cufo-Foil sheathing process described in the section on sheathing hulls. Once the nickel content exceeds that of copper it is technically a nickel copper alloy, the best known of which is Monel, containing only thirty percent copper. These are extremely strong and corrosion resistant materials, but also very expensive. 'K Monels' contain some aluminium and are even stronger.

Table 9 indicates the composition and relative strengths of the principal copper alloys.

Lead

Lead is a very dense metal with a low melting point which makes it ideal for casting ballast keels or blocks. It corrodes very slowly if left exposed to sea water but is a soft weak metal that tends to 'creep' or sag if insufficiently supported. It is commonly strengthened by adding small quantities of antimony or tin.

Density: 0.41 lbs/cu in or 11.35 gms/cc
Yield stress: 0.5 tons/sq in or 7.7 N/mm^2
Ultimate tensile strength: 1 ton/sq in or 15.4 N/mm^2

Table 9 Copper and nickel based alloys (All have a density around 0.3 lbs/cu in or 8.3 gms/cc)

Identification	Composition						Yield stress		Ultimate tensile Strength		Comments
	% Cu	% Zn	% Ni	% Sn	% Al	Other	Tons/ sq in	N/mm²	Tons/ sq in	N/mm²	
Copper	99.9						4-6	60-90	14-16	210-240	Nails, piping
'Brasses' — dezincify underwater:											
Red brass 85	85	15					8	130	20	310	
Cartridge brass	70	30					8	120	20-30	300-450	more ductile
Admiralty brass	70	29		1		As	7	110	21	320	inhibited
Muntz metal (Brass)	60	40					8-12	120-180	20-30	300-450	
Naval brass (Tobin Bronze)	60	39		1			9	140	24	370	
Aluminium brass	76	22			2	As	9	140	21-35	320-550	inhibited
Manganese bronze	58	39			1	Mn	14-16	210-240	28-32	430-500	inhibited
'Bronzes' — safe underwater:											
Gun metal (G bronze)	88	2		10			8-12	120-180	13-20	200-310	casts
Gun metal (M bronze)	88	4		6			8-9	130-140	16-21	250-320	well
Silicon bronze	96					Si	7-9	110-140	17-23	260-350	bolts,
Aluminium bronze	88				9	Fe	10-15	150-230	23-32	350-490	fittings
Nickel aluminium bronze (NAB)	80		5		10	Fe	16-26	250-400	40-45	610-690	etc.
Nickel/aluminium/manganese bronze	75		2		8	Mn	18-22	280-340	42-47	650-730	propellers
Phosphor bronze	90			10		P	10	150	27	420	springs and bearings
Copper nickel alloy	90		10			Fe	4-8	60-120	20-21	310-320	piping
Copper nickel alloy	68		30			Fe	10-14	150-220	25-28	390-430	
Nickel/copper alloys:											
Monel	30		67				11-22	170-340	31-40	480-610	
K Monel	30		67		2.8		18-23	280-350	40-50	610-770	

(Cu = Copper, Zn = Zinc, Ni = Nickel, Sn = Tin, Al = Aluminium, As = Arsenic, Mn = Manganese, Si = Silicon, Fe = Iron, P = Phosphorus)

3. Fastenings

Fastenings, as their name implies, hold things together. They do this in one of two ways: either they are driven into a 'blind' hole and rely on friction with the timber to hold them there; or they pass right through the materials and hold them together with some sort of swelling at either end. Words used to describe individual fastenings can be misleading, but in general terms nails and screws are driven from one side only, while bolts and rivets are through fastenings.

As a general principle fastenings should be hidden where possible. As screws (and nails) are only seen from one side, hiding them is often simply a matter of driving them from the less visible side. When this is not possible they can either be disguised by counterboring and filling, or made into a decorative feature, using devices that are described below. For a neat appearance fastenings should always be evenly spaced, and staggered to reduce the likelihood of splitting the timber.

The construction industry mostly uses fastenings made of mild steel, although in some exterior situations they are galvanized, and for better quality interior joinery brass is used. Boatbuilders only use steel fastenings for jig making; on the boat itself more corrosion resistant materials are necessary, as has been explained in the last section. Brass is generally used for interior work, but for exterior use, copper, bronze, Monel, or stainless steel fastenings should be used. On work boats heavily galvanized fastenings are acceptable. Silicon bronze screws and bolts are widely available; stainless steel should be at least type 304 and preferably type 316.

Driven Fastenings

Staples, all types of nails, and drifts come into this category. Nails are sold by weight, and as an aid to estimating requirements Tables 10 and 11 give the average numbers per pound for various types of nails and tacks.

Table 10 Copper boat nails and bronze ring nails - approximate numbers per pound (Multiply by 2.205 for numbers per kilogram)

Copper boat nails

Length in	mm	16	15	14	13	12	11	10	9	8	7	6
6	150											16
5	125											19
4	100							48		30	27	
3½	88							54	44	40		
3	75					80	76	64	52	36		
2½	62					120	90	78				
2¼	56					128	100	82				
2	50					136	110	91				
1¾	44			272	200	160	126					
1½	38		416	320	230	182	144					
1¼	32		490	384	268	216						
1⅛	28			416	312							
1	25	800	608	480	352							
⅞	22	940	670									
¾	19	1000										
⅝	16	1200										
½	13	1370										

Bronze ring nails

16	15	14	13	12	11	10	9	8	7	6	Length in	mm
								41			3½	88
						68		48			3	75
				145		82		55			2½	62
				161		102		75			2	50
				183		111		89			1¾	44
		400		205		135		95			1½	38
		552		254		155					1¼	32
924	705	571		350		188					1	25
1000		584									⅞	22
1136	956	714		416							¾	19

Gauge

Table 11 Copper roves, copper tacks, and brass panel pins - approximate numbers per pound (Multiply by 2.205 for numbers per kilogram)

Copper roves (burrs)

Rove dia in inches	3/16	1/4	5/16	3/8	7/16	1/2	9/16	5/8	3/4
in mm	4.8	6.3	7.9	9.5	11.1	12.7	14.2	15.9	19.0
Suitable for nail size	16	15	14	13	12	11,10	9	8,7	6
Approx number per lb	5250	2144	1056	654	432	320	240	182	108

Pins and tacks

Length inches	mm	Copper tacks	Brass panel pins (brads)		
			gauge 18	gauge 16	gauge 14
½	13	1507	2550	1720	1100
¾	19	720	2200	1275	830
1	25	452	1520	980	600

178

Staples

Steel staples are cheapest, but are only usable as temporary fastenings while glue sets; they should then be removed. If they are to be left in place silicon bronze or Monel should be used. Staples are inserted with a staple gun, which is fast and efficient, but removal is a very slow and tedious job, especially if care has to be taken not to damage the wood. Stapling through cardboard reduces damage. Several tools are available to aid staple pulling, and one type is shown in Plate 2.2.

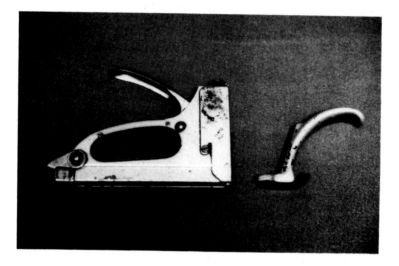

Plate 2.2 A staple gun for driving staples, and a tool for removing them.

Pins and Tacks

There are many patterns of small nail, each with a different shaped head. Tacks have a large flat head and are used for holding down copper plate or felt. Escutcheon pins have a smaller domed head that can be decorative, while panel pins, or brads, have a small head that is easily punched below the surface with a pin punch, the hole can then be filled with a plastic wood (such as 'Brummer') before varnishing. Panel pins are useful for holding wood trim while the glue cures. It may be necessary to drill hardwood before driving brass pins which bend easily.

An alternative way to hide pins is to lift back a curl of timber, drive the pin beneath it, then glue back the shaving to hide the panel pin. This takes time and is reserved for perfectionists.

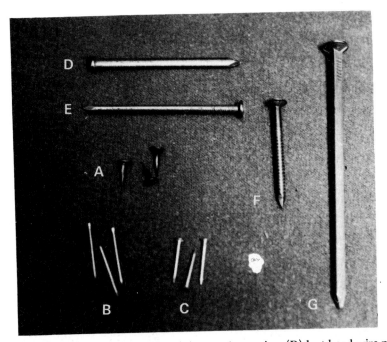

Plate 2.3   (A) tacks, (B) panel pins, (C) escutcheon pins, (D) lost head wire nail, (E) round head wire nail, (F) bronze ring nail, (G) copper boat nail.

Nails

Nails are described by their length and gauge. The standard wire gauge is used, Table 12 showing the actual diameter for gauge numbers. These figures should only be taken as a guide as different manufacturers have slightly different sizes. The important thing to remember is that the higher the gauge number, the smaller the diameter.

Wire nails can be round with a flat head, or oval with a very small head called 'lost head' nails. Flat headed copper wire nails can be obtained, but the most widely used nail for traditional boatbuilding is the copper boat nail. This is a square sectioned nail with a countersunk head. It has no sharp point but tapers slightly before being rounded. Copper nails are clenched (riveted or turned) where possible, and this is described when considering rivets, but they can be used as ordinary nails, although the grip is poor with small sizes. Very large nails can be driven into a predrilled blind hole, and used as drifts.

Drifts

Drifts, or drift bolts, are simply outsized nails. They can be galvanized iron or copper. Copper drifts can be made in the workshop

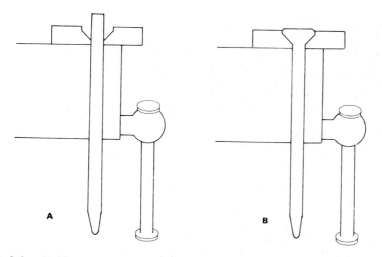

Fig 2.6   Making a copper drift:(A) copper rod is held in the vice with one end protruding through a steel mould; (B) when heated the copper can be hammered until it fills the mould, making a neat countersunk head.

from bar, tapering it at one end and working a head at the other. The best heads are made by using a heavy piece of steel plate that has a countersunk hole drilled in it as a mould. The copper bar is held in a vice and the steel plate slid over it so that a length equal to the rod's diameter protrudes. This is heated with a blow torch, and hammered repeatedly until the countersunk hole is filled, as shown in Fig. 2.6. The rod can then be removed from the steel plate and the head cleaned up. Light rod can be worked cold.

Holes should be predrilled for drifts, about 1/16 in (1.5 mm) less than the bolt diameter, although for long bolts through hardwood it may have to be larger.

Ring Nails

Nails are quicker and easier to drive than screws, but they cannot be easily removed. Easy removal is an advantage when repair work has to be carried out, but with many modern construction methods everything is glued, so whether or not a fastening will unfasten is immaterial. In these situations nails may just as well be used and the stronger their grip the better. Ring nails, sometimes called barb or threaded nails, have better holding power than ordinary smooth nails. There are several brands available (such as 'Gripfast' and 'Anchorfast') and they can be made from silicon bronze or Monel, with both flat or countersunk heads.

Ring nails do not have the holding power of screws, so more should be used; extra strength can be added by driving the nails at different angles to obtain a dovetail effect. Holes for ring nails should be predrilled, and should be about three quarters of the nail's diameter in hardwood, and half in softwood. The holes should only be three quarters as deep as the nail will be driven. Nails are hidden by punching below the surface and filling.

Some heavy fastenings are square sectioned, but with a slight twist from end to end. These rotate as they are driven home, and are called drive screws.

Trenails

Trenails (or trunnels) are a very ancient form of fastening, with the great advantage that they do not corrode. They are simply a wooden dowel, held in place by splaying the ends with wedges. They can be through fastenings, wedged inside and out, or driven into a blind hole.

Wedging is done by making a saw cut in the trenail and then, after it has been hammered home, a hardwood wedge is driven into the cut. The wedge should be aligned across the grain so that it does not start a split in the timber. Even when driven into a blind hole the inboard end can still be wedged. The dowel is cut and a short wedge inserted prior to driving, as shown in Fig. 2.7. The wedge is forced into the dowel by the bottom of the hole. This method is called blind wedging or 'foxtailing'.

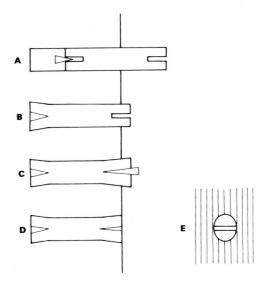

Fig 2.7   Blind wedging trenails: (A) with a wedge inserted in the trenail it is positioned in the hole; (B) then driven home; (C) a second wedge is driven in the outboard end; (D) and finally cut off flush. (E) The wedges should be aligned across the grain to avoid splitting the wood.

Unwedged dowels used with modern glues, such as epoxy, make good fastenings if the dowels are of sufficient diameter.

Screws

Screws are not sold by weight, but by number; a box usually contains 200, although less than this can always be bought. Their size is described by length and gauge number, but the screw gauge works the opposite way to the wire gauge: for screws, the larger the number the larger the screw. On boat work, only even numbered screws are customarily used, and Table 12 gives the actual shank diameter for these from gauge 4 to 16.

Table 12 Screw and nail sizes

Nails (shank diameter)			Gauge numbers	Screws (shank diameter)		
inches (fractions)	inches (decimals)	mm		inches (fractions)	inches (decimals)	mm
15/64	0.232	5.892	4	7/64	0.108	2.743
3/16	0.192	4.876	6	9/64	0.136	3.454
5/32	0.160	4.064	8	5/32	0.164	4.166
1/8	0.128	3.251	10	3/16	0.192	4.877
7/64	0.104	2.640	12	7/32	0.220	5.588
5/64	0.080	2.032	14	1/4	0.248	6.299
1/16	0.064	1.625	16	9/32	0.276	7.010
Larger the gauge number, smaller the nail.				Larger the gauge number, larger the screw.		

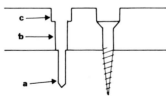

Fig 2.8   A correctly drilled screw hole is in three parts: (a) pilot hole, (b) clearance hole, and (c) counterbored hole.

To fasten two pieces of timber together a clearance hole should be drilled through the first, and a pilot hole into the second, as shown in Fig. 2.8. The clearance hole should be the same size as the screw shank and is most easily discovered by slipping the screw into the holes in the box of bits to find which it neatly fits.

The pilot hole should then be about ³⁄₆₄ in (1 mm) smaller than the clearance hole. The exact size of pilot hole depends on the hardness of the wood, and is best discovered by trial in scrap wood to ensure that the screw can be driven right home, without splitting the timber.

If the screw is to be countersunk or counterbored this entails a third drilling operation, but by using special combination bits the three operations can be combined in one. The problem with these bits is that in the large gauge size (10 and 12) they tend to be longer than is required for boatwork. By removing the pilot bit they can still be used to counterbore and drill the clearance hole, the pilot hole again being drilled in a separate operation.

The Gougeon Brothers suggest a startling way of increasing fastening performance by drilling an exceptionally oversize hole, perhaps ⅛ in (3 mm) or more larger than the screw. This is then filled with epoxy resin which the screw is simply pushed into while still wet. Once the resin has cured it is as strong as the fastening, and effectively increases the fastening's diameter, spreading the load further and so improving holding power. Advantage can also be gained by saturating the ordinary pilot and clearance holes with resin before inserting the screw: this both improves performance and allows the natural grip of the screw to pull the parts together as the fastening is tightened.

Screw Types
There is a wide variety of screws available with different threads, heads, and slots. Figure 2.9 illustrates the different types of head available: pan and round head do not need countersinking; the flat countersunk head is a normal wood screw, while the raised countersunk head looks better on a metal fitting.

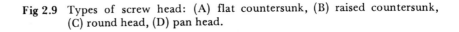

Fig 2.9 Types of screw head: (A) flat countersunk, (B) raised countersunk, (C) round head, (D) pan head.

The simple slot is the most common type of screw although other patterns shown in Fig. 3.12 are available. These give a better grip if the correct type and size of screwdriver is available, the problem is that often it is not. A screw with no slot but a square or hexagonal head designed for use with a spanner is called a lag bolt, and is a strong heavy duty fastening. Another less common fastening is a 'hanger',

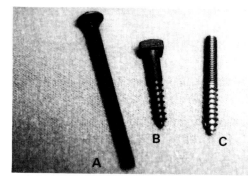

Plate 2.4
Less common fasten-ings: (A) coach bolt, (B) lag bolt or coach screw, and (C) hanger bolt.

which has no head as such, but is machine threaded instead, that is it has a machine thread one end and wood screw the other. A fitting or machinery can be bolted to it with a nut, and easily removed again without having to extract the 'hanger'.

Screws have several thread patterns, but the principal types are the wood screw, and the self-tapping screw. As its name implies, the wood screw is best for fastening two pieces of timber together, as it is only threaded for part of its length; the remaining unthreaded shank passes cleanly through one piece of timber, allowing it to be firmly pulled against the other by the screw's head. If a self-tapping screw, threaded for its entire length, is used for this purpose, the clearance hole either becomes a water trap, or if drilled smaller the thread grips both pieces of wood and actually prevents them being pulled together. A self-tapping screw is good for fastening metal plates or small fittings to timber as no shank is necessary and the entire length of the screw grips, but its main use is for fastening to metal: it will pull its way into a pilot hole drilled through aluminium or metal plate where a wood screw could not.

Disguising Screws
The usual way to hide a screw head is to sink it into a counterbored hole, and cover this with a dowel. Dowel cutters are available that match the sizes of counterbore on combination bits. When gluing the dowels into the hole, care should be taken to align the grain with that of the surrounding timber. If possible dowels should be taken from an offcut of the timber to be plugged, as this ensures a good colour match. Poorly matched dowels can sometimes show more clearly than the screw would, although they are still preferable to an exposed screw head. If the timber is to be painted, screws can be lightly countersunk and filled with stopping.

In some cases such as very thin ply, or timber surfaced with a laminated plastic (Formica), the screw cannot be counterbored or even countersunk. For interior joinery, appearance is improved if the screw sits in a screw cup or finishing washer. Alternatively it can be covered by a snap-on cover with a plastic or metal finish. Special screws can be obtained that have a tiny threaded hole down their centre into which is screwed a flat or domed brass cover, either of which gives a pleasing decorative appearance. Plate 2.5 shows all these methods.

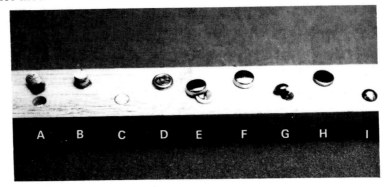

Plate 2.5   Screws are usually hidden by a dowel: (A) counterbore hole, (B) with dowel glued in, and (C) cleaned off flush. Other methods are: (D) screw sitting in a cup washer, (E) snap covers are pressed over plastic washers, (F) and can have a metallic finish, (G) expensive screws have a threaded hole that accepts (H) brass discs or (I) brass dome covers.

Bolts

Bolts are normally through fastenings, with the head at one end and a nut at the other, although on machinery they are often screwed directly into a tapped hole, no nut being necessary. Around the world there are many different thread patterns, and in Britain alone BSW, BSF, BSP (British Standard Whitworth, Fine, and Pipe, respectively) and metric are all in common use. The important thing is that the bolt and the nut have the same screw thread. A bolt with a fine thread is stronger than a coarse threaded one as less metal is removed, leaving a thicker and stronger core.

Bolts are only threaded for part of their length; if the thread extends to the head it is called a machine screw. Threads can be made in two ways; cut or rolled. This makes no difference on a machine screw, but does on a bolt as a rolled thread actually has a larger diameter than the unthreaded shank. Consequently the bolt is slightly loose in its clearance hole, which both makes the fastening weaker, and can allow water to leak in.

186

Boats often require exceptionally long bolts. These can be ordered specially, or the boatbuilder can make them himself. Studding is rod threaded for its entire length, and this can be cut to size and a nut used at both ends. Alternatively plain rod can be used and threaded with a die. Copper or bronze rod can be threaded easily, and one end can have a countersunk head worked onto it in the manner already described for drift bolts.

Head Types

Although bolts normally have a hexagon head, for use with a spanner, they can just as easily be obtained with any of the heads described for screws. Small 'bolts' need have no head at all but a socket instead, and are tightened with Allen keys; these are called socket set screws, or grub screws.

Coach bolts are for use in timber, and have a dome head hiding a short square section of shank. The square section is pulled into the timber and prevents the bolt turning while the nut is tightened (see Plate 2.4).

Nuts

The full hexagon nut is the most common, but the others are useful in particular situations: wing nuts, tightened and loosened by hand,

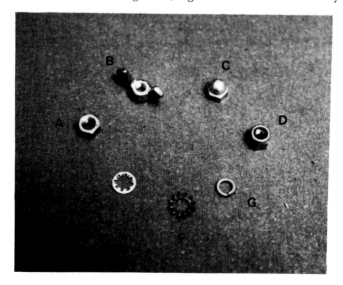

Plate 2.6 Some types of nut and washer: (A) ordinary hexagon full nut, (B) wing nut, (C) dome nut, (D) self-locking nut. Nuts are also locked with special washers: (E) and (F) are inside and outside toothed washers, (G) is a spring washer.

are useful if the nut has to be removed frequently, dome nuts (or cap nuts) give a more attractive finish and can be used when heavy bolts unavoidably protrude into cabin interiors. Half nuts (or jam nuts) can be used as lock nuts, or where a low profile is necessary, although if used alone they are obviously less strong than a full nut. Some of these are illustrated in Plate 2.6.

Locking a nut, preventing vibrations working it loose, is usually necessary. If the nut is in tension it will not work loose, so nuts tightened against each other are locked, and special nuts can be obtained that lock themselves, such as the 'lock nut' and castle (or slotted) nut. A castle nut is actually locked by drilling the bolt and inserting a split pin against which the slots cannot turn. Alternatively locking washers can be used that bite into the nut preventing it turning. These are in two patterns, the spring washer or toothed washer. A tab washer also prevents a nut undoing, even if it has to be only lightly tightened, as with the nuts on some seacocks.

Other methods to lock nuts are to use a chemical adhesive, such as 'Locktite', or to split the bolt and open it slightly, as in Fig. 2.10, or even to cut it just above the nut and burr it over. This is a fairly final method, as removal of the nut even intentionally becomes difficult.

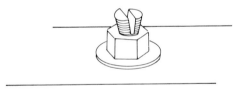

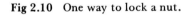

Fig 2.10   One way to lock a nut.

Apart from plain washers, and locking washers already mentioned, oversized or 'penny' washers can be obtained. These are particularly useful when it is necessary to spread the load of a bolt, as on timber or ferrocement. Even penny washers are often not adequate and a proper backing plate should be used in many situations.

Washers designed to be used when riveting copper nails are called roves or burrs.

Rivets

Rivets are through fastenings usually used to join sheet metal together. The rivet has a head one side, the other side being splayed in some manner after insertion, to form a permanent fastening.

Conventional rivets can be made of mild steel, aluminium, copper, etc., and are splayed or clenched by striking with a hammer or pneumatic tool; if the metal rivet is inserted hot it is both easier to work and grips tighter as it cools. Conventional rivets need to be set by two workers (one either side) and have for the most part been superseded by welded joints, but the 'blind rivet' is a very quick and handy fastening, and is widely used.

Blind rivets, or pop rivets, are made from aluminium, stainless steel, or Monel, and their great advantage is that they are fastened from one side only. This means they can be used to fasten fittings to alloy masts and in other situations where access is impossible. Fastening is simple: a hole is drilled, the rivet inserted and splayed with a riveting tool. This tool looks a little like a pair of pliers and works by pulling the mandrel through the hollow rivet until the mandrel's head breaks off, leaving the rivet firmly fastened. Of the many types of blind rivet available, Fig. 2.11 illustrates three. The first two are the most commonly used type, the 'breakhead' leaving a hole, whereas the 'breakstem' does not. In either case a sealant should be used to insulate the rivet from the surrounding metal. Blind rivets with countersunk heads are also available.

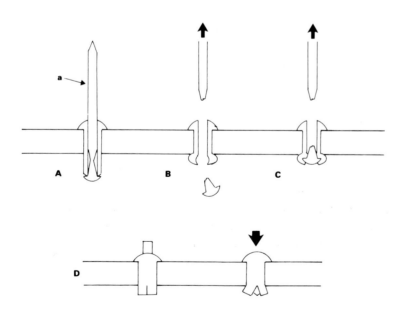

Fig 2.11   (A) Blind rivets are placed in a predrilled hole and set by pulling the mandrel (a) with a special tool. (B) 'Breakhead' rivets leave a through hole, (C) 'breakstem' rivets do not. (D) Drive pin rivets do not need a special tool but are set by striking with a hammer.

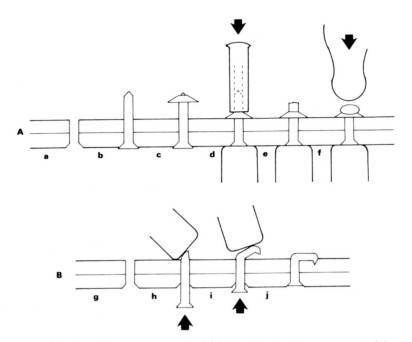

Fig 2.12   (A) Clenching a copper nail: (a) hole drilled and countersunk, (b) nail inserted, (c) rove positioned, (d) with dolly held against nail head rove is driven with a rove punch, (e) nail cut (one nail thickness above the rove), (f) nail clenched or burred over with a light ball peen hammer. (B) Turning a nail: (g) hole drilled and countersunk, (h) nail driven with dolly held inside to deflect tip, (i) dolly gradually brought perpendicular to plank, (j) nail re-enters timber and is drawn tight.

In traditional wooden boat building, copper rivets are the standard method of fastening the planks to timbers or frames, and also of fastening planks to each other in clinker, or lapstake boats. The method of riveting copper nails is illustrated in Fig. 2.12, as is the simpler technique of turning the nail. Turning the nail is quicker and easier, but is not as strong as a nail properly clenched or riveted over a rove. A turned nail ends up flush with the surrounding wood which is an advantage if something will have to be fitted at that point. Thinking ahead and turning instead of clenching nails where floors or knees will be sighted can save some work.

4. Adhesives

Gluing technology is a very complex subject about which several books have been written. Despite this, many people fail to inform themselves about the basics of adhesives, or if they do attempt to, are quickly swamped by the vast amount of irrelevant information, and give up. After all, we all know how to glue: a dash of this mixed with a gloop of that, spread it on and clamp it up. Usually it works, but if it does not, it is because 'that glue is useless'.

Because the adhesives used by the boatbuilder are limited in number, the relevant information is not that extensive. A full understanding of it and careful consideration when planning and setting up the workshop and gluing procedures, can make gluing almost as simple as the description above, with the difference that success is assured. The basic concepts are set out here, but once the type of glue has been decided upon, close attention should always be paid to the manufacturer's instructions.

At the end of this section adhesives for use in special situations, for gluing to metal, ferrocement, and fibreglass are dealt with, but the main consideration for the boatbuilder is the successful bonding of timber.

Waterproof Wood Glues

The high specification required for glues used in boat construction limits the choice to three types: urea formaldehyde, resorcinol formaldehyde, and epoxy. In addition to the comments following, comparative details of these are provided in Table 13.

Polyvinyl acetate, or PVA, (a commercial example is Evo-stick Resin W) is the ordinary wood glue found in most carpenters' and joiners' shops. It is cheap, easy to use, and needs little clamping, but is unfortunately not suitable for boatwork. Its main disadvantage is that it is not resistant to moisture, but it also creeps if tensioned under sustained loads, so is unlikely to be of use even in jig construction. It is best left in the garden shed for home use only.

Urea Formaldehyde
(Commercial examples: 'Cascamite', by Borden UK Ltd., and 'Aerolite', by Ciba-Geigy.)

This takes the form of a white powder to which water is added to make a paste. With 'Cascamite' the glue is then activated, and is applied to both surfaces before clamping. 'Aerolite' is activated by a clear liquid hardener which is applied to one surface, the paste to the other. When the two are brought together curing commences. This means that 'Aerolite' has in practice no 'pot life', but remains workable indefinitely, whereas the activated 'Cascamite' cures in the pot after a few hours. A liquid hardener can also be used with 'Cascamite' to reduce clamping times.

Urea formaldehyde is a good general purpose glue for non-critical situations. It is cheaper than resorcinol or epoxy resin, and easier to use as neither their mix ratios (powder to water) nor the curing temperature are critical. It also produces invisible glue lines. Disadvantages are that it is not as durable as the other glues, and should not be used where it will be exposed to continuous severe weathering or high humidities.

It is normally used for building dinghies that are not to be kept continually afloat, and for interior joinery on larger craft.

Resorcinol Formaldehyde
(Commercial examples: 'Cascophen' by Borden UK Ltd and 'Aerodux' by Ciba-Geigy.)

Resorcinol formaldehyde is a dark chocolate-coloured resin that is activated by mixing with a hardener: 'Cascophen' is a powder hardener, 'Aerodux' comes as two liquids mixed in a 1:1 ratio. This glue produces a very strong joint whose great advantage is its outstanding durability. It can stand severe weathering and prolonged immersion, even in boiling water. It also has reasonable gap-filling qualities, quite sufficient for laminating work, but ⅟₃₂ in (1.5 mm) should be considered the maximum possible. For gaps of this size ten percent filler (supplied by the manufacturer) may be necessary to help retain the glue in the joint until cured.

Drawbacks with this glue are the very dark and visible glue lines and the care needed when working with it: mixing ratios must be accurately observed, and temperatures should not be allowed to fall below 60 degrees Fahrenheit (16 degrees Centigrade) during the initial cure of sixteen to twenty-four hours.

Resorcinol resins are used for all structural and exterior work, and for cold moulded and laminated structures. When laminating heavily stressed members clamping pressure should be maintained for up to four times as long as normally recommended. Resorcinol glue is successful with teak and other oily woods without the need to degrease, provided the surfaces have been freshly cut. On the other hand the acidic nature of oak makes this a difficult timber to glue with resorcinol, and extra high temperatures (100 degrees Fahrenheit or 40 degrees Centrigrade) should be maintained while curing.

Epoxy Resins
There is a vast range of epoxies available, designed with different properties, and to suit different needs. They can be obtained as liquids, thixotropic pastes, and putties, with fast or slow setting times, and have remarkable strength and good bond with a very wide variety of materials. The Gougeon Brothers have explored and developed the use of epoxy resin in conjunction with wood as a raw material for boatbuilding. In their typically practical way, they have produced a basic resin and hardener to which can be added a variety of fillers to obtain an epoxy of the required consistency and properties for each job. Rather than providing a large range of products for every situation, they supply the basic materials and good detailed advice. As already discussed, the WEST System is more than a gluing method, but here it is examined as an example of epoxy resin used as a waterproof wood glue.

WEST Epoxy (available from Borden UK Ltd) is in the form of two liquids, mixed by volume in the ratio 5:1. This activated resin can then be used itself as a glue, but to prevent glue starvation in the joint (caused by excessive absorption of resin into the wood) fillers in the form of micro fibres are added; these conduct resin to the dry areas by capillary action. Alternatively unfilled resin can first be painted onto the mating surfaces, and before it has cured, a putty of resin filled with colodia silica is applied. The two parts are then brought together and pressure applied to ensure complete surface contact.

The advantages of epoxy glues are many. First, the glue has superb gap-filling qualities without any reduction in strength (¼ in (6 mm) or more is quite acceptable,) and so a good fit is required only for appearance, not for strength. Secondly, the minimal clamping pressures mean that in many cases actual clamps are unnecessary; simpler systems using staples or stretched rubber can be devised that provide adequate pressure during cure. Finally, the clear nature of the resin means that glue lines are discreet, unlike the prominent ones produced by resorcinol resin.

There are drawbacks in the use of epoxy resin, the most obvious of which is the price, being considerably more expensive than the other glues discussed. It is also liable to be dermatitic, particularly the hardeners, so extra care is necessary when handling, including the use of barrier and cleansing creams and gloves when possible. Epoxy resin is not easy to work with either: it requires accurate measuring of mix ratios by volume (WEST supply dispensers to simplify this). Temperatures should preferably be controlled between 60 and 80 degrees Fahrenheit (16–26 degrees Centigrade); and it is more difficult to clean from tools, solvents being necessary instead of water as used with the other glues. WEST epoxy also has a very short pot life, only ten to twenty minutes under normal working temperatures, and even with their slow hardener this is only extended to about thirty minutes. Because epoxy cures by an exothermic reaction (i.e. giving off heat) a volume of activated resin will cure quicker when concentrated in a mixing bowl than when spread out, where the larger surface area keeps it cooler. This results in the 'open joint' time, before which the two parts have to be brought together, actually being longer than the pot life, the opposite of resorcinol resin which stays fluid in the pot for several hours, but skins up in a matter of minutes once spread. Pot life of epoxy can be lengthened by cooling the mix, most simply accomplished by standing the pot in a bowl of cold water, or pouring the mixed resin into a flat dish whose larger surface area will mean an extension of the pot life. Polythene bowls make the best mixing containers as they are one of the few things epoxy will not bond with; excess glue can be easily cracked out after curing.

The WEST system uses epoxy in every gluing situation, but for builders who are mainly using resorcinol resin for construction, epoxy is invaluable when wood has to be glued to other difficult materials, especially metal, glass fibre, or ferrocement.

Comparative Table of Timber Adhesives

The details in Table 13 apply to the commercial examples 'Cascamite', 'Cascophen', and 'WEST Epoxy', (all available from Borden UK Ltd). Other brands of the same types of glue will behave similarly, although the mixing ratios and curing times may vary slightly, and in the case of epoxy can be entirely different.

The terms used in the table have the following meanings:

(i) Moisture content: percentage of water in the wood, relative to dry sample as explained in Section 1: Timber.

Table 13 Adhesive comparison

	Urea formaldehyde	Resorcinol formaldehyde	Epoxy resin
Commercial example	'Cascamite'	'Cascophen'	'WEST'
Description	Powder and water	Resin and powder	Resin and resin
Mix ratio: by weight	2:1	5:1	-
by volume	(3½:1)	(2¼:1)	5:1
Tool cleaner	Soapy water	Warm water	Solvents
Timber moisture content	12½% - 15%	15% - 18%	less than 12%
Glue line appearance	Clear	Dark brown/black	Clear
Gap filling (max)	0.01 in (0.25 mm)	0.05 in (1.25 mm)	¼ in (6 mm) or more
Durability classification	MR	WBP	WBP
Pot life	50° F (10°C) 9 hours 60° F (16°C) 3½ hours 70° F (21°C) 1½ hours	60° F (16°C) 9 hours 70° F (21°C) 3½ hours 80° F (27°C) 1¾ hours 90° F (32°C) ¾ hour	50° F (10°C) approx 2 hours (with slow hardener) 80° F (27°C) approx 10 mins (with fast hardener)
Minimum clamping times	50° F (10°C) 18 hours 60° F (16°C) 7 hours 70° F (21°C) 3 hours	60° F (16°C) 18 hours 70° F (21°C) 7 hours 80° F (27°C) 4 hours 90° F (32°C) 1⅓ hours 100° F (38°C) 1 hour	at 70° F (21°C) approx 5 hours with fast hardener and 9 hours with slow hardener, reduced with heat

(ii) Durability: as specified by BS 1204, which classifies glues as follows:

INT: interior joints, resist cold water but not bio deterioration. PVA has this classification.

MR: moisture resistant, withstands exposure to limited weathering and bio deterioration, but not boiling water.

BR: boil resistant, withstands boiling water and limited weathering.

WBR: weatherproof and boil proof, highly resistant to boiling, biological organisms, prolonged weathering and dry heat.

(iii) Pot life: period during which activated resin is usable. Once it ceases to be a liquid, and starts to gel it should be discarded.

(iv) Minimum clamping times: period pressure should be maintained. These times should be multiplied by a factor of four for heavily stressed laminated structures.

Procedures when Gluing Timber

Timber Preparation

The timber should have a suitable moisture content, as shown in Table 13 and its surface be clean, dry, and free from grease. With the exception of epoxy, a good fit is important as the thinner the glue line the stronger the bond. For this reason timber should not be sanded prior to gluing, a smooth planed surface giving better results. Where possible surfaces should be recently cut, as ageing can adversely affect the bond.

Application

Glue can be applied by a number of methods: brush, spreader, roller, or special applicators. Brushes are the least efficient as they tend to spread unevenly over large surfaces: hard bristles are better than soft. Foam rollers spread more evenly, but are more difficult to clean. WEST supply cheap disposable foam rollers for applying epoxy resin. Both brushes or rollers should be cheap as, despite thorough cleaning, they rapidly become unserviceable with repeated use due to a build up of cured glue. For large areas spreaders are very effective. These spread the glue quickly and evenly; they can be made of plywood or Formica, one edge serated with a series of short saw cuts. Formica or other plastic is better than wood as it can easily be cleaned either before or after the resin has cured.

In industries that have continual gluing processes glue is often applied to one or both sides of the timber by passing it through rollers that automatically and evenly apply a controlled quantity. Most boatyard gluing is a spasmodic event, not justifying the investment in this equipment.

Glue Starvation

It has already been stated that the thinner a glue line, the stronger the joint. This is true, provided the glue has effectively penetrated the timber pores in both members. Glue starvation is when this is insufficient, and results in a poor bond. It can occur in two apparently contradictory ways. First, if the timber is particularly oily, or non-porous, the glue only penetrates slowly. If the two parts are brought together and clamping pressure is applied immediately, the glue is squeezed from the joint before it has penetrated the pores. When gluing 'difficult' timbers, time should be allowed for this penetration to occur before applying pressure. With resorcinol resin the two glued faces should be brought together quickly but a minimum 'closed assembly period' of about thirty minutes allowed before pressure is applied.

Glue starved joints can also occur because the timber is too porous. This is particularly a problem with WEST epoxy, as it has been specially formulated to penetrate the wood as thoroughly as possible. When applied to end grain the resin is absorbed so effectively that the surface is left dry. This can be overcome manually by repeatedly applying glue until absorption ceases, or more simply by the addition of micro fibres as a filler to the resin; these conduct resin to the dry areas by capillary action, ensuring adequate resin remains in the joint.

Applying Pressure

Generally, the better gap-filling qualities of a glue, the lower the clamping pressure required, so for epoxies it is minimal, but for ureas, should be quite high. Even for urea formaldehyde little pressure is needed in non-critical situations. For example, gluing back into place a splinter of wood for cosmetic purposes is most easily accomplished by holding it in place with masking tape while the glue sets.

Where possible it is easiest to hold parts under pressure by mechanical fastenings: staples, panel pins, or screws. Screws provide considerable pressure, while staples do not do much more than hold the part in place, unless many are used. The advantage gained by using mechanical fastenings is that work can continue on the part while cure takes place without heavy clamps causing an obstruction to progress. Once the glue has cured the fastenings can either be

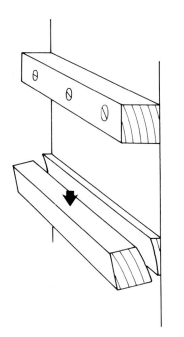

Fig 2.13   Even though a glue joint is stronger than the wood, screws may still be necessary to provide strength across the grain.

removed and the holes filled, or left in place. Removal is sometimes necessary to allow machining, or as with cold moulded structures, removal from a jig. Sometimes removal is desirable simply to save weight, as on a racing dinghy. On the other hand leaving fastenings in place saves time, and can add strength across grain that may be liable to fracture if a glued surface joint is the only connection, as shown in Fig. 2.13.

The usual way to provide pressure is with clamps, and even when the glue itself requires little force, clamps are often needed when laminating to bend the timber to shape. Every boatbuilder has a good collection of clamps, but never enough. Improvisation with such items as bolts and wedges is often necessary. There are many types of clamp available (see Part 3 Tools), but the ordinary 'G' clamp is the most used. 'Sash' clamps are necessary when a long reach is required, but often of more use to the boatbuilders are clamps with a deep bite that can reach well toward the centre of a panel. When gluing panels (such as scarfing plywood) one method of applying pressure at the centre of the panel is to use a clamp at each end with bowed lengths of wood between, as shown in Fig. 2.14. As the clamps are tightened, pressure is first applied to the centre of the panel and only reaches the edges once the bowed boards have been straightened.

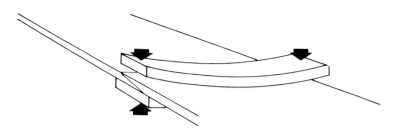

Fig 2.14 Pressure can be applied to the centre of wide panels by using curved boards and clamping at the edges.

Clamps should always be used with wooden 'toes' or pads to spread the load and prevent the metal damaging the wood surface. Clamping pressure should be sufficient to bring the parts firmly into contact, but not so heavy as to distort the timber. For the same reason clamps should always be sited as close to the glued joint as possible, as demonstrated in Fig. 2.15. Figure 2.16 shows another form of clamping distortion that should be avoided when edge-joining boards.

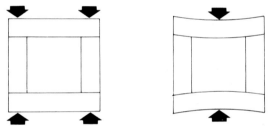

Fig 2.15 Clamping pressure should be applied as close to the joints as possible to avoid distortion, as with this simple frame.

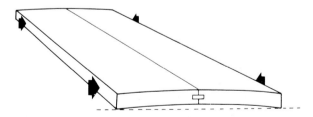

Fig 2.16 When edge-joining boards, care should be taken that clamping pressure does not cause bowing.

Pressure can be provided in other ways, one being the use of a vacuum or pressure bag to force laminates against a solid form of the required shape. These systems are again of more use to industries where a large number of identical parts have to be laminated, but

199

in certain circumstances could be very successfully applied in boatbuilding, in particular 'vacuum bagging' for the construction of 'Constant Camber' panels.

Vacuum Bagging

Vacuum bagging was used to apply pressure to the first moulded hulls in the 'forties and 'fifties. Powerful pumps had to be used with those early glues, but the low pressures now required with epoxy make the method possible with much smaller and cheaper pumps which are readily available as spare parts for industrial vacuum cleaners. The simple shape and small radius of curvature required for laminated or cold moulded 'Constant Camber' panels, make them ideal for this method of pressure application.

The vacuum bag itself simply consists of a sheet of heavy polythene, sealed around its edges with either a Plasticine-like mastic, or, for a more sophisticated set-up, an aluminium channel into which a rubber bead is inserted that holds and seals the edge of the plastic sheet. To ensure that air is drawn from all parts inside the bag, measures are taken to prevent the bag 'choking' around the extraction point: inside the length of the bag a pipe is led, with many holes to suck in air, and between the bag and the panel a wire or fibreglass mesh is laid to allow air to 'bleed' from the entire panel area, or alternatively strips of foam or lengths of rope can do the same job.

Once parting films are taken into account as well it will be realised that the vacuum bag actually consists of several layers. These layers are shown in Fig. 2.17; the first is the mould itself, solid enough to accept staples, and sealed with several coats of epoxy to ensure it is airtight because it is actually the bottom half of the 'vacuum bag', and around its edge is the mastic seal. Onto the mould is placed a sheet of light polythene to act as a parting film to release the cured panel from the mould, and onto this the laminates are positioned; all are glued and stapled in place at one time, so that they all cure simultaneously. Finally over the top the last three layers are positioned: a second polythene parting film, 'bleeder' mesh with pierced pipe, and final heavy polythene sheet. These can all be kept rolled together and positioned by unrolling along the panel. The top sheet of polythene, the actual 'bag', is pressed into the mastic to form the seal, and the header pipe connected to the vacuum pump with mastic, again ensuring a good seal where it leaves the bag. Once the pump is switched on, a check should be made for leaks, then the motor left running until the glue has cured, about six to ten hours for epoxy.

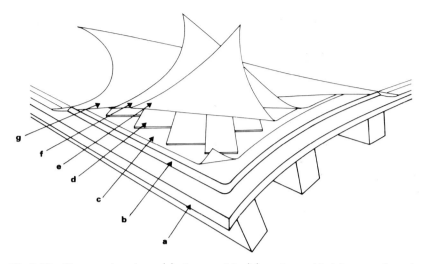

Fig 2.17 Vacuum bagging: (a) the mould; (b) seal provided by mastic strip; (c) polythene sheet as a parting film; (d) glued veneers; (e) top parting film; (f) mesh to allow air to bleed from entire area; (g) heavy polythene forming top half of the vacuum bag.

Centrifugal pumps need some air passing through them, so it may be necessary to incorporate a valve to allow the entry of air when pressure drops below a certain level. The valve should be adjusted so that the pump just operates correctly; when too little air is in the system it can be heard racing.

Advantages gained by vacuum bagging are the application of an even pressure over the entire panel which ensures a better bond and reduces the quantity of glue required, and the minimal use of staples so less staples have to be pulled, saving considerable time. Time is also saved as all the laminates are glued at once, saving the repeated curing interval required for conventional cold moulding where each layer has to be cured before the staples can be drawn, and the next glued.

Gluing Different Materials

Epoxies form excellent bonds with a wide range of materials. Boat-builders will most commonly have to make joints with fibreglass, steel, and ferrocement, and in all these cases epoxy is a good choice. Where the mating surfaces are very uneven, as when bonding two fibreglass mouldings, an epoxy putty may be more suitable than the filled epoxy resin supplied by WEST, which is primarily formulated for use with wood.

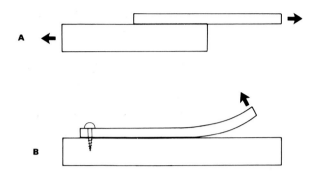

Fig 2.18   (A) Glued joints are strongest in shear, but (B) weak when peeled. A mechanical fastening at the end of a glued strip prevents the start of a failure due to peeling.

Where possible a joint should be designed that allows the adhesive to work most efficiently. Adhesives are strongest when a shearing force is applied to the two parts, and weakest when 'peeled', as illustrated in Fig. 2.18, which also shows how the onset of peeling can be avoided when long strips are glued, by mechanically fastening their ends.

When fastening to fibreglass or metal it is important to thoroughly degrease and abrade the surface. Initially using a coarse sand paper and then a finer one (180 grit), cleaning with solvent after each, produces a good surface for bonding. With steel this surface should be glued to immediately.

Ferrocement should be prepared by scrubbing clean with detergent, then rinsing thoroughly with water, and allowing to dry.

When fitting out the galley and 'heads', it is common to use laminated plastics (e.g. 'Formica') to provide wipe-clean surfaces. Gluing these plastics to plywood is best done with a contact adhesive, similar in nature to the glues used for repairing inflatables. Although these glues make bonds with little strength they are quite adequate for this purpose as they are subject to hardly any stress.

Contact adhesive is spread on both surfaces and allowed to dry. When the parts are brought together an immediate bond is made. For this reason the 'Formica' should be cut oversize to allow some latitude when positioning, as once contact is made it cannot be moved. Newspaper placed between the two surfaces allows accurate positioning, and it is then slid out to bring the glued parts into contact. Trimming the 'Formica' back to the same size as the plywood can be done with an electric router fitted with a trimming blade, or simply with a sharp plane. The plastic dulls tools quickly.

202

Special trimming tools can be obtained, some of which automatically cut a tiny chamfer on the laminate edge. This can equally well be done by hand, and makes a good finish as it looks tidy and avoids a corner which can sometimes be sharp enough to cut the skin.

One other type of adhesive which should be mentioned is the Anaerobics (commercial example: 'Superfast' range by Locktite). These cure in the absence of oxygen and are used to lock nuts chemically, instead of using locking washers.

5. Sealants

Ensuring joints are watertight is an important consideration for every boatbuilder, and an obsession for the boat owner. Avoiding leaks, which are at the very least a worry below the water line and an irritation above, is reason enough to attempt to seal all joints, through-hull fittings, and fastenings, but a second reason is to protect the wood. Even small fittings that are simply screwed in place should be bedded to avoid water getting into unprotected end grain, and this is of particular importance when dealing with plywood.

A well designed joint with a good waterproof glue will be watertight, but is not always possible. Timber that is likely to move through shrinkage and swelling, or that may have to be removed at a later date for maintenance or repair cannot be glued. Similarly joints or fittings that will be heavily stressed are through bolted, making glue unnecessary. In these situations sealants are used — some sort of gooey substance that will fill any gaps, and stay there, keeping water at bay.

Matching Sealants to Situations

Because of the wide choice of materials available and the fact that none is perfect, selecting which sealant for a given situation can be difficult. It helps to understand their properties and the job they have to do but often the decision is a matter of personal preference. Most boatbuilders have their own favourite brand of 'gunk', but no one sealant can be ideal in every case and several different types should be to hand.

Although the next two sections are labelled 'Traditional Seals' and 'Modern Compounds', these should not be seen as exclusive choices: the sensible builder selects the most suitable solution to each problem as it arises. For example the main frame joints of a hull may be luted with white lead but the decks caulked with polysulphide rubber, or conversely the builder of a fully laminated hull that uses much epoxy or resorcinol resin may still choose to bed the

204

ballast keel on a strip of bituminous felt. It is not a choice of either traditional or modern, but what is right for the job.

There are two different types of joint in which sealants are used. Either the joint squeezes the mastic during assembly, or the joint is filled with mastic after. In the first the tighter the joint the better, but in the second, although part of the joint is tight, a seam is deliberately left to be filled. The second type of joint demands more of the sealant as it must be adhesive enough to stay in place, and flexible enough to allow the parts on each side both to swell and contract, squeezing or stretching it in between.

The terms describing the use of sealants in various situations are many and confusing, but these are the interpretations that will be used in this book: 'luting' and 'bedding' are both inserted in the 'squeeze' situation, but luting is a sealant thinly spread in a timber joint, while bedding is a thicker mastic placed under fittings or between prebuilt parts; 'caulking' and 'stopping' both fill seams, but caulking is expected to keep out the water, whereas stopping is of a more cosmetic nature, intended primarily to fill the holes and accept paint. These four different situations are illustrated in Fig. 2.19. As is often the case with boats and boatbuilding, words change meaning with locality and no doubt these words are sometimes used differently, or others in their place.

Which sealant to use in a given situation is a decision based on many factors, but the following descriptions of methods and materials together with the accepted applications as laid out in Table 14 should help make that choice.

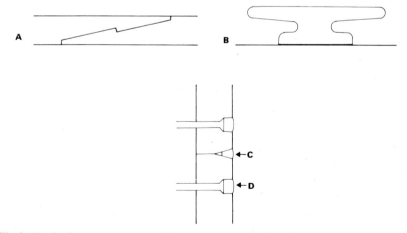

Fig 2.19 Sealants as used in different situations: (A) luting in a timber joint; (B) bedding under a fitting; (C) caulking seals a seam but (D) stopping serves a more cosmetic purpose, filling nail holes etc.

205

Table 14 Sealant selection

Material	Description				Method of application			Situations used					Comments
	one part	two part	prime with paint	special primer	knife	gun	other	luting joints	bedding fittings	caulking hull	caulking deck	stopping	
Pitch	✓						✓			✓	✓	✓	Cheap
White lead putty		✓	✓		✓				✓	✓			
Linseed oil and white lead		✓			✓			✓					Good preservative
Butyl rubber	✓							✓	✓				Reasonably priced
Polysulphide rubber	✓	✓		✓		✓			✓	✓	✓		Expensive - but superior performance
Silicone rubber	✓			✓		✓			✓				Expensive - good for special applications
Foam tape	✓						✓		✓				Clean
Pliable mastics	✓						✓		✓				
Solid stopping (P 38)		✓			✓							✓	

Traditional Seals

Young boatbuilders may have a favourite brand of gunk, but the old boys usually have a favourite recipe, whose special ingredients are sometimes a jealously guarded secret. With patience a sample may be obtained, but not the formula! Most of these mixtures are made from a combination of some of the following ingredients: raw linseed oil, ground white (or red) lead, putty, and grease. With these four items in the workshop a paste can be made to suit most situations, adding putty where body is needed, adding grease to prevent the paste ever drying.

These apparently old-fashioned concoctions should not be dismissed out of hand. They have been proved over a very long time, and the inclusion of lead in the mixture makes them excellent wood preservatives, though also poisonous, so they should be handled carefully.

Luting and Bedding

A thinnish mixture of raw linseed oil and ground white lead makes an excellent luting composition wherever wood meets wood. The two ingredients should be well mixed and have no lumps of white lead remaining preventing the joint closing. It is best used fairly fresh as with time a skin forms, but this can be removed and additional oil added before mixing again.

The same mixture, but thicker, can be used for bedding, especially where metal fittings are tightly fastened to wood. There is no advantage in using this mixture, as opposed to a modern compound, when bedding two components which are not wood. Bedding an item with a doubtful fit, where the mastic is expected to bridge large gaps, can be achieved if putty is added to the brew.

Bedding between the wood and metal ballast keel was normally tar, although this inevitably weeps through any number of coats of paint. If the top face of the ballast keel is uneven, a strip of bituminous felt, as used for roofing or damp-proof courses in the construction industry, can be painted with tar, then laid between the two. This compresses where necessary as the bolts are tightened.

Caulking a Carvel Hull

The traditional way of sealing the joint between planks on a carvel hull is by driving caulking cotton into the seams. Although the seam is then filled with some form of stopping — usually a mixture of linseed oil, putty and a little ground white lead — it is not this that seals the joint but the cotton fibres. When they get wet they swell

207

against the planks on either side preventing any further penetration of water.

Care must be taken when caulking a hull: sufficient cotton must be driven into the joint to prevent leaks, and driven hard enough to ensure it is not squeezed out when the planks swell, but if driven too hard the cotton may be forced right through, or planks dislodged from the frames. Effective caulking strengthens the hull by tightening the planking. As caulking progresses this tensioning of the hull can be heard; dull thuds in the early stages progressively rise in pitch until the whole hull rings.

A proper caulking mallet has a long head made from a heavy timber such as lignum vitae. The head has slits on each side of the handle to give it spring, and is bound with metal ferrules. Although this is the proper tool for the job, an ordinary wooden mallet is quite adequate, and probably easier to handle for the inexperienced with only a limited amount of caulking to do. Similarly there is a very wide range of caulking irons available although for much boat work one or two will be sufficient.

Caulking cotton is bought in balls that contain six strands. These are separated and an appropriate number re-twisted together. Depending on seam width, two or three strands are usually all that are used. Twisting the strands together is simply accomplished by holding a hook of wire in the chuck of an electric drill, then looping a long strand of the cotton sufficient for the seam over the hook. With the other end held the drill is run, quickly twisting the strands together. The drill is stopped as soon as the cotton starts to make secondary twists.

The cotton is driven into the seams in two stages, illustrated in Plates 2.7 and 2.8. First a bight is driven in about every 2 inches (50 mm) leaving loops of cotton hanging loose between; then the caulker returns and picks up these loops, driving them in to fill the entire length of seam. As already explained, while the cotton must be driven in firmly, it must not be forced right through the planks. Tight seams are caulked first as this will close the wider ones. Planking butts and the entire length of the rebate are also caulked.

Before filling the seam with stopping, it should be painted with primer as it adheres better to this than to the untreated timber surface.

Caulking with cotton (or on fishing boats the much coarser oakum), then stopping with linseed oil putty is the traditional method of making a carvel hull tight. The development of modern materials has made alternative systems available; sheathing the hull

Plate 2.7 Caulking: first a bight of cotton is driven into the seam every 2 in (50 mm).

Plate 2.8 Then the loose loops are driven home.

with nylon or epoxy resin and fibreglass as described in the next section, practically guarantees a watertight hull. It is more questionable how much advantage is gained by simply using a modern mastic, such as polysulphide rubber, in the seams. Although it adheres well to the timber, forming a seal in itself, caulking is still wise as a back up system, and also necessary to prevent the rubber reaching the bottom of a 'V' seam, which weakens it, as explained

209

fully when dealing with this rubber. Polysulphide rubber is also thin when being applied, although it finally sets to a very firm rubber. Persuading this thin mixture to stay in the overhead seams of the bilge is very difficult; or else very easy if the hull is built and caulked upside down. The same problem is encountered when pitch is used to fill the seams of workboat hulls: a mop is used to swab the hull repeatedly with hot pitch which quickly cools and solidifies. Eventually an adequate amount is retained in the seams. By then of course there is a surfeit of the stuff everywhere else!

As some of the strength in a carvel planked hull is derived from the tightening achieved by driving something between the planks, whether it is cotton, or timber splines, this process should not really be omitted, even if the entire hull is to be sheathed.

Paying Decks

After caulking deck seams with cotton, the traditional way to fill or 'pay' the seams was to pour hot pitch into them from a narrow spouted ladle. Sometimes the ladle was a square shape with a spout at each corner, enabling two seams to be filled simultaneously. Any width of plank (narrower than the ladle) could be accommodated by angling the ladle appropriately. Once the pitch had cooled the surplus was cleaned off.

Decks are subjected to frequent wetting and drying, resulting in considerable movement, which tests the pitch considerably; inevitably leaks occur. Polysulphide rubber which has greater adhesion and elasticity than pitch is generally accepted as a vast improvement, and has in this situation (unlike hull seams) superseded the traditional solution.

Modern Compounds

Of the many materials available today, and described as sealants, three types are generally accepted for marine use. These three rubbers are butyl, polysulphide, and silicone. Before examining them in detail a brief comparison of their suitability can be made: butyl is cheapest and is good as a general purpose bedding compound, but unsuitable for caulking applications; polysulphide is more expensive but is excellent for both bedding and caulking; silicone is best suited for special situations, as will be described. These three are all applied by gun from a cartridge, but other materials used differently and of particular interest will also be examined.

210

Butyl Rubbers

Butyl rubbers set by the gradual evaporation of a solvent. A skin forms first, then the remainder gradually thickens, though it never drys completely. As a result it cannot be sanded. Cleaning up is best done with a knife or chisel after about a week, but it can also be done immediately after application with a cloth moistened with white spirit. This tends to leave smears, although these dry quickly and can be easily sanded off timber the following day.

Butyl rubbers can be used as a luting in wooden joints, or as a bedding when fitting hatches, fastening deck fittings etc. Joints should be well fitting for two reasons: the rubber shrinks while setting, and it perishes or oxidises with time where exposed to the air. Tight joints minimise the problems arising from this, while caulking is obviously out of the question.

Applications: luting joints; bedding fittings, hatches etc.
Resistance to solvents: poor.
Commercial examples: Flo Caulk (Boatlife UK), Secomastic (Expandite Ltd).

Polysulphide Rubbers

These are available either as a single part mastic, cured by moisture in the air, or in two component packs which have to be mixed very thoroughly. The two part types have a better performance, but are extremely messy to use. Empty cartridges can be obtained, and the worst mess is kept to a single bench if one person mixes the components and loads the tubes, while another applies the mastic with a gun. This is only practicable for large jobs and one part compositions make more sense in most cases.

Adhesion is poor unless a primer is applied, and this is essential when the rubber is to adhere to oily timbers, such as teak, or to metals. Polysulphide rubbers cure slowly over a period of a week or more, finally setting to a firm rubber. Excess can then be removed with a knife or chisel, or by sanding.

It is more expensive than butyl rubbers, but its better performance makes it worth using as a bedding wherever the seal is important or difficult. Its durability and good resistance to both salt water and solvents make it very suitable for deck caulking. Whenever any movement is likely in a joint it is better to have a wide seam than a narrow one, as there is then more rubber to stretch as the wood contracts. For this reason polysulphide rubber should not be used alone to caulk a 'V' shaped seam as the rubber at the bottom is easily stretched

211

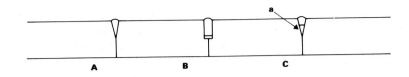

Fig 2.20 Caulking seams with polysulphide rubber: (A) the rubber at the
bottom of a 'V' seam is easily stretched beyond its elastic limit
causing failure of the seal; (B) a rectangular seam, lined at the bottom
is far better; (C) the same effect is achieved by traditional techniques,
a 'V' seam caulked with cotton (a) before applying the rubber.

beyond its elastic limit, causing a complete failure. A rectangular
seam is better, but it must be lined at the bottom so that the rubber
is only adhering to the sides as shown in Fig. 2.20. A narrow piece
of masking tape is sufficient lining. Alternatively traditional caulking
procedures, (a 'V' seam with caulking cotton at the bottom of the
seam,) actually produce the same result. Even if the planks are laid
on a plywood subdeck, 'V' seams should be caulked with cotton
if polysulphide rubber is to be used.

Applications: paying decks; bedding in important situations,
   sometimes used to caulk carvel hulls.
Resistance to solvents: good.
Commercial examples: Life Caulk (Boatlife UK), PRC (Berger
   Paints).

Silicone Rubbers
These have properties very different from the two sealants already
described, which make them most useful in some unusual situations,
though their poor adhesive qualities (improved with primers) and
inability to sand smooth make them unsuitable for caulking.

Silicone rubbers are very durable and resistant to solvents, fuels,
and oils. As they are also resistant to heat (up to 250 degrees Centigrade or 480 degrees Fahrenheit) they are a good choice for use
in the engine room.

Once silicone rubbers have set they maintain their form well.
This means that it is possible to tailor-make gaskets, or bed awkward
shapes that have no flat faces to help form a natural seal. When
used in these situations the rubber is applied and the two parts
brought together, but only partly tightened. Final fastening is done
after the rubber has cured, the pressure squeezing the solidified
rubber to form a very effective seal. If a gasket is literally being
formed, and the parts are required to separate easily, one face is

smeared with grease before being positioned on the wet rubber. Once it has cured the part is removed and wiped free of grease; the gasket is cleaned up before final fixing. Silicone rubbers cure in a matter of hours, so this process does not entail much delay.

This mastic is also a good sealant for windows as it can be obtained in a clear form and adheres reasonably to glass.

Applications: in situ gaskets; bedding windows; engine room applications and deck fuel fillers.

Resistance to solvents: very good.

Commercial examples: Marine Silicone Rubber (Boatlife UK), Silicone Sealant 33 (Expandite Ltd).

Other Bedding Materials

One effective and clean way to bed fittings is to use a plastic foam tape. It is placed between the fitting and deck, bolts or screws then being driven straight through it. As the fastenings are tightened it is tightly squashed, the foam protruding around the edge is trimmed with a knife. This method is quick, effective, and clean, and is particularly useful for small fittings being simply screwed into place.

At the other extreme, very large areas, such as ballast keels, can be bedded into the Plasticine-like mastics used in the building trade as 'strip sealers'. These mastics have much more body than those described above, but they do not cure at all, maintaining the same consistency in service as they have when applied. They are too thick for most applications, but the power exerted by ballast keel bolts soon squeezes out unwanted excess, leaving a difficult joint well sealed and a good insulation between the metal and wood keels.

Solid Stopping

When little movement of the wood is anticipated a stopping or filler can be used that sets hard. This is suitable when finishing the hull for filling all the small imperfections in the wood such as plucked grain or poorly dowelled fastenings. Similarly the seams of a carvel hull that is to be sheathed could be filled with a hard stopping as the sheathing prevents the penetration of water and so little movement is expected. Materials suitable for this are those used by car body repairers and sold in auto accessory shops. One example is Isopon's P38.

6. Sheathing Systems

Adding a supplementary skin to the hull or deck of a finished craft has been standard boatbuilding practice for many centuries. Recent technology has provided new materials, but the two principal reasons for sheathing remain the same. They are to protect the timber from damage and to improve watertightness.

A boat lives in a hazardous and hostile environment. At some stage during its life it will inevitably be liable to mechanical damage, such as grounding, collision with floating debris, or chafe against another boat or harbour wall. In addition, a wooden boat afloat in salt water is under perpetual threat from marine borers. A sheathing that toughens the surface protects a hull from abrasion or impact damage, while marine borers are deterred by a barrier that is either physically impenetrable, or chemically poisonous to them.

Covering decks with canvas laid in paint or white lead was a traditional way to ensure leak-proof decks and drip-free bunks. With time, canvas rots and peels away from the deck; modern materials and resins are used for the same purpose but with greater durability and effectiveness. In fact so effective are today's glues that not only the deck, but also the hull can be made watertight by sheathing. This is an advantage with carvel hulls as it reduces maintenance by eliminating the need to renew caulking, or even to caulk efficiently in the first place. Entirely sealing the hull is of particular advantage on a plywood or laminated hull where the penetration of water through scratched paint could be the start of more serious problems, such as delamination or rot.

Sometimes an old hull, in such bad condition as to be unseaworthy, is entirely clad with either fibreglass or ferrocement. Although often referred to as 'sheathing', this is really a misnomer. It is rebuilding, for most of the hull strength has to be replaced by the new skin. The old hull is essentially a mould, even if it remains inside the new hull as an aid to fitting out. The sheathing systems examined below do add useful strength in some cases, but this is a bonus and not the primary reason for sheathing.

214

Reinforced Resin Systems

Most modern sheathing methods are a thin skin of resin reinforced with fibre. The choice of which resin and which fibre to use affect the cost, application techniques, strength/weight advantages, and appearance of the end product.

The three systems described below have been developed, tested, and promoted by the manufacturers of the resin or reinforcing used, and all have proved successful in the past. No guarantees can be given as effective sheathing is dependent on good preparation, and application in a warm enough environment. Clean dry timber, free from oil or grease is of prime importance in all cases, and for this reason sheathing a new hull in the workshop before it has come into contact with paint or the elements is always more successful than covering an old hull. This can be done, but the timber must be allowed to thoroughly dry out, and much time must be spent scraping and preparing the hull. All surface imperfections and fastenings are filled and sanded.

An old boat is also more work because it is necessary to remove all fittings. Sheathing should be applied to a clear deck and hull; everything else is then bedded onto it. This is straightforward with a new hull, simply a matter of slotting the sheathing process in at the appropriate point in the building schedule. On an older hull, removal of cleats, winches, stanchions, skin fittings and so on considerably adds to the work. On a deck the sheathing should turn up at the cabin sides or coamings for about 1 in (25 mm) and then be covered with a cleat. Similarly it turns down the hull sides and is covered by the rubbing strakes.

Temperatures should be kept up both during application and the intial cure. This is of particular importance with the 'Cascover' system, where temperatures should not be allowed to fall below 60 degrees Fahrenheit (16 degrees Centigrade) for at least sixteen hours after application.

Of the three systems described below, 'Cascover' is the most expensive and difficult to apply, but it is widely accepted as a very high quality sheathing, applicable to both hull and decks. The epoxy/glass cloth sheathing can also be used on both and is certainly far easier to apply. The excellent adhesive qualities of epoxy make it a good choice where materials other than wood are involved, such as sheathing a plywood deck on a ferrocement hull, or where metal fittings cannot be removed on an older boat, they can be sheathed instead. Clear epoxy can also be used for a bright (varnished) finish.

The third system, 'C-Flex', is for hulls only. It is cheaper, but the difficulties of obtaining a good finish make it more suitable for work boats than yachts.

'Cascover' Nylon Sheathing

This system was developed twenty-five years ago and so has a proven life of at least that, although it is no doubt much more. As well as efficiently sealing the hull or decks, it affords excellent protection from marine borers. Conventional antifouling is still necessary as it does not prevent the growth of marine life on its surface, but should the antifouling get tired or damaged, the borers cannot penetrate this skin.

'Cascover' is a process by which nylon cloth is attached to the wood by a very thin layer of resorcinol glue, then impregnated with a vinyl resin by the application of several coats of vinyl paint. The method was developed by Borden (UK) Ltd who supply all the materials necessary, including the special paint, a resorcinol resin that wets well with the nylon cloth (which is so tightly woven that it is watertight even before impregnation), and all the tools necessary.

Because the cloth can stretch slightly it will easily accommodate the hull's compound curves. An excellent bond is made between the wood and cloth, but the very thinness of the resin membrane between them allows considerable flexibility. The hull can move without danger of delamination. For this reason this system is ideal when sheathing a carvel hull as well as the more rigid structures of a plywood or laminated one.

The 'Cascover' sheathing process is demonstrated in Plates 2.9 to 2.16, in this case covering a coach roof. It is important to realise that with this method the resorcinol resin does not saturate the cloth. Other reinforced resin systems require complete impregnation, but with this the glue should remain under the cloth; any that does get onto the surface spoils the job as the vinyl paint adheres badly to it.

Gluing progresses in sections: an area is painted with glue, the cloth unrolled over it, gently flattened down, then the glue is spread as far as possible beneath the cloth with a 'scraper'. This is a piece of Formica or light plywood with smooth sanded edges. It is the same size, and used in a similar manner, to a cabinet scraper. Pushing it across the cloth, a small ripple is formed in front of it full of glue or air. Glue can be spread beneath the cloth in this way until an area twice the size of that originally painted is stuck down. The cloth darkens slightly when effectively glued, but 'scraping' should

Plate 2.9 'Cascover' sheathing *Tirrick's* coach roof: the surface is prepared by filling, sanding and wiping clean. Tape is used to mark the limits of the area to be sheathed and newspaper protects other surfaces from dripping glue.

Plate 2.10 After cutting the cloth roughly to size, dry, it is rolled back and gluing proceeds in sections. Glue is painted thinly over an area, then the cloth rolled out over it.

Plate 2.11 Using a Formica 'scraper' over the cloth, the glue beneath it is stretched over as large an area as possible, usually twice that initially painted with glue. Stapled battens then hold the cloth in position until the glue has cured.

Plate 2.12 To ensure that temperatures remain adequately high for the initial 16 hour curing period a polythene tent is erected over the work with fan heaters or lights providing a heat source.

218

Plate 2.13 The first coat of vinyl pain should be applied within 24 hours.

Plate 2.14 This binds the cloth into a flexible rubbery sheet, enabling overlaps to be cleaned up easily without leaving frayed nylon strands.

Plate 2.15 Edges are best cut after the timber trim has been fastened in place.

continue to ensure that all air bubbles are pushed out, together with any excess glue. Once the cloth pores are effectively filled with glue, the less that remains the better. Glue is most likely to be transferred to the surface when working near the edges, inadvertently

219

Plate 2.16 Sheathing should be continuous under deck fittings: in this case the chain plates will be let into the deck.

getting some onto the 'scraper' and smearing it with the following stroke. If the cloth gets wet the glue tends to penetrate it and for this reason sweat dripping onto the cloth can be a nuisance. Yes, spreading the glue under the cloth is hard work. Stapled battens hold the cloth in position while the glue is curing.

Where two sheets of cloth meet they should overlap by 2 in (50 mm). To obtain neat laps, tape is positioned where the joint will come, and the cloth fitted oversize. When the first piece of cloth is glued down it will reach beyond the tape, and is then trimmed back to it. The tape is then removed and a second piece stuck over the glued cloth 2 in (50 mm) back from the cut edge. Gluing the second cloth over the first as far as this piece of tape produces neat parallel sided butts once it has been trimmed. The first cloth can be trimmed with the glue still wet, in order not to delay progress, but the overlapping cloth is left until after the first coat of vinyl paint has been applied, and then trimmed along with all the other edges. Trimming the cloth after painting is necessary as the vinyl binds the nylon into a clean plastic sheet which is easily cut, whereas trimming the nylon first produces many tatty ends. Butt joints inevitably leave a slight ridge; on the decks they should be neat and square across the boat for appearance sake, but on the hull run fore and aft for fairness.

Sheathing a hull is the same process as for the decks, although in concave curves the battens have to be stapled very close together, even adjacent to each other. The cloth will not adhere to a metal ballast keel. In order to ensure protection from marine borers, the underside of the wood keel should be sheathed before fastening the ballast keel, so that only the metal is outside the protective envelope.

Epoxy/Glass Cloth Sheathing
This system is quicker and easier than the 'Cascover' method, as scraping and battening are unnecessary. A carefully prepared timber surface is primed with epoxy resin; this is allowed to cure before being covered with glass fibre cloth. When working on relatively flat surfaces this can be done by laying dry cloth on the primed timber, then working resin into it with a brush, roller, or plastic spreader, ensuring that the cloth is completely wetted out and that no dry spots are left. This method is preferable as there is no danger of the resin partially curing before wetting out is achieved. Where the surfaces to be sheathed are vertical or overhead, a coat of resin is painted onto the surface, the cloth is then pressed onto it and impregnated with more resin. In order to avoid the resin under the cloth curing too soon, small sections of about one square yard (1 m^2) should be worked on in turn.

At least two further coats of epoxy resin are applied, sanding if necessary, or filling if the weave of the cloth is still visible. As with the 'Cascover' system, fittings should be fastened after sheathing, and edges should be hidden by timber trim, rubbing strakes etc. The cloth is also initially cut oversize, but with this system accurate trimming is done when the first impregnation coat is partially cured. If the right stage is caught it cuts easily and pulls away without difficulty; if left too long it is much harder and may need heavy sanding.

Joints in the cloth can be lapped, and then sanded smooth, which requires a lot of work. Alternatively butting can be neatly accomplished by first lapping the cloth, and when the right state of partial cure is reached, cutting down the centre of the overlap. By peeling back one side the two cut ends can be removed, letting the two pieces meet in a tidy joint. (Fig. 2.21.)

International Paints supply both resin composition and a compatible cloth, but if a clear resin such as that supplied by WEST is used with a light-weight cloth a remarkable effect can be achieved. It is invisible, yet it still has the advantages of sheathing, a watertight hull with a tough abrasion-resistant surface. When wetted out

221

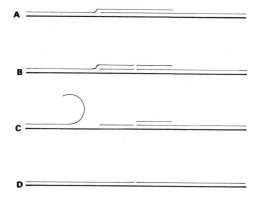

Fig 2.21 Making a butt joint in epoxy sheathing: (A) the two sections are overlapped; (B) when partially cured a cut is made down the centre of the lap; (C) one side is pulled back so that the two excess pieces can be removed; (D) allowing a neat butt joint to be formed.

with clear resin the glass cloth becomes transparent itself, allowing the natural wood to show clearly through. If this method is to be used, much more careful surface preparation is required, and the cloth weave has to be entirely filled with the second and third coats of clear resin. Ordinary fillers cannot be used. If possible when this finish is used the clear resin and wood should be protected from sunlight by applying further coats of varnish containing ultraviolet filters, as sold for use on spars.

The superior adhesive qualities of epoxies make this a good system to choose for sheathing a plywood deck on a ferrocement hull; it will bond well with properly cleaned cement ensuring a good seal where the sheathing runs down the hull beneath the rubbing strakes.

Glass Fibre Sheathing and 'C-Flex'
Cheaper materials and a more widespread familiarity with the techniques of application tempt many to sheath a hull or deck with the standard fibreglass formula of polyester resin and chopped strand matt. This is unfortunate as it gives a poor performance compared to the systems already described. Excessive stiffness in the cured glass fibre sheathing, and an inadequate bond between it and the wood make delamination almost inevitable. If it does not occur as the resin contracts while curing, it will probably result later as the hull works, or is subject to unavoidable impacts. Once delamination has occurred, moisture in the void leads to further delamination or rot.

222

The manufacturers of 'C-Flex' have devised a system that overcomes these problems and still allows the cheaper polyester resin to be used. 'C-Flex' is a series of thin glass rods loosely held together by glass fibres. As the rods are free to move individually these planks easily conform to a hull shape. The new ingredient of the 'C-Flex' system is a rubberised mastic that is thickly spread over the hull. 'C-Flex' planks are then bedded into this and stapled to the hull. Once the mastic has cured, the glass is saturated with resin, and an additional layer of chopped strand matt added and also impregnated. This helps to even out the corrugations due to the glass rods. Two gel coats finish the process. This still inevitably leaves a very irregular surface, but for the old wooden fishing boats for which this process was devised it is quite adequate. Yacht finishes would require much filling and sanding before applying the gel coats.

This system is an improvement on simple glass fibre sheathing as the staples and adhesive mastic enhance the bond between glass and wood, but allow some movement without delamination. ('C-Flex' is distributed in Britain by GRP Material Supplies Ltd.)

Alternative Combinations
Other combinations of reinforcing and resin can be used, and many systems have been tried successfully using epoxy resin with alternative reinforcing, in particular polypropylene. If an entirely new mixture is to be tried, test samples should be made. Effectiveness can then be examined, particularly the strength of bond when the sample is flexed, subjected to impact, and the reinforcing 'peeled' from the wood. Other considerations would be cost, weight, and ease of application.

Other Sheathing Methods

Sacrificial Wood
This was one of the earliest methods tried to protect a hull from marine borers. A skin of wooden planks was fastened over the heavily tarred hull, hoping that the sheathing would be eaten, but not the structural timber. As a protection from *Teredo* it still does not work today, but easily replaceable timber can be usefully employed to protect areas liable to severe mechanical damage, which is unavoidable on some workboats. Areas of hull which are scraped or knocked by fishing gear are often protected in this way, as are the sides of pilot boats whose horizontal and vertical rubbing strakes take the worst punishment when alongside much larger vessels.

223

Copper Sheathing and 'Cufo-Foil'

Due to its poisonous nature copper sheathing below the water line did prove effective against marine borers, and was the standard protection until the development of antifouling paints.

Although this method is now considered prohibitively expensive, here is a brief description of the process. The copper sheets are shaped to ensure each fits closely to its section of the hull, and are bedded on bituminous mastic and felt. Each sheet is fastened by copper nails every 1½ in (37 mm) around their edges, and tacks are spaced 3 in (75 mm) vertically and 6 in (150 mm) horizontally over their entire surface. Work starts from the water line aft, and progresses down and forward, so that laps face aft and upward, with a single piece wrapped under the keel, reaching above the rebate line each side if possible.

It is now realised that cupro-nickel alloys resist the attack of marine borers and the growth of barnacles and weed as effectively as pure copper does. The greater strengths of these alloys have allowed hulls to be not merely sheathed, but actually built from them, ensuring underwater surfaces that are very slippery and never need antifouling. A new system called 'Cufo-Foil' enables owners to take advantage of these alloys considerably more cheaply. A thin foil of the alloy is glued to the hull with a bituminous adhesive that both seals the hull and insulates it from the foil, enabling this sheathing to be used on any type of hull without fear of galvanic action. Although the process has only recently been developed the manufacturer (Fredk C Mitchell, of Dorset) guarantees it for eight years, and expects a longer service life in practice. 'Cufo-Foil' sheathing, as shown in Plate 2.17, looks similar to the old copper system, but not only does it protect the hull from marine growths and borers, it effectively seals the hull and provides a tough skin that can prevent some mechanical damage.

'Limpetite' Sheathing

'Limpetite' is a self-curing synthetic rubber (manufactured by Protective Rubber Coatings (Bristol) Ltd) which was originally intended as a protective coating for harsh industrial situations. It is now being promoted as a marine sheathing system as well. It effectively seals a hull, protects timber from marine borers, and steel from corrosion, but does not prevent fouling, so it has to be overcoated with conventional antifouling paints. Its remarkable resistance to abrasion and many chemicals and solvents makes it a good choice for particularly severe environments.

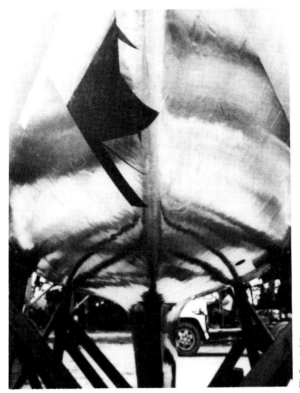

Plate 2.17
'Cufo-Foil' sheathing: a
cupro-nickel alloy that
is applied as a thin foil.

Sheathing a hull is straightforward as the materials are painted on,
but the surface must, as usual, be well prepared, dry and free from
oil, grease, paint, and dust. It will not adhere to traditional stoppings
such as white lead putty, so these must either be sealed with shellac,
or removed and replaced with a synthetic rubber caulking compound.
Different primers are provided for timber above and below the water
line, and for other materials. Two priming coats are necessary,
followed by as many as ten coats of 'Limpetite' in order to obtain
the recommended thickness of 0.03 in (0.75mm). Although each
coat must dry before the next is applied, at least three coats can be
applied in a day and a period of more than twenty-four hours should
not be allowed to elapse between any two coats. In order to ensure
an effective covering with each coat, the manufacturers provide it
in two colours, black and grey, which are applied alternately until
the last three coats which are all grey. This avoids the black dis-
colouring other paints applied later. 'Limpetite' can be applied
quickly by roller, but a better finish is achieved if a good quality
brush is used.

225

The manufacturers recommend the whole hull being coated at one time, and suggest that enough labour be obtained to ensure this is possible. If it has to be done in sections, each should be painted with the full number of coats and finished neatly with a taped square edge, the next section lapping over this. A feather edge is not possible as the overlapping coat will tend to lift the one below.

'Limpetite' cures as solvents evaporate from it, and as these solvents are highly flammable the working area should be well ventilated. At the same time it should be realised that excessive drafts can cause the solvents to evaporate too quickly and make work difficult. Containers should always be kept covered when not in use to prevent the solvent evaporating.

Part 3
Tools

1. General Comments

Purchasing Tools

A difficult job is simplified enormously if the right tool is available; if it is not, a simple task can sometimes seem impossible. It will be seen by flicking through the pages of any tool dictionary that there is a 'right tool' for absolutely every conceivable job. The tools described here are only a small portion of those that are available, but it is the portion that has proved useful for boatwork. It is reasonably comprehensive but inevitably incomplete, as is even the best of tool kits, to which another tool can always be added.

Acquiring tools is an expensive business, and it is not suggested that those mentioned here are the minimum requirements: but knowing what is available, and its usefulness, can save a lot of time and cursing. One way to buy tools economically is to search through second-hand tool shops. The tools may appear battered but are often better quality than their modern counterparts, and some useful ones may be found that are no longer available. But beware! The fascination of old tools is almost addictive. Together with the reasonably priced tools that are needed will be acquired a boxful of fascinating devices that will probably never be used!

When working in a boatyard, if a particular tool is needed it can often be borrowed, but be sure to return it promptly in a clean and sharp condition. Better not to abuse the privilege by frequent or 'permanent' loans either. When working alone, so much time can be wasted by trying to borrow, or even hire a particular tool that a policy of buying each tool as it is needed makes a lot of sense. Having obtained a tool, it is surprising how much more often it is used than was anticipated, and for this reason it is wise to buy better quality tools whenever possible. Similarly, if building anything larger than a dinghy, electrical tools should be of industrial quality (rather than domestic) if they are to survive the heavy and prolonged demands made on them.

This is undoubtedly an expensive philosophy, but then if the bad workman blames his tools, which are usually a poor selection of blunt and rusting implements, the good workman's craftsmanship is reflected in his: they are not only shining and sharp, but the right one is always ready to hand.

Tool Storage

Tools, whether bought, borrowed or made, have to be stored somewhere. The worker with his own lockup workshop can have open racks, shelves, and cupboards where they can be left safely at night, but in many circumstances a locking *toolbox* is an advantage. Traditionally one of the apprentice's first jobs was to make his own, and with modern training schemes it is still retained as an early exercise.

Putting all tools away each evening is a worthwhile habit, whether working alone or with others. If each tool is in its place at the beginning of the day, it can always be found. Tools not put away one day may not be put away the next, and by the third are entirely forgotten, unless required. Unfortunately, by then they cannot be found.

It is wise to allocate a place for everything, even if it seems rather vague, such as 'the right-hand tray'. Although that may be overflowing with other things that also belong in the right-hand tray,

Plate 3.1 Two common patterns of toolbox.

it will be quickly located amongst them. Certainly more quickly than if it has no home at all and could be almost anywhere. Tobacco tins are the usual receptacle for small items, and it is useful to have several tins to separate drill bits from nail punches, from dowel cutters and so on.

Toolboxes are sometimes of the suitcase type, opening at the front, and sometimes of the trunk type, opening at the top, both shown in Plate 3.1. The trunk type holds a larger quantity of tools more easily, but needs two people to move it. Then again, even the suitcase pattern gets pretty heavy when well stocked. A much smaller box can be useful for carrying selected tools to a job and is kinder to them than canvas carrying bags which tend to pile the tools together in the bottom when lifted.

Workshop Safety

Equipment can help prevent injury and ill health, but safety is primarily a matter of sensible procedures, and a constant awareness of possibly dangerous practices.

Keeping the workshop and bench clean and tidy removes a lot of risks. Treading on even a small block of wood can twist an ankle, and if operating a portable saw at the time the possibilities are horrendous. Then again, in the shavings covering an untidy workbench several sharp blades may be lurking unnoticed, until one is found in an unpleasant way. They should be sharp of course, because the extra effort needed to cut wood with a blunt chisel is much more likely to result in an uncontrolled slip: even a blunt chisel can easily cut flesh.

Correct practices are safe practices, and using any equipment in a way for which it was not intended is asking for trouble. Removing safety guards, taping pistol grip switches open and similar apparently time-saving tricks may save seconds in the short run, but lose weeks in the long term if the result is hospitalisation. By the same token a few minutes spent on simple maintenance should not be put off. If a chafed cable is not replaced as soon as it is realised that it is damaged, it is quickly forgotten that it needs attention and its unsatisfactory condition is regarded as normal.

Perhaps the best piece of safety equipment is a vivid imagination, the ability to visualise the possibilities in any situation. No hazards are too far-fetched, for real accidents are often even more unlikely.

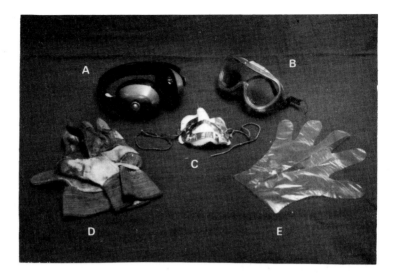

Plate 3.2 Protective clothing: (A) ear muffs, (B) goggles, (C) face mask, (D) heavy gauntlets, (E) disposable glove.

Protective Clothing

Of course good practice involves using protective equipment. The uniform of the construction site, safety helmet and steel toe caps, are hardly necessary in a boatyard, but it is sensible to wear practical clothing: a pair of overalls, or at least clothing with no loose ends to get caught in machinery, and tough shoes. Shoes should not be too heavy though when working on the finishing stages of a smart yacht, as they themselves can cause damage.

In certain situations particular parts of the body are at risk and need special protection. When using any machinery that is sending out a shower of wood or metal, *protective goggles* should be worn. Those who normally wear glasses should not simply rely on these, as the glass can easily shatter. Wrap-around goggles that protect the eyes from every angle are best.

Hearing can also be damaged when using loud machinery. If exposed to noise for sustained periods *ear muffs* should be worn. It is worth noting that blunt tools make far more noise than sharp ones, and one indication that the blades of a portable planer need attention, is the excessive din it makes.

Many modern materials (and even some timbers) cause irritation to exposed skin, and with time can produce dermatitis. Dust from these substances, if inhaled can cause lung infections, quite apart from being unpleasant. A *face mask* can protect the lungs from dust

232

and droplets of sprayed paint, the replaceable gauze pad being renewed as necessary. This type of face mask does not prevent the inhalation of toxic fumes for which a proper respirator is needed with appropriate filters.

Hands should be protected from irritants, especially those with known dermatitic properties such as epoxy resins. The most effective protection is to wear gloves, and very cheap *disposable gloves* can be obtained that are so thin they interfere little with the work. In some situations even these are a nuisance and then a barrier cream can be used instead, applied before starting the work and removed afterwards with the aid of a cleansing cream. The manufacturers of the particular chemicals being used should be consulted for advice on suitable creams to use in conjunction with their products.

Basic Workshop Equipment

For boatbuilding work a *workbench* has to be solid and strong, but need not be very fancy. Some of the intricate machines illustrated in tool catalogues would be rather wasted in the boatshop as the workbench is often subject to undignified treatment. It may be used as a paint bench, gluing bench, or even simply as a gantry support when working on the hull. All that is required is a large work surface with a good vice. It must be sturdy though, as it is very annoying when tackling delicate work to have the bench joggle at every thrust of the chisel. Portable workbenches such as the Black and Decker 'Workmate' are useful additional equipment, but not a substitute for a proper bench as they are too light to hold items steady when heavy work is under way.

When using the workbench for woodwork an oilstone is always close to hand, ensuring that blades are never dull. Woodworkers often make their own *oilstone box,* as illustrated in Fig. 3.1.

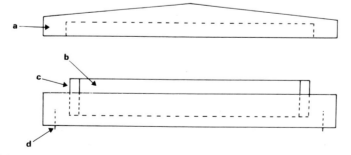

Fig 3.1   An oilstone box: (a) lid, (b) oilstone, (c) softwood end blocks, (d) nails nipped off to provide points that hold the box firmly on the workbench.

The oilstone is one item that craftsmen are reluctant to let others use, because it can be ruined by incorrect practice. To sharpen wide chisels and plane blades the stone's surface needs to be quite flat. Whenever it is used, care should be taken to work over its whole area to avoid wearing a dip toward the centre. Small chisels can cause damage particularly quickly, and some workers have a separate stone for sharpening these. The softwood blocks at each end of the stone in Fig. 3.1 allow its entire length to be used with confidence: if the tool does slip off the end it digs into the wood, not the stone, causing no damage.

Finally an adaptable system that can supply light and power in awkward corners is indispensable, even in a workshop that is amply provided with electric sockets and lights. An *extension lead* can be made up easily. It is worth including multiple sockets as illustrated in Plate 3.3, so that several tools and lamps can be used at once. When using an extension lead it should not be left coiled, but unwound even if the entire length of wire is not required. This is because the coiled wire uses more electricity, and can become a fire hazard if it overheats.

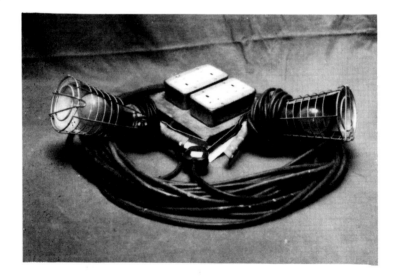

Plate 3.3 Extension lead with multiple sockets, and gripper lights.

Gripper lights are useful, both for providing light and localised heat to cure glue. Laminated members can have a light placed beneath them, and are then covered with a sheet of polythene to raise the temperature appreciably. Care should be taken to ensure that there is no fire risk here either, by keeping the polythene well away from the bulb, and preferably switching off at night when the workshop is unattended. Gripper lights have a built-in spring clamp, and so can be attached anywhere, but the jaws can leave nasty marks on timber unless protected with a piece of heavy cardboard.

2. Marking and Measuring Tools

Marking

Of course *pencils* are the easiest way to mark wood; they can be kept sharp, and their marks are easily removed by sanding. An HB or H pencil is most satisfactory. A softer pencil blunts too quickly, while harder ones leave too faint a line.

Both chalk and thick waterproof felt tip pens are also handy for marking clearly and boldly. *Chalk* can be used on part finished work as it wipes off easily, perhaps for assembly order numbers on glued structures. *Felt tips* can be used to mark jigs and other rough work that will be needed at some future date; without a bold label it may end up on the fire.

A *scriber* or *scratch awl* makes a clear and precise mark; the problem is that the marks are too permanent, and can only be removed by heavy scraping. Lines to be cut to can be marked with a scriber, but generally a sharp pencil is more satisfactory. When a mark is actually required to be permanent, such as the water line, it can be deliberately cut into the wood. A *scribing knife* is designed to do this, although it can be done with other tools, such as a very narrow chisel, or even the edge of a screwdriver.

Straight lines are usually obtained by marking against a *straight edge,* which can be either metal or plywood. Several straight edges of different sizes are useful in any boat shop. Longer straight lines, such as the grid on the loft floor are best marked with a *chalk line.* The versions sold in shops are neatly designed so that the line coils into a holder, and is automatically rechalked as it is pulled out for use, but a piece of string rubbed with chalk or charcoal works equally well, and is much cheaper. The line is simply stretched tight at the desired place, and plucked like a guitar string: as the line strikes the ground it leaves a straight line marked in chalk.

Methods of drawing curved lines are described in the early sections of this book, but if the curve is part of a small circle, obviously a pair of *compasses,* or *dividers* can be used. Dividers that can be locked open are particularly useful. Larger circles can be drawn by using *trammel points*. These are adjustable points attached to a wooden beam, similar to a draughtsman's beam compass. One point can be replaced by a pencil if necessary.

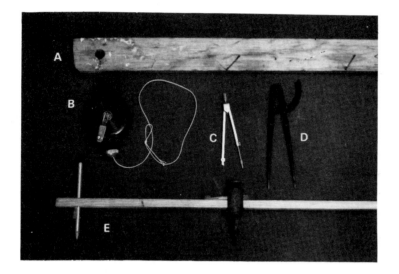

Plate 3.4 Marking straight lines and circles: (A) plywood straight edge, (B) chalk line, (C) compasses, (D) dividers, (E) sliding trammel point and pencil making up a beam compass.

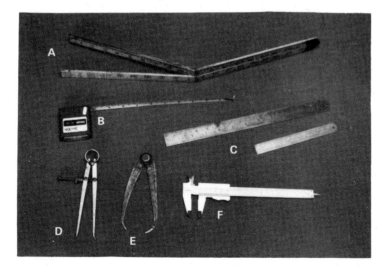

Plate 3.5 Measuring tools: (A) folding rule, (B) extendible rule, (C) large and small metal rules, (D) inside callipers, (E) outside callipers, (F) vernier callipers.

237

Rules

A carpenter's *folding rule* is the general purpose tool for most measurements, but when doing bench work it is often easier to use a *metal rule*. A 1 ft (300 mm) rule is a good size, but a smaller one, 6 in (150 mm), can often take measurements in awkward corners that are impossible with larger rules. An *extendible rule* or metal tape is also useful in tight corners, as well as its more obvious use for measuring longer distances. Extendible rules should be used with care though, as their floppy nature often makes precise measurements difficult to obtain.

Woodworkers' *inside, and outside callipers* look similar to dividers, but with curved legs, and can be used for measuring mast diameters and suchlike. For measuring bolt diameters, or the inside diameters of pipes, greater precision is needed and an engineer's *vernier calliper* is used. This can take both inside, outside, and depth measurements very accurately, but does not have the extended reach of the woodworker's tools.

Squares and Bevels

For marking right angles a *tri square* is used, and for forty-five degree angles a *mitre square*. A *combination square* combines both of these,

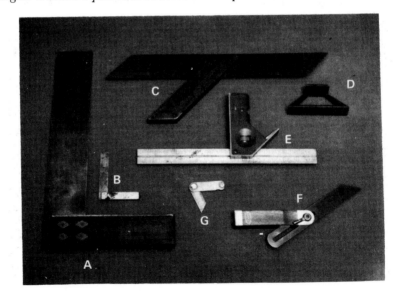

Plate 3.6 Squares and bevels: (A) large tri square, (B) engineer's tri square, (C) mitre square, (D) old-fashioned mitre template, (E) combination square, (F) sliding T bevel, (G) small home-made bevel gauge.

and is often a rule and spirit-level as well. Once again several sizes of square are useful; for precision work a small *engineer's square,* and a large tri square for marking out heavier work. A square measuring several feet in each direction can be useful when lofting, although once a right angle is needed on that large a scale it is better to use the *horning rod* described in the Horning and Levelling Section.

Angles that are neither forty-five degrees nor ninety degrees are measured and marked with a *sliding T bevel.* This is an indispensable tool for the boatbuilder, and should incorporate a locking lever so that the required angle can be held indefinitely. Even with the locking lever it is wise to mark the angle onto a piece of scrap wood soon after measuring it, in case the sliding bevel is knocked. For tight corners a much smaller bevel can be made from scrap pieces of brass, with a clenched copper nail for the pivot.

Gauges

For marking a line parallel with the edge of a piece of timber, a *marking gauge* is used. This can be set very precisely and scribes the line accurately. When using it, pressure should be applied against the timber, and the line scribed in one continuous movement. In many cases a pencil line is preferable to a scribed line, and for lines up to about 1½ in (37 mm) from the timber edge, the *'finger gauge'* can be

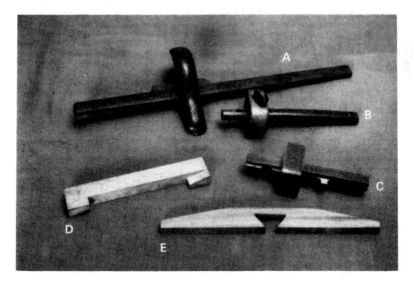

Plate 3.7 Gauges: (A) panel gauge, (B) marking gauge, (C) mortise gauge, (D) spar gauge, (E) trimming gauge.

Plate 3.8
With a little practice
the 'finger gauge' prod-
uces quick and accurate
results.

used. Holding the pencil as illustrated in Plate 3.8 can produce
accurate results with little practice. For lines further from the edge
a pencil used together with a combination square produces good
results. A *panel gauge* is designed to scribe lines at up to 2 ft (600 mm)
from the timber edge, but it is rarely used now.

A *mortise gauge* is similar to a marking gauge, but has two scribing
points which can be set independently. It is used to mark out both
mortises and tenons.

The *trimming gauge* and *spar gauge* are both simple workshop
made tools, and have already been described in Part 1, Sections 2
and 3.

Levels

Levels are used to obtain perfectly horizontal or vertical surfaces.
Of course the oldest way of checking if something was vertical
was not with a spirit-level at all, but with a *plumb bob*. A plumb
bob is still a useful tool, particularly for transferring the centre
line on the keel to deck beams, and other similar situations, but

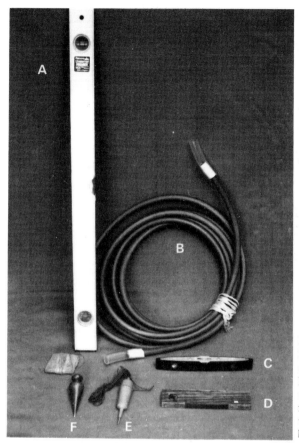

Plate 3.9
Levels: (A) standard spirit-level, (B) water level, (C) torpedo level, (D) pocket level, (E) modern shot filled plastic plumb bob, (F) older brass plumb bob.

in most cases a *spirit-level* is easier to use. A standard spirit-level is two or three ft long (600 or 900 mm), and generally the longer it is the better the accuracy obtained when setting up large members. A small *pocket level* about six inches long (150 mm) is useful for small shelves etc. A *torpedo level* is similar to a pocket level, but rounded at the ends. Very small levels can be obtained, that check surfaces are flat in both directions simultaneously, but this is just as easily done with a pocket level, by moving it through ninety degrees.

The *water level* described in Horning and Levelling is used to level two points separated by a considerable distance, or an obstruction.

3. Cutting Tools

Saws

It is the teeth of a saw that do the work, and different teeth are for different jobs. Fine teeth cut very accurately and cleanly, but are slow; coarse teeth cut through heavy timber quickly and efficiently, but leave a rougher face. The size of teeth is described by the number of points per inch (or per 25 mm): hand saws may have as few as five points per inch, and a fine dovetail saw sixteen or more points to the inch.

Saws intended for cutting with the grain, rip-sawing, have teeth that act like tiny chisels, each taking a shaving in turn. Saws for cross-cutting have teeth that act like knives, and are designed to sever each fibre. These two different shapes are illustrated in Fig. 3.2. The top half of both types of teeth are 'set', bent slightly in alternate directions. This ensures that the cut is fractionally wider than the metal saw blade, giving it clearance room, and allowing it to slide freely.

Saw sharpening is a skill that takes time to learn, but is worth practising. Every time a saw finally gets sharpened you wonder why it was not done much earlier, because every minute spent sharpening saves so much hard labour. Modern handyman saws can be bought with hardened teeth; these stay sharp longer, but once blunted they cannot be resharpened, and have to be thrown away. Better to get a good tradesman's saw and learn how to sharpen it.

Saws with coarse teeth are easier to sharpen than fine toothed ones, and at first it may be sensible to sharpen only larger saws, paying a 'saw doctor' to do the fine toothed ones until more confident. A good tool shop should be able either to provide a saw sharpening service itself, or direct customers to a private 'saw doctor'.

There are four stages to sharpening: levelling, shaping, setting, and sharpening. The first two, levelling the teeth, and shaping them, are only necessary if a saw is very worn, and such saws would be best handed to an expert to work on. A saw in good condition, but blunt, only needs to have the teeth set and sharpened.

242

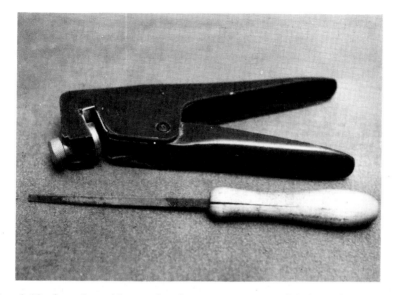

Plate 3.10 Saw sharpening tools: above, a saw set, and below, the triangular sectioned saw file.

Teeth are set with a *saw set* shown in Plate 3.10. This is a hand held tool that can be adjusted for different sized teeth by turning a small wheel until the number of points per inch required lines up with the plunger. The saw set is then used on each alternate tooth in turn, and by squeezing the handles the tooth is set correctly. Every other tooth is set from one side, then the saw is reversed, and the intermediate teeth are set in the opposite direction.

Once the teeth have been set, the saw is held in a set of *saw chops* for sharpening. Saw chops are a simple wooden clamp that holds the full length of the saw blade close to the teeth; the saw chops may be freestanding or held in the bench vice. The teeth are then sharpened with a triangular *saw file,* which is held in both hands as illustrated in Plate 3.11. The teeth are sharpened by placing the file in a gullet, and pushing it away for two or three even strokes. Alternate teeth are filed from one side, the saw is reversed, and the remaining teeth filed from the other. In every case the file must be positioned in a gullet so that the neighbouring tooth on the side nearest the saw's handle points toward the operator. The angle that the file is held at is different for a rip-saw or a cross-cut saw. A rip-saw is filed square, but for a cross-cut, the file is angled at about seventy degrees as shown in Fig. 3.2. It is also angled upward, the operator lowering the file handle slightly.

243

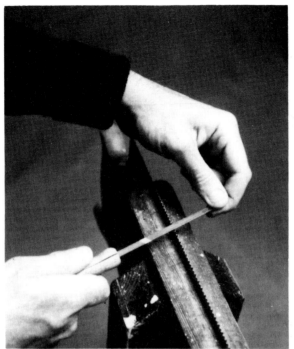

Plate 3.11
Sharpening a saw: the saw is gripped in the saw vice while each alternate tooth is filed in turn.

The traditional range of saws are these:

Hand saw, which is up to 26 in long (650 mm) and may be a rip-saw with five or seven points to the inch, or a cross-cut with six or eight points.

Panel saw, this is a finer cross-cut saw, usually 20 in long (500 mm) with ten points.

Tenon saw, or back saw, is from 8 to 14 in long (200 to 350 mm) and may have twelve or more points. The stiffened back allows accurate straight cuts, and is used for cutting joints.

Dovetail saw, is a small back saw which may have a handle either like the tenon saw or like the gent's saw; it can be from 6 to 10 in long (150 to 250 mm) and have from fifteen to twenty points.

Gent's saw, is a very small fine saw with a straight handle; it may have as many as thirty-eight points to the inch, and some have a horn at the end of the blade which is held between the finger and thumb of the left hand to obtain greater accuracy.

All the above saws are designed for cutting straight lines; other saws have to be used for cutting curves. The *compass saw,* or *keyhole saw,* (sometimes called a *pad saw*) has a very narrow blade to allow holes and curves to be cut. More intricate shapes can be obtained with a *coping saw.* The wire blade is replaceable, and tensioned by

244

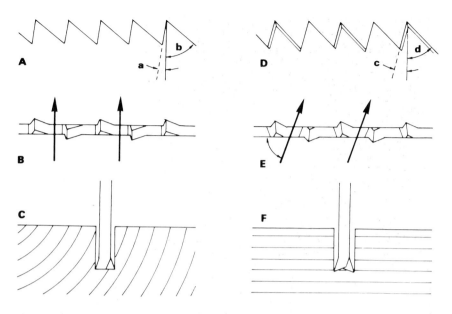

Fig 3.2 Sharpening saw teeth: on the left a rip-saw, on the right a cross-cut. (A) Rip-saw teeth are steeply angled, (a) and (b), being 8 and 52° respectively. (B) The teeth are filed square across the saw so that (C) each acts as a tiny chisel when cutting with the grain.
(D) Cross-cut teeth are more shallowly angled, (c) and (d), being 15 and 45°. (E) The file is held at an angle of 70° when sharpening so that (F) each tooth acts like a knife, cutting the timber fibres when sawing across the grain.

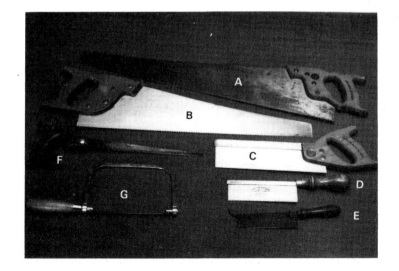

Plate 3.12 Saws: (A) hand saw, (B) panel saw, (C) tenon saw, (D) dovetail saw, (E) gent's saw, (F) compass saw, (G) coping saw.

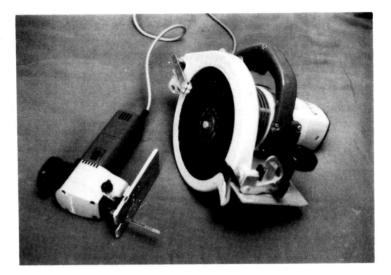

Plate 3.13 Powered saws: on the left a jig-saw, on the right a portable circular saw.

tightening the handle.

Most intricate work is now cut with a powered *jig-saw* or *sabre saw*. These are very useful in all boatwork, particularly for cutting out shapes such as bulkheads from large sheets of plywood. Jig-saws are excellent for cutting curves, but poor at cutting straight lines. It is sometimes suggested that the saw should be held against a straight edge, clamped in position as a guide. This is not in practice very effective as the flexible blade can still wander, even if the saw's shoe is being guided correctly. Better to cut as close to the line as possible freehand, then plane it true afterwards. Some jig-saws have a shoe that can be tilted to allow bevels to be cut. These are useful, but the design should be such that the shoe can be positively locked in the normal position, and not just held there by tightening a nut: the nut can vibrate loose and a bevel be cut quite unintentionally, ruining the work.

For heavier work a *portable circular saw* is required. A good industrial one is essential for construction of any boat over about 18 ft (5.5 m), as it can be used to cut out the keel, stringers, gunwales, planking and so on. The circular saw is excellent for these jobs as it not only rip-saws quickly, but can accommodate the gentle curves of these members, actually giving a fairer line than would be obtained on a band saw. Portable circular saws should be treated with respect as they are potentially very dangerous. Always keep both hands on the machine until the blade has completely stopped turning.

246

Extra care is required when cross-cutting, support being provided to the timber on both sides of the cut. If this is not done the danger is that as the cut progresses the unsupported timber will drop, jamming the blade and causing it to try to jump out of the operator's hands. The jolt can be unexpectedly powerful.

Different blades are available for circular saws, designed for rip-cutting, cross-cutting, or general purpose work, as shown in Fig. 3.3.

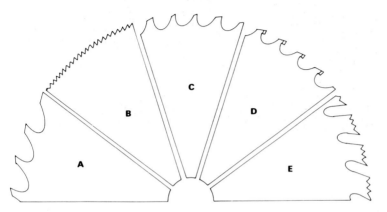

Fig 3.3   Some of the blades available for a portable circular saw: (A) rip-cut, (B) cross-cut, (C) combination, (D) carbide tipped, and (E) a planer blade which leaves a very clean finish.

Carbide tipped teeth are much more expensive, but last far longer before needing sharpening, which has to be done by a specialist. Other blades can also be obtained for cutting metal or even stone.

Pit saws were the two-man saws used in the past to cut out keels and planking. The timber was either supported on trestles or placed over a pit, with the craftsman working on top and his apprentice below. The craftsman ensured that the line was followed, the apprentice did most of the hard work, and got covered in sawdust for his effort. Fortunately the circular saw now makes this unnecessary, and even substantial thicknesses can be cut if the saw is used first from one side 'burying' the blade as deeply as possible, then from the other to finish the cut.

Two other saws that are useful to the boatbuilder are the metal cutting saws: the *hacksaw* and *junior hacksaw*. The junior hacksaw can be used in awkward corners as its blade is only 6 in long (150 mm) whereas an ordinary hacksaw can take blades of 8, 10 or 12 in (200, 250, 300 mm). When fitting a blade, ensure that the teeth are pointing away from the handle. Blades can be obtained with from fourteen to thirty-two points to the inch. Coarse teeth are used on soft metals like aluminium; fine teeth are used for hard metals and thin sheet material. When cutting sheet material the blade should be angled to keep as many teeth in contact with the work as possible.

Chisels

The wood chisel is a tool with a long metal blade attached tradition-ally to a wooden handle, although modern handles are made of impact-resistant plastic. The blade is sharpened at the end on one side only, the other always being maintained flat, and it is normally used with the flat side against the work. Chisels can be square edged or bevel edged, and the handle connected by either a tang or socket, as shown in Fig. 3.4. A square edged chisel is stronger, but a bevel edged blade can be used on undercuts such as dovetail housings.

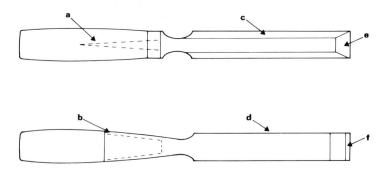

Fig 3.4 Wood chisels: the blade can be attached to the handle by either a tang (a) or socket (b) and be either bevel edged (c) or square edged (d). Some workers sharpen their chisels with a single bevel (e), and others with a double bevel (f).

The two principal categories of chisel are the firmer chisel and the paring chisel. The *firmer chisel* is generally used with a *joiner's mallet,* and is for most general purpose work. It is available in widths from ⅛ in (3 mm) to 2 in (50 mm), and is sharpened with a cutting angle of twenty degrees. A *framing chisel* is similar, but for heavier work, sometimes having a metal ferrule on the handle to prevent it splitting. It is sharpened to an angle of twenty-five degrees. The *paring chisel* is longer and lighter than the firmer chisel, and is used by hand only, without the aid of a mallet. It is available in sizes up to 1½ in (37 mm) and is sharpened with a cutting angle of only fifteen degrees. A *slick* or *slice* is a giant paring chisel with a long

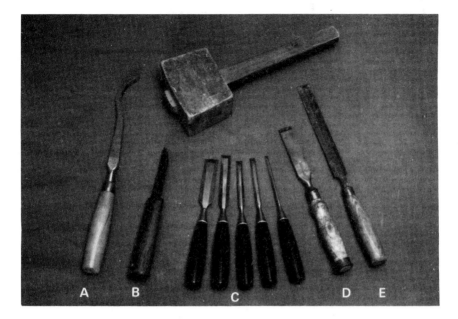

Plate 3.14 A joiner's mallet and several types of wood chisel: (A) swan necked mortise chisel, (B) ordinary mortise chisel, (C) set of bevel-edged firmer chisels, (D) framing chisel, (E) paring chisel.

handle and exceptionally wide blade that can be from 2 to 4 in (50 to 100 mm). Although a traditional boatbuilder's tool it is rarely used now.

In practice most boatwork can be accomplished with a good set of bevel edged firmer chisels, including a large one of perhaps 1½ in (37 mm). Additionally a single heavy framing chisel set aside for rough work, and a long paring chisel for working on very wide joints would prove useful.

Many special purpose chisels are made, and one example is the *mortise chisel*. This is designed solely for cutting mortises and is very stout, the blade's cross-section being almost square and therefore strong. For cutting deep mortises a *swan necked mortise chisel*, sometimes called *lock mortise chisel*, can be used. This has a curved blade which is used as a lever to cut the mortise deeper as shown in Fig. 3.5. For letting in small fittings, particularly butt hinges, a *butt chisel* is used. This is a very short chisel with a wide blade — often an old firmer chisel that has been ground so often it is too short for most work, but set aside especially for this purpose.

Chisels are sharpened in one of two ways. Some workers use a double bevel, and others a single bevel, also illustrated in Fig. 3.4.

249

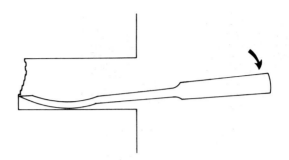

Fig 3.5   Using a swan necked mortise chisel to cut a deep mortise.

Both are equally satisfactory, provided the cutting bevel is at the correct angle and absolutely flat; a rounded cutting bevel is difficult to work with. A chisel is sharpened with a double bevel by grinding one bevel on a rotating grindstone, then sharpening the cutting bevel on an oilstone. Subsequent sharpening, on the oilstone only, is then quite quick as little metal has to be removed, but regrinding is necessary fairly frequently. A chisel with a single bevel is slower to sharpen, but it is easier to maintain the correct angle with the oilstone alone, and grinding down on a rotating grindstone is only necessary when the tool is actually damaged by striking a nail or suchlike.

The method of sharpening a chisel on an oilstone is illustrated in Plates 3.15 to 3.17.

Before starting to sharpen, a little oil is put on the stone and the chisel's bevel rocked in it slowly. Oil is squeezed out from under the blade until the bevel is flat against the stone. By watching carefully while rocking, the bevel angle can be found. The wrists are 'locked', held firmly in that position, while the blade is sharpened, thus avoiding rounding the bevel. The burr is taken off the back of the blade by holding it flat on the stone and rubbing two or three times; finally the sharpened blade is stropped on the hand, or slid across a piece of softwood, to clean up the cutting edge.

In the long run it is easiest to learn to sharpen chisels and plane blades in this way freehand, but devices are available that hold the blade steadily at the correct angle while being sharpened on an oilstone. Some of these devices are very compact and have rollers that run on the stone itself, but a better type is larger and the roller runs behind the oilstone box on the bench. With these there is less likelihood of wearing a trough down the centre of the oilstone.

Always maintaining a good edge on chisels is essential for high quality work. When working with hardwood this may entail a

Plate 3.15
Sharpening a chisel: the wrists are 'locked' to maintain a constant angle to the bevel, and firm pressure is applied while sharpening the chisel, using the whole area of the stone.

Plate 3.16
With the back of the blade pressed flat against the stone a few strokes remove the 'burr'.

sharpening several times in an hour, and this in itself is a good reason to learn to sharpen freehand as then there is less reason to delay: as soon as the blade is found to be getting dull the oilstone box is opened, and in a matter of seconds the edge is good again.

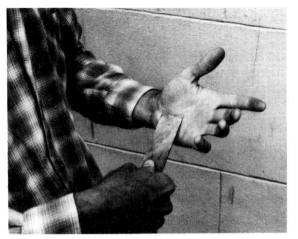

Plate 3.17
Finally the blade is stropped on the hand to remove the paper-thin metal at the tip of the freshly sharpened blade.

Gouges are chisels with the blade curved down their longitudinal axes. They can be obtained in similar sizes to ordinary chisels, but because there are a variety of different curves a large range of blades are available. In practice they are needed little in boatwork, although two or three of different sizes and shapes will prove useful on occasions.

Plate 3.18
Gouges, showing the alternative bevels to the blade: on the left an out-cannel gouge, on the right an in-cannel gouge.

Gouges can either be sharpened with the bevel on the inside of the curve, called *in-cannel gouges* or conversely sharpened with the bevel on the convex side, and then called *out-cannel gouges*. An out-cannel gouge can be sharpened on an ordinary oilstone, by continually rolling the wrists, but a small curved oilstone called a *slip* is needed to sharpen an in-cannel gouge.

Other Tools for Cutting

Hacksaws have already been mentioned for cutting metal, and they can equally well be used for hard plastics, but when cutting

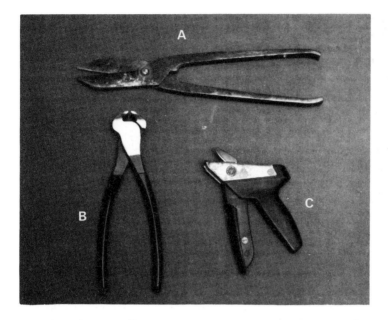

Plate 3.19 (A) Snips or shears, (B) nippers, (C) double cutting snips for cutting laminated plastics.

thin rod or thin sheet, whether metal or plastic, other tools are often quicker than a saw.

When clenching copper nails, they have to be cut above the rove, and this is done with a pair of *nippers*. These look similar to pincers designed for extracting nails, but have sharp and hardened jaws. For cutting heavy nails, nippers with long handles are needed to obtain the necessary leverage, or better still nippers with a 'box joint' can be obtained. These have a double pivot (like bolt cutters) so that added leverage is obtained without extending the handles.

Thin sheet metal can be cut with *snips* or *shears;* heavy cutting tools that work like scissors. For cutting laminated plastics, such as Formica, snips are needed that operate from one side of the material only, called *double cutting snips,* or sometimes by their trade name of 'Goscut'. Laminated plastics can be cut with an ordinary saw, but double cutting snips simplify things enormously.

4. Planes and Shaping Tools

Bench Planes

Bench planes are used for obtaining a flat surface or straight edge on a piece of timber. The longer the base of a plane, the more effectively it does this, as short planes just follow the humps instead of removing them. Large long planes are heavy and cumbersome to use though, so a large plane is used to true up the timber, then a small plane to obtain a smooth finish.

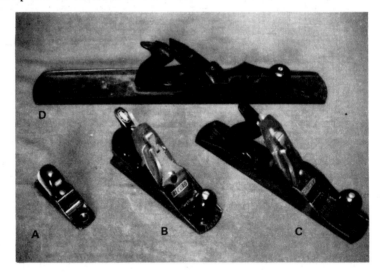

Plate 3.20 Metal planes: (A) block plane, (B) smoothing plane, (C) jack plane, (D) the largest hand plane, a trying plane.

There are four sizes of bench plane: the largest is the *trying plane,* or *jointer* which is 22 in (550 mm) or more long; next is the *fore plane* at about 18 in (450 mm); then the *jack plane* at 14 in (350 mm); and finally the *smoothing plane* at 10 in (250 mm).

If timber is purchased thicknessed to size, or the workshop has a bench planer and thicknesser, only the smaller smoothing plane and jack plane will normally be used. The standard width of these

Plate 3.21 Wooden planes: (A) smoothing plane, (B) jack plane, (C) rebate plane, (D) compass plane, (E) round bottomed compass plane.

planes is 2 in (50 mm) but professionals often use heavier planes which are 2⅜ in wide (60 mm).

Modern planes are metal but the old-fashioned *wooden planes* are still widely available in second-hand shops. Although more difficult to set up they can be useful, especially the smaller sized ones which are light, and so can be worked continuously in awkward positions, or even overhead with less effort. They also tend to have a wider mouth, so can be set with a lot of blade out and used as a scrub plane to remove quickly a large amount of timber. Finally their shape can be altered to produce special purpose planes; for example a gentle round can be put on the plane's sole, and the iron blade ground to the same curve to make an ideal plane for hollowing the bilge planks on a carvel hull.

Adjustment of the blade depth on a wooden plane is accomplished by tapping the end of the blade to make more blade protrude. If too much is out, the blade has to be removed, reset further back, and tapped down again until correctly positioned. The blade is held in position by a wooden wedge, which is removed by loosely holding the plane in one hand and striking it sharply with a mallet: a small plane is hit at its back end or heel; a large plane is hit on the forward end where a 'striking button' is sometimes located, as shown in Plate 3.22.

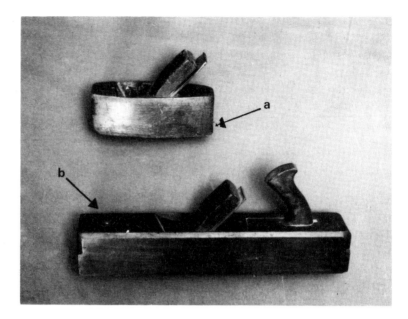

Plate 3.22   To remove the blade in a wooden plane the wedge is loosened by striking the plane's body: small planes are struck on their heel (a) while larger planes are hit on the 'striking button' (b).

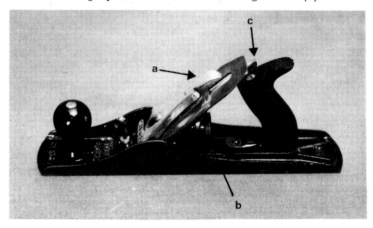

Plate 3.23   On an iron plane the blade is removed by lifting the lever (a). Depth adjustment is made with the adjusting nut (b) and the lateral adjusting lever (c) controls the angle of the cutter.

Adjusting a metal plane is easier and more precise. Plate 3.23 shows the adjusting screw for raising and lowering the blade and the lever for setting it parallel to the plane's sole. The blade is removed by lifting the lever on the lever cap, so loosening the assembly. Plane blades are sharpened with an angle of 25° in the same manner as chisels, and equally frequently. When repositioning the cap iron it should be about ¹/₁₆ in (1.5 mm) from the blade edge, although less may be necessary for very fine work. It should lie flat against the blade as shown in Fig. 3.6, and in order to ensure that it does, may very occasionally need sharpening itself, otherwise shavings get trapped between it and the blade, blocking the plane's mouth.

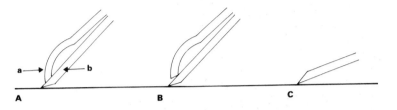

Fig 3.6 (A), the cap iron (a) should rest flush on the blade (b). (B), if there is a gap between the two, shavings get caught in it, jamming the plane's mouth. (C) Planes with the blade set at a shallow angle, such as block planes, have no cap iron, but are used with the bevel side uppermost.

Plate 3.24 The correct grip when using a plane.

The correct position for holding a plane is illustrated in Plate 3.24, and as with other tools that are gripped, only three fingers clasp the handle, the index finger pointing along the side of the tool, as this gives better control.

Planes can be obtained with a grooved sole for use on resinous timber, but simply rubbing an ordinary sole with a piece of candle wax effectively prevents the plane from sticking.

257

Plate 3.25   Special purpose planes: (A) bench rebate plane, (B) rebate plane with fence and depth gauge — an alternative position for the blade allows it to be used as a bull nosed plane, (C) small bull nosed plane, (D) adjustable compass plane, (E) shoulder plane, (F) side rebate plane.

Specialised Planes

As with other tools, planes have been developed to do particular jobs, and many of these specialised tools are used by boatbuilders.

Rebate planes are designed to cut rebates, so the blade extends the full width of the plane sole, to allow it to cut down into the timber with each pass. A *bench rebate plane* is similar to a jack plane, and is used for cutting wide rebates. It has to be used against a straight edge as a guide, but the smaller rebate planes have an adjustable fence and depth gauge to allow accurate cutting of rebates.

Block planes are designed to plane end grain, and have the blade set at a shallower angle than the normal forty-five degrees. Usually they are set to twenty degrees, although some may be as little as twelve degrees. Block planes (and other planes with a shallow angle of cut) have the blades inserted with the bevel upwards, and do not have a cap iron. The difference between these and ordinary planes is shown in Fig. 3.6. Block planes can be of simple design with manual adjustment of the blade, or sophisticated tools with adjustment screws for both the depth of cut and size of mouth opening.

Other small specialised planes are *shoulder planes, bull nosed planes* and *side rebate planes*. The shoulder plane is a small rebate plane used to trim the shoulders of large joints, while the bull nosed plane has its blade position very far forward to allow planing close

258

into corners. If it has no 'nose' at all it is called a *chisel plane*. Many special purpose planes are designed with two positions for the blade; one for normal use and one for use as a bull nosed plane. A side rebate plane is used to remove timber from the sides of grooves or rebates.

For planing a gently curving surface a *compass plane* is used. These have a flexible sole that can be adjusted to any reasonable curve, either convex or concave. They are difficult to use as every time the curve of the sole is altered it effectively alters the depth of cut of the blade, but with patience they can be set up correctly and made to function adequately well. As already mentioned, wooden planes can have their sole altered, curving either fore and aft or athwartships (so to speak) to make permanently curved compass or round bottomed planes.

Spokeshaves

The compass plane just described is expensive and difficult to use; in contrast spokeshaves are relatively cheap and a pleasure to use. They are designed to finish curved pieces, of almost any shape, and are made in several patterns, although the simple *flat faced* and *round faced spokeshaves* are usually all that are required.

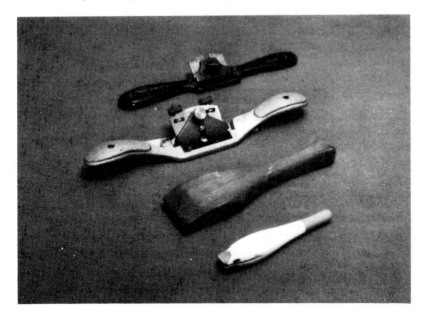

Plate 3.26 Two patterns of spokeshave, and holders used when sharpening their blades.

The round faced spokeshave is used for concave curves, the flat faced spokeshave for convex curves, spars, chamfers, and so on. Spokeshaves used to be made of beech or boxwood and were very delicate and gracefully shaped; now they are metal. Simple ones are adjusted by tapping the blade; more expensive versions have two adjusting screws.

The blade of a spokeshave is so small that it is impossible to hold for sharpening. This problem is overcome by using a wooden handle with a slot at one end into which the blade is pushed. These handles can be purpose made, but an old paint-brush handle with a slot cut in it serves quite adequately.

Spokeshaves are normally used by pushing away from the worker.

Traditional Tools

Two tools associated with boatbuilding are the draw knife, and of course the adze. They are both very efficient tools, and can quickly remove a large amount of timber; but the portable planer

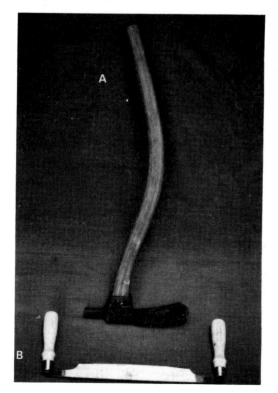

Plate 3.27
The traditional boatbuilder's tools: (A) a shipwright's adze and (B) a draw knife.

260

(described next) removes it even more quickly, and has superseded their use in many situations. They can still be useful though, particularly when working on concave curves, where the planer is unsuitable.

The *draw knife* has been made in various patterns and sizes from about 6 in wide (150 mm) upwards. The largest is the sparmaker's draw knife which can be as wide as 2 ft (600 mm), although half that size is adequate for most work. The handles may be cylindrical or egg-shaped, but in either case the worker's thumbs are hooked over the back of the metal blade during use. It is pulled toward the operator in a series of firm strokes, usually with the bevel up, but can be used the other way when working in concave curves. The secret is not to be too greedy, but to take reasonably sized shavings with repeated strokes.

The *adze* is also made in many shapes and sizes, but the distinguishing feature about a *shipwright's adze* is the spur or pin on the back of the poll. This was used as a punch for driving in fastenings when the adze was being used to scrub off the hull of wooden boats. For the occasional use that an adze gets in the modern boatyard, any pattern would do.

The adze can be used with great accuracy to shape up concave faces which are impossible with a plane. To obtain this accuracy the blade has to be very carefully controlled, despite requiring some momentum in order to cut effectively. To achieve this control the adze is held with both hands, one near the head and the other at the extreme end of the handle. The hand positions are interchangeable, but it is the hand at the handle end and farthest from the adze head that really controls the blade. In order to maintain accuracy it is never allowed to move freely, but always held against another part of the body. The hip is the most comfortable position, but it can be held anywhere from the knee to the chest, according to the dictates of the work. With the handle end held steadily in this way, the other hand lifts and drops the adze head to pare away the timber. As progress is made, the position of the hand against the body is gradually moved, higher to cut more shallowly, lower to cut deeper, and although the rhythm of the cutting is not broken, a blow is never actually struck until this hand is again secure in its new position.

Electric Tools

The *portable planer* is an excellent tool for rapidly removing large quantities of wood, and can remove ⅛ in (3 mm) with each pass

Plate 3.28   Electric tools for shaping timber: on the left a portable router and on the right a portable planer.

if required. The blades can be set very finely for accurate finishing work, but it is common practice to use the electric planer only for quick rough work, finishing with a hand plane.

The electric portable planer can save a lot of hard graft in certain situations, but its use is fairly limited. In contrast the *portable router* is an extremely adaptable and versatile tool. The router has a vertical spindle to which a wide variety of cutters can be attached; manufacturers supply specification sheets of their range of standard cutters, although they will also make special shapes to order. Cutters are normally made of high speed steel, but when tungsten carbide tipped they maintain their edge far longer.

Figure 3.7 shows some of the shapes that are possible with router cutters. When using the router for any type of edge cutting (rebating, chamfering, bevelling, or trimming) the cutter itself has a guide in the form of a round stud at its end. This follows the edge of the timber, and allows beautifully neat beads to be cut on curved as well as straight edges. On hardwood the stud can tend to burn the timber due to friction heating; this can be avoided by using cutters with a ball-bearing mounted guide pin shown in Plate 3.29, although these are expensive. When cutting along an edge the router is always pushed against the turn of the spindle, as this ensures greater control; if work proceeds in the opposite direction the cutter can grab, pulling the router down the work in a jerky haphazard fashion, failing to cut the correct depth, and possibly damaging the work.

When using the router to cut a groove across work, a guide is provided by clamping a straight edge to the work against which

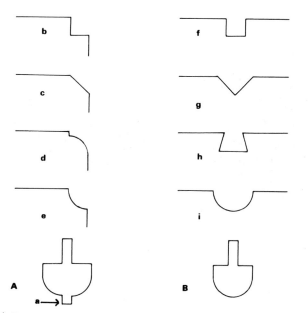

Fig 3.7 (A) For working along the edge of timber, router cutters have a guide pin (a) and can be used to cut (b) rebates, (c) chamfers, (d) beads, (e) coves. (B) Cutters without the pin are used to cut various grooves: (f) dado, (g) 'V' groove, (h) dovetail, (i) core box.

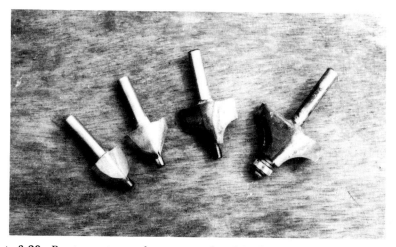

Plate 3.29 Router cutters: the one on the right has a ball-bearing mounted guide pin which will not cause friction burns to the timber.

the base plate is held. Curved guides can be used to produce complicated shapes.

263

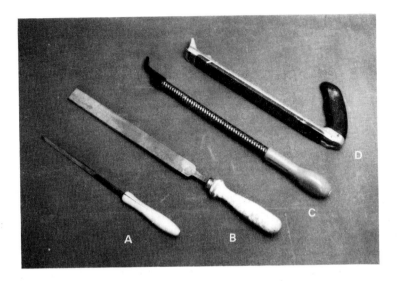

Plate 3.30   Files and rasps: (A) triangular file, (B) flat file, (C) round surform rasp, (D) plane surform rasp.

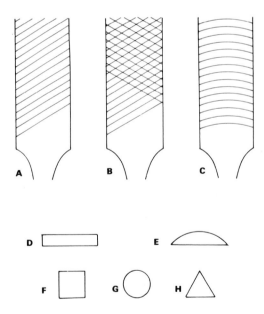

Fig 3.8   Files: the grooves can be in three different patterns, (A) single-cut, (B) double-cut, and (C) curved-cut. Some of the cross-sectional shapes available are (D) flat, (E) half round, (F) square, (G) round, and (H) triangular.

Files and Surform Rasps

Files are used for shaping and smoothing metal. They are made from hard steel and have a series of grooves across them which may be in three patterns as shown in Fig. 3.8. The more grooves, the finer the cut, and files are divided into three categories of coarseness: bastard (with twenty-six teeth per inch or per 25 mm), second cut (with thirty-six), and smooth (with sixty).

Files can be obtained in a range of sizes, and with different crosssections (also shown in Fig. 3.8), but for general use in the workshop a 10 in (250 mm) double cut flat file is all that is required. It should not be too coarse, second cut, or even smooth being suitable.

Rasps are used for roughing out fancy shapes in wood, or opening out tapered holes and so on. Traditionally they looked similar to files, but with raised spikes or teeth instead of grooves. These old fashioned rasps are now replaced by the *surform tool* which works on the principle of a cheese grater. They are also available in several shapes, including round, half round, and flat. The blades can be replaced once they become worn.

5. Drills and Bits

Drills

Woodworkers make holes in timber by using a 'drill' to turn a cutting tool called a 'bit'. Unfortunately metal workers call the 'bit' a 'drill', so inevitably the two terms are commonly confused. Here, the drill is the tool that does the turning, not the cutting.

For very small holes a drill is not needed at all. Pilot holes for small screws can be made with a *bradawl*, a metal point on a round wooden handle, which is pushed into the wood, twisting backwards and forwards. A *gimlet* can be used to make slightly larger and deeper holes, its screwed point pulling into the wood as the 'T' handle is twisted in a clockwise direction.

Another simple tool that can be used to quickly drill pilot holes for small screws is a *push drill,* which is similar to a pump screwdriver: the bits are in fact interchangeable. This is a superior tool to the gimlet as a series of special straight-sided bits called 'points' can be obtained, so that the correct point can be fitted for different sized screw holes.

The normal drill used for boring holes up to ¼ in (6 mm) diameter is the *hand drill.* This has a gearing mechanism which turns the chuck at quite high speeds, allowing twist bits to be used effectively. Some hand drills are open framed, but modern versions enclose the gear mechanism in a plastic case to protect it from dust. Some hand drills such as the *leytool* are shorter than normal allowing them to be used in awkward corners, but the altered handle gives a less precise grip than the standard type. A larger version of the hand drill is called a *breast drill* which has a saddle shaped plate to push with the chest for increased pressure. It often has two gear ratios for different speeds, and will turn larger drill sizes.

Holes of a larger diameter than can be bored with a hand drill are made with a brace and bit. The brace turns slowly, but the sweep of the handle allows considerable power to be put into it. The *plain brace* is the simplest type, but a *ratchet brace* is a much more useful

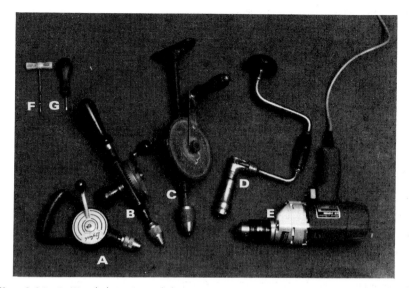

Plate 3.31 Drills: (A) leytool, (B) hand drill, (C) breast drill, (D) ratchet brace, (E) electric drill. (F) and (G) are a gimlet and bradawl.

tool, as the ratchet allows the brace to be used even when a full sweep is impossible. For confined spaces a *joist brace* can be used. This is a ratchet brace with a single lever handle that is operated by moving it back and forth, so turning the bit.

Of course the drill in widest use today is the *electric drill* which speeds up all drilling operations enormously. Modern drills are often two speed with 'hammer action'. This last facility is only necessary when drilling through concrete or masonry and is not necessary for most boatwork, with the exception of work on ferrocement hulls. Drills are available with chuck capacities of up to ½ in (12 mm) for domestic use, and larger for industrial use. Normally the bigger the chuck size the more powerful the drill. A drill with a ½ in chuck is adequate for most occasions, although when drilling for keel bolts and similarly large sized holes a heavier duty drill may have to be borrowed or hired.

An electric drill is normally used with a twist bit, but larger diameter holes can be drilled into solid timber with a spade or flat bit, or through panels of plywood or fibreglass with a hole saw.

Bits

Twist Bits

The *twist bit* (or *morse bit*) with a diameter of up to ¼ in (6 mm) can be used in a hand drill, and up to ½ in (12 mm) in a domestic

267

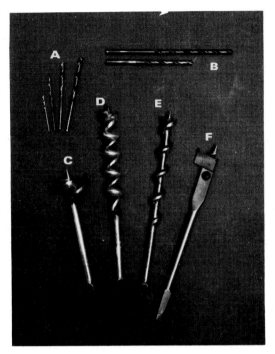

Plate 3.32
Bits: (A) twist bits (or morse bits) and (B) the relative sizes of a 'long series' and standard twist bit. Various patterns of auger bits are: (C) centre bit, (D) Jennings pattern, (E) solid centre, (F) expansive bit.

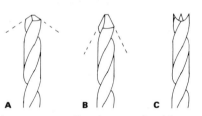

Fig 3.9 (A) Twist bits are normally sharpened with an angle (between the dotted lines) of 118°, but (B) for wood working a sharper point enclosing an angle of 55° is better. (C) A superior tool altogether is the dowel bit with a diamond point and twin spurs.

electric drill. Larger bits can be obtained, but need industrial drills to turn them. The standard length of bit is often too short for boatwork, but 'long series' bits can be obtained which are about one and a half times as long. It is sensible for a boatbuilder always to buy these in preference to the ordinary size. Twist bits are normally bought with the point sharpened to an angle of 118 degrees, as in Fig. 3.9. Although this does drill timber adequately it is an angle designed for metal working. A sharper point is better for woodworking, fifty-five degrees being the correct angle. Twist bits with a double spur produce even better results, and these are called *dowel bits* or *brad point drills*.

Auger Bits

The auger bit gets its name from the old fashioned *auger,* which had a lead screw and helical twist like the modern bits, but was used without a drill: its long handle ended in an eye into which a wooden handle was inserted, like a giant gimlet. Augers are still available, but no longer used in boatbuilding.

Many patterns of *auger bit* have been made, differing in style of lead screw, helical twist, and number of spurs. Three types are readily available today. The *Jennings pattern* or *double twist,* has a double helical twist which clears shavings from the hole quickly. The *solid centre* has a similar lead screw and twin spurs, but only a single helical twist around a solid centre; this makes a stronger bit better suited to drilling long holes. Both are available in diameters up to 1½ in (37 mm). The *centre bit* is available up to 2¼ in (56 mm) but is only for drilling shallow holes as its short helical twist allows it to wander in a deeper hole. It only has one spur.

The lead screw on an auger bit pulls the cutting blade into the wood so that little pressure is needed. It should always be protected from damage when not in use, and one way is to store bits with the screw embedded in an old cork.

The spur, or spurs, are designed to score the surface grain before the bit enters, avoiding unsightly plucking or splintering around the hole. Once the bit has entered the timber the spurs are not necessary and they can, together with the lead screw, tend to pull the bit off a true line when boring deeply. In the past, boatbuilders had their own patterns of auger bit for boring the shaft log and other long holes. The *ship auger* had no spurs, and a very open helical twist, while the *barefoot ship auger* had neither spurs nor lead screw. It would produce the most accurate hole, but be hard work to use. An auger bit similar to the ship auger is still available, but called the *Scotch auger bit.*

Auger bits are expensive, and a full set is a considerable and unnecessary investment, as their use is only occasional. Better to buy each size as and when it is needed to avoid buying sizes that will probably never be used. A cheaper alternative is the *expansive bit,* a gouge-shaped bit for drilling end grain, and the *taper bit* meters from ⅝ in (15 mm) to 3 in (75 mm). This bit is only a lead screw and single spur, with no helical twist. It is a poor alternative to a proper auger bit, but can be used instead of the centre bit for shallow holes.

Other bits that can be used with a brace include the *bright spoon bit,* a gouge-shaped bit for drilling end grain, and the *taper bit* which is used to cut tapered holes. Both are more likely to be found in a second-hand shop than a modern tool catalogue, but the taper bit can be useful to the boatbuilder. Dead knots in planking are liable to fall out as the timber shrinks and swells; one solution is to fit a backing pad, but it is neater to cut a tapered hole and plug with a tapered dowel.

Bits for Power Drills

The twist bit already described is the usual type of bit to be used with a power drill, but larger diameter holes can be cut with the *spade bit,* sometimes called a *flat bit.* These are suitable for drilling into both cross and end grain, but have to be turned at high speeds. They can be used with an *extension bit holder* to drill holes of considerable depth, although the accuracy of alignment will be poor. When this is not a consideration they are a good inexpensive bit for both large diameter and deep holes.

At the other end of the price range is the *Forstner bit,* a very accurate and clean cutting bit. It is normally used in a drill press, but can be used with care with a hand held power drill. Its principal advantage is that it produces a flat bottomed hole, with no lead screw or spur cutting deeper into the timber. This means that it is ideal for drilling shallow holes in thin timber where other drills would penetrate right through. Another advantage is that it can cut parts of a circle, or be used at an angle to the timber surface,

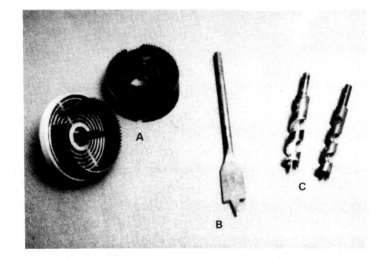

Plate 3.33   Some bits for use with an electric drill: (A) a set of hole saws and their backing plate, (B) a spade bit (or flat bit), and (C) auger bits with a diamond point (in place of the lead screw).

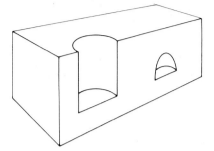

Fig 3.10 A Forstner bit will drill parts of a hole, or holes angled to the wood's
surface, both difficult operations with other bits.

as shown in Fig. 3.10. These unique qualities make the Forstner bit
an excellent tool, but its application in boatwork is limited.

In contrast the *hole saw* can be used extensively when fitting out
a boat, as it cuts both plywood and fibreglass panels cleanly. They
are available in diameters up to 4 in (100 mm) and are particularly
useful when cutting holes for piping through bulkheads and the
like. Hole saws can be a solid cup shape, or a curved strip which
is pressed into a backing plate in any of several different diameters.
In either case it is used in conjunction with a twist bit at its centre,
and turned at the slow speed on a two speed electric drill.

Countersinks and Counterbores
Fastenings are said to be 'countersunk' when they are set flush
with the surface of the timber, and 'counterbored' when let in
below the surface and the hole plugged with a dowel or filled with
stopping.

A *rose countersink* is a bit that can be used in a hand or electric
drill to make a small conical depression to accept the head of a
wood screw. As already described when dealing with fastenings, a
correctly drilled screw hole is in three parts; a pilot hole, clearance
hole, and countersunk or counterbored hole. A *combination drill
and countersink bit* does all three operations at once, providing a
perfect hole for a flush finished screw. The *combination drill and
counterbore bit* does the same, but the hole can be counterbored
deep enough to accept a dowel, which is cut with a matched *dowel
cutter*. Both types of combination bit and the dowel cutters can
only be used at the high speeds provided by an electric drill.

The combination counterbore has three rings marked on it
so that the depth of counterbore can be accurately controlled.

271

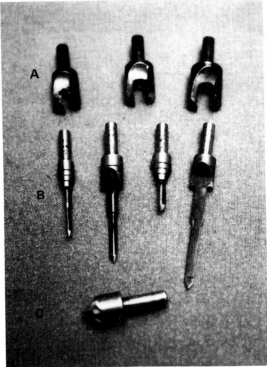

Plate 3.34
(A) dowel cutters, (B) combination counterbore bits, and (C) rose countersink.

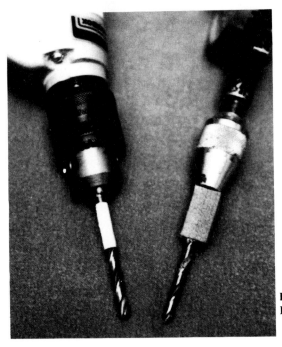

Plate 3.35
Improvised   depth   gauges.

Drilling to a specified depth with other bits is often necessary and several types of *depth gauge* are available. Some fasten directly to the bit, others fasten above the drill chuck with an adjustable rod that slides down beside the bit. Simple depth gauges can be improvised quite easily: a piece of masking tape wrapped around the bit is a visual indication of the required depth, although it cannot be used on very many holes before it gets dislodged. Drilling through a scrap of wood, so that it can be pushed up the bit to rest firmly against the chuck is a more durable gauge for a large number of holes. It is cut so that the required length of bit protrudes beyond it.

6. Tools for Fastening

Hammers

From the wide range of hammer patterns manufactured, three are generally used by the boatbuilder: the ball peen, cross peen, and claw hammer.

A light *engineer's ball peen* hammer is used specifically for clenching copper nails, the rounded striking surface being essential to burr the rivet correctly. An 8 oz (0.2 kg) hammer is quite heavy enough for this job, although on very large nails a slightly heavier hammer could be used.

The *joiner's cross peen* is used for light work, the cross peen itself being used to start small panel pins while they are held in position with the other hand. Again a small size, perhaps 10 oz (0.25 kg) is adequate.

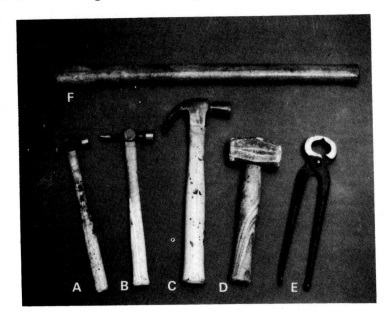

Plate 3.36 (A) ball peen hammer, (B) cross peen hammer, (C) claw hammer, (D) lump hammer, (E) carpenter's pincers, (F) shipwright's pin maul.

274

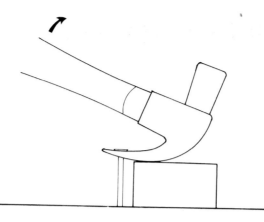

Fig 3.11 To extract long nails a piece of timber is positioned under the head of the claw hammer.

For most work the *claw hammer* is used, a 16 or 20 oz (0.5 or 0.6 kg) hammer being a good size, although professionals often prefer the extra clout in a 24 oz (0.7 kg) hammer. Metal or wooden handles are equally satisfactory, the traditional wooden handled tool being correctly called an *adze eye claw hammer,* referring to the extended sleeve (similar to that on an adze) into which the handle fits.

The claw is used for pulling nails, but the timber should always be protected with a scrap of plywood. If the nail is long it can be withdrawn in stages, slipping larger pieces of wood under the hammer head with each successive pull, as shown in Fig. 3.11. *Carpenters' pincers* can be used in a similar way to remove nails.

Heavier hammers can be useful on occasions for demolishing jigs, driving wedges, or even driving large sized bolts. A 2½ lb (1.1 kg) *lump hammer* (sometimes called *club hammer*) usually proves adequate, but removing bolts, particularly old keel bolts, is another problem. For this the boatbuilder's ultimate weapon is his own version of the sledge hammer: the *shipwright's pin maul.* If there is enough room inside the boat to wield it, this can be used to start the bolt moving, a good initial blow being necessary to break the bond of rust between the bolt and keel. The nut should of course be loosened, but not at first removed if it is hoped to re-use the bolt, as any damage to the bolt's thread is corrected when the nut is removed. To continue driving the bolt below the level of the timber a *punch* is used.

Punches are made in a variety of sizes, and not only used to remove bolts, but to drive the heads of nails below the surface too.

The smallest is a *pin punch,* larger sizes are *nail punches.* They have a flat, or even slightly hollow tip to prevent them slipping off the nail head when struck. A pointed punch is called a *centre punch* and is used to make a starting hole when drilling metal. A *rove punch* has a hole down its centre and is used to drive the rove over a copper nail before it is nipped and clenched. Several sizes of rove punch are necessary as the hole should only be slightly larger than the nail.

Whenever clenching, or driving a nail into any part of a boat, a *dolly* should be used; this is held behind, and firmly against the member being struck to prevent excessive vibration. Although a hull may appear solid it is surprising how much flexing occurs when hammering, and the weight of a dolly at the relevant point not only makes it easier to drive the nail, but prevents damage occurring to other parts of the hull. A dolly can be any heavy piece of metal, and often surprising items are made to serve, but the simplest is a length of 1 in (25 mm) diameter steel rod perhaps 8 in (200 mm) long, with the ends smoothed and slightly bevelled to prevent marking the timber.

Screwdrivers

The ordinary screwdriver can be bought with two types of handle; a bulbous oval sectioned pattern made from wood or plastic, or a fluted plastic type. The fluted plastic would appear to give a better grip,

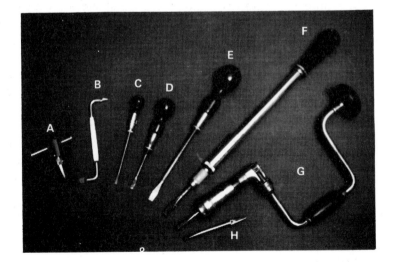

Plate 3.37   Screwdrivers: (A) stubby, (B) offset, (C) ratchet, (D) medium cabinet, (E) large cabinet, (F) pump action, (G) brace with screw driver bit, (H) alternative bit.

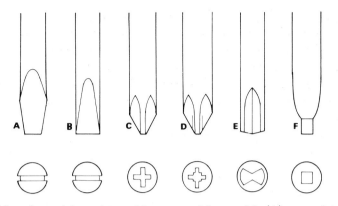

Fig 3.12   Screwdriver tips: cabinet screwdrivers with (A) ground taper, and (B) parallel tips, (C) Phillips, (D) Pozidrive, (E) clutch, (F) square.

but in practice the reverse is true: the larger surface area of the traditional shape fitting snugly into the palm provides a superior grip. Also, when many screws have to be driven, the fluted handle soon chafes the hand, while the smooth bulb can be held and used continuously for prolonged periods, provided it is undamaged and clean.

Many varieties of tip are available for use with particular patterns of screw, and these are illustrated in Fig. 3.12. The most widely used type is the flat tip for use with slotted screws. To avoid damage, the screwdriver should fit the slot correctly; if it is too large the surrounding timber is damaged, and if too small the screwdriver is liable to slip, both damaging and failing to tighten the screw. The tip can be maintained by occasionally grinding the end square, as a tip with rounded corners easily slips from the slot.

The most common *cabinet screwdriver* has the tip flared and then ground back to a taper, but a parallel tipped version is available which can tighten a deeply counterbored screw without tending to open out the hole.

For confined spaces a *stubby screwdriver* is necessary, although it is difficult to put much power into tightening with these. Some have a tommy bar which helps, or alternatively an *offset screwdriver* can be used.

Using a *ratchet screwdriver* saves having to relocate the tip after each turn, and this is particularly useful on small sized screws or awkwardly positioned ones when repeatedly repositioning the blade is difficult.

Driving a large number of screws is a slow job and several methods have been devised to speed the process. The *pump screwdriver* (sometimes called *Yankee* or *spiral screwdriver*) has interchangeable screwdriver bits for different sized screws. Pressure on the handle turns the bit, rapidly tightening the screw. This is a very fast way to drive screws, but the main drawback is that if the bit jumps from the screw it continues to turn in the neighbouring timber causing damage. To prevent this the chuck should always be held over the screw with one hand while pressure is applied to the handle with the other. Even with this precaution it is advisable not to use this type of screwdriver on high quality work, where bruised or damaged timber will be visible.

Screwdriver bits can be obtained to fit either a brace or an electric drill. When a brace and bit are used to drive a screw an excellent combination of power and control is achieved. This is often the only way to drive into hardwood the large gauge screws used in many situations in boatbuilding. If an electric drill is to be used to drive screws, it really needs to be one of the more recent models with a variable speed controlled by the trigger. Two-speed drills, used on the slow speed, can be used to produce quick results, but the likelihood of damage is even greater than when using a pump screw driver.

A useful item to keep in the tool box for use whenever driving large screws is a small tin of grease. A smear of grease on the tip of each screw greatly reduces the need for elbow grease.

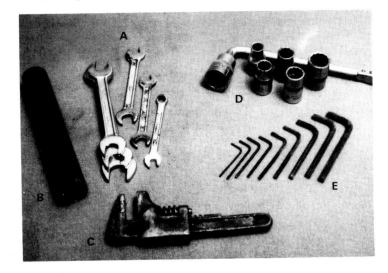

Plate 3.38   Spanners: (A) set of open ended spanners, (B) pipe to add leverage when necessary, (C) adjustable spanner, (D) socket set, (E) Allen keys.

Spanners

Bolts are used as fastenings in many situations on a boat, but for the most part a small set of *open ended* spanners, or even a good *adjustable spanner* is all that is required. A *socket spanner* is necessary where nuts or bolts are set in counterbored holes, and often a ratchet handle to turn them is useful for keel bolts set between deep and narrow floors. To add extra leverage for tightening or loosening a nut a length of pipe can be slid over the spanner to effectively increase its length.

These few spanners, perhaps with the addition of a set of *Allen keys* for maintaining other tools, are all that are likely to be required for actual boatbuilding. Of course if the boatbuilder is involved in the machinery installation, plumbing, and so on, a more complete kit of engineer's and mechanic's tools will be necessary.

Dies

Boatbuilders often require extra long bolts that cannot be bought as standard. Sometimes the length required is so long that they are not called bolts at all, but 'tie rods'. Tie rods are lengths of metal, threaded at each end to accept nuts, and are used to hold members in tension. Their most common position is between the carlings and gunwale, but they are also used on occasion right across the hull, and with a keel stepped mast both between the main deck beams and these beams and keel itself.

It is easier for the boatbuilder if he can buy lengths of rod and cut them and thread them as required, rather than having specially manufactured tie rods and bolts for every situation. Dies are used to thread rod; their counterpart, a tap, is used to cut the matching internal thread, but these are not usually required as suitable nuts can easily be bought.

The usual type of die is a *round split die* which is held in a *die stock*. The die stock has three screws which both hold the split die in position, and open or close it to control the depth of cut. The thread is cut by positioning the die on the end of the rod (a slight taper may be filed on it first) and while pressing down firmly, turning slowly. Once the die begins to bite pressure is unnecessary. Cutting continues by turning half a turn down, then backing off a quarter turn to release the swarf. Some lubricant should be used during cutting, either oil, grease, or a cutting paste.

Die stocks are reasonably priced, and each can be used for several

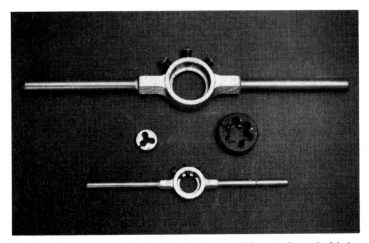

Plate 3.39 Two sizes of round split dies, and the stocks to hold them.

sizes of split die, but the dies themselves are expensive. Normally they are made from high speed steel, but if only a limited number of threads need to be cut, carbon steel dies can be obtained that are about one third of the price.

A *die nut* is a solid nut containing the same cutters as a split die. It is not intended to be used to cut a new thread, but to clean up damaged or rusty threads.

7. Clamps

Clamps, or cramps, of almost any shape or size, are an invaluable asset to a boatbuilder. Apart from their obvious uses for temporarily holding parts together while permanent fastenings are driven or glue cures, they are often used as extra hands, holding sprung parts in place while the fit is examined. For many jobs, particularly laminating, there never seem to be enough and however many clamps a boatbuilder has, he can always use more. Reasonably sized metal clamps are expensive, and often it is possible to improvise by using bolts, wedges, shores, or even a loop of string tightened as a 'spanish windlass'.

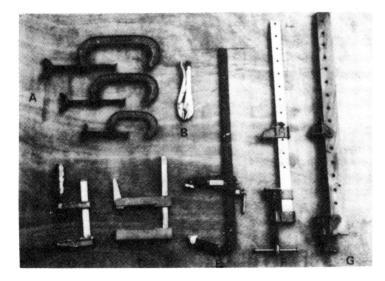

Plate 3.40 A few of the many types of clamp: (A) three sizes of standard G clamp, the smallest has a knurled wheel in the frame allowing single-handed operation; (B) mole grips, which can be used as a hand vice; (C) standard fast action clamp with notches filed in bar to improve locking action; (D) clamp with pressure applied by lever-operated cam; (E) fast action clamp with serrated bar; (F) bar clamp; (G) bought clamp heads fitted to a wooden bar.

Of the manufactured clamps the most useful is the standard *G clamp*. This is available in a range of sizes, up to a capacity of 12 in (300 mm). It should always be used with a pad of wood between the clamp and work as its small sized shoe easily bruises the timber. G clamps are available in several patterns including a long reach clamp and a clamp that can be easily held and tightened with one hand, by turning a knurled wheel incorporated into the clamp frame.

Edge clamps are similar to the G clamp but have an additional screw thread at right angles to the work. These are helpful when fastening trim to the rounded edge of a plywood bulkhead, but otherwise have little use in a boatshop.

Adjusting G clamps to suit the work is slow because of the long screw that has to be wound down to the appropriate size. Several types of *fast action clamp* are available that have a sliding jaw. This quickly adjusts to the correct size, then pressure is applied by turning a screw. In theory the sliding jaw is locked in position as the clamp is tightened; unfortunately on the most common pattern with a smooth bar there is a tendency for the jaw to creep, gradually relieving the pressure. This can occur very rapidly if the clamp is vibrated, perhaps due to hammering taking place elsewhere on the boat. This problem is easily overcome if a series of notches are filed in the bar, which the sliding jaw can lock against. Better quality fast action clamps are designed with a serrated or indented bar, and with some the pressure is not applied by the normal screw, but by a lever operated cam.

Some fast action clamps may have a jaw capacity of 3 ft (900 mm) but for even larger spans a *bar clamp* (sometimes called *sash clamp*) is required. These have movable clamp heads that can be positioned as required on a long bar. There are several varieties; some have a flat iron bar with drilled holes, others a 'T' bar, and others again slide on a length of pipe. All are expensive, but a cheaper alternative is to just buy clamp heads which can be fastened to a wooden bar. These have the added advantage that practically any span can be accommodated by using larger timber bars.

Two other tools can be used as clamps. For large and awkwardly shaped pieces the very adaptable jaws of the Black and Decker *Workmate* are ideal. Lugs can be inserted in the top surface that allow it to grip almost any shape. At the other extreme, small parts, especially metal ones, can be difficult to hold by hand while they are worked on, perhaps filed or cut. A *hand vice* is a small clamp that grips the piece firmly and is then itself held comfortably. Rather than purchase this particular tool which has no other purpose

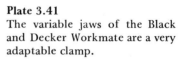

Plate 3.41
The variable jaws of the Black and Decker Workmate are a very adaptable clamp.

a pair of *mole grips* can be made to serve equally well, and have a wide variety of additional applications. It is worth noting that mole grips are available with many different patterns of jaws (including an approximate G clamp shape), as well as the standard plier style.

When planking a clinker hull, clamps are needed to hold each plank against the last while it is riveted. These clamps need to have an extended reach, and be fastened and released quickly. Boatbuilders have developed several patterns of *boatbuilders' grips,* all of which are made of timber to avoid damaging the planks. They are easily made in the workshop, the mechanism for tightening them being simply a wedge.

Plate 3.42 Two types of boatbuilder's grips used in clinker work. Pressure is applied to both with wedges.

8. Finishing Tools and Abrasives

Scrapers

On some softwoods sanding alone may produce a satisfactory surface for painting or varnishing, but with most timbers scraping is necessary first. With some hardwoods a superior finish may be achieved if the surface is only scraped and not sanded at all.

The traditional tool used for surface preparation is the *cabinet scraper,* and although it is nothing more than a rectangular piece of thin steel, it does the job excellently. To be effective it must be sharp, and its main drawback is that it blunts rapidly, and requires a certain knack to sharpen again. It is well worth learning to sharpen though, as a cabinet scraper is more effective than the other types, and can be controlled with great precision to tidy up small patches of 'wild' grain that cannot be tackled with other tools.

A cabinet scraper works by having a slight burr along the edge of the blade. Normally only the long sides are sharpened (although the short sides can be used in restricted places) and as each side actually has two edges with a burr as shown in Fig. 3.13, the scraper can be used in four ways. As one burr is dulled the blade is turned and another used until all four need sharpening again.

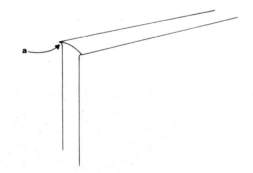

Fig 3.13   An enlarged view of one corner of a cabinet scraper; the work is actually done by the burr (a) along both faces of each edge.

Plate 3.43 Using a cabinet scraper, the blade is curved slightly with the thumbs, and pushed away from the worker.

The blade is held in both hands as shown in Plate 3.43, the thumbs bending it into a slight curve. The tighter the curve, the smaller the area scraped. The blade is angled away from the worker and pushed firmly so that shavings are peeled from the surface. The scraper must actually obtain shavings if it is being used correctly; if only dust is produced it is either angled incorrectly or blunt.

Wheel burnishers are available that quickly and accurately sharpen the scraper, but the usual hand method is illustrated in Plates 3.44

Plate 3.44 Sharpening a cabinet scraper: first the edges are filed flat.

Plate 3.45
Then each edge in turn is stropped with a burnisher to draw out the burr.

Plate 3.46 Finally the burr is turned with a single firm stroke of the burnisher.

to 3.46. First with the scraper held in a vice the edges are filed flat. Then, using a *scraper burnisher*, (which can in fact be any rounded

286

piece of steel such as the back of a gouge, or a screwdriver blade) the burr is drawn out by holding the scraper flat on the work bench and stropping repeatedly with the burnisher. Finally it is returned to the vice to turn the burr, but as both edges are to be sharpened (on both sides) it is necessary at this stage to hold the scraper between two scraps of wood to prevent the sharpened edges being damaged. With the scraper held firmly the burnisher is pushed down onto the blade at the angle shown in Plate 3.46 and slid once across the edge. The most common mistake is to repeat this action several times, which turns the burr too far, making it unusable. One firm stroke is all that is required, and even if success is not obtained every time, at least two of the four possibilities should be satisfactory at each sharpening. As already said, the blades dull rapidly so plenty of practice is guaranteed.

Cabinet scrapers can be held in holders, either like planes or large spokeshaves, and are then called *scraper planes*. Once adjusted correctly these are effective for large flat surfaces, but setting them up takes time, whereas when using a hand-held scraper the angle and degree of curve in the blade can be continually altered with each stroke to obtain the best results.

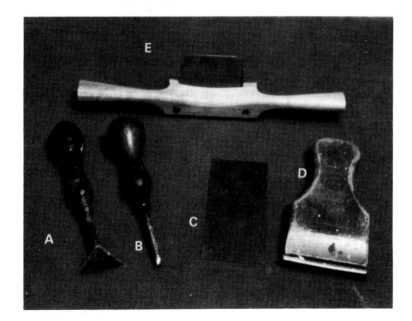

Plate 3.47 (A) shave hook, (B) scraper burnisher, (C) cabinet scraper, (D) Skarsten scraper, (E) scraper plane.

287

Perhaps because the cabinet scraper does require a certain knack to keep sharp, other scrapers are often used in preference, but none is quite so effective. The *Skarsten scraper* (or *hook scraper*) can be used for finishing work, and its blades do not need sharpening as they can be replaced instead. A variety of blades are available with various curves, as well as a serrated blade that breaks up old paint to make it easier to remove.

The *shave hook* is not suitable for finishing, but can be used for preparatory work such as removing glue. Several blades are available, the most common being the triangular one. The shave hook is sharpened by bevelling the outside of the blade with a file. The steel used in the blade of the purchased shave hooks fails to hold a very good edge, but a superior scraper can be made by cutting the blade off an old one and brazing in its place a short length of blade taken from an old hand plane. This blade can then be sharpened on an oil stone, and if used with both hands — one pulling, the other pressing the shank to add weight to the blade — can even be used for finishing. A home-made scraper of this type with its rectangular blade is very similar to a *ship's scraper,* which is a large version of the shave hook, but with a longer handle and square blade, intended for heavy work.

Sanders

Sanding is the final preparation of timber before painting or varnishing, and between subsequent coats; rubbing down with various grades of abrasive paper to provide a smooth surface. Between-coat sanding not only removes any imperfections, dust particles, raised grain, (perhaps even drips!) but provides a mechanical 'key' for the next coat to adhere to.

Abrasive paper should always be used with some sort of backing pad, even if it is only a scrap of timber. Rubbing by hand produces an uneven result, sanding being good under each finger tip, but not between them. Occasionally when sanding a very curved section, perhaps a spar, the paper can be held in the palm of the hand which adapts easily to any shape, and in this case the fleshy palm is itself the backing pad.

Purpose-made *sanding blocks,* around which to wrap the abrasive paper for hand sanding, used to be made of cork. The modern ones are a hard rubber and have spikes protected by a flexible flap at either end to hold the paper. For large curved areas a *sanding plane* can be made from a length of plywood: handles at each

Plate 3.48 Sanders: (A) electric drill with disc sander fitted and foam drum sander alongside, (B) finishing sander, (C) belt sander, (D) cork sanding block and (E) modern rubber sanding block.

end allow it to be pushed firmly against the curve while sanding, as shown earlier in Plate 1.35.

Sanding by hand is hard work; power sanders can reduce time and effort, and on flat surfaces can produce a better result. There are three types of power sander; the disc sander, belt sander, and finishing sander.

A simple rubber backing pad can convert an ordinary electric drill into a *disc sander,* but this is a very unsatisfactory tool. The drill is used at an angle, the flexing rubber in theory following the timber surface, but in practice rubbing rounded scallops into the surface due to the uneven pressure. More sophisticated disc sanders have some sort of 'floating' head; the disc is fitted to a ball joint that allows it to follow the timber surface with even pressure all over. This is a better sander, and if used with a soft backing pad and care can produce good results; the problem is that some cross grain scratches are inevitably left by the circular action. These have to be removed by hand sanding.

The *belt sander* leaves no cross grain scratches as it continually turns in one direction. It is an efficient sander and with coarse paper can rapidly remove a considerable depth of timber. It can usefully be used to clean up large areas of discoloured or blemished wood, but its very effectiveness can be a drawback: if it is left running in one place it quickly eats out a trough in its surface. Generally it is rather too large and clumsy for finishing work, especially as it cannot sand right into corners due to the rollers at each end.

The *finishing sander* (or *orbital sander*) is, as its name implies, designed for finishing work. The abrasive paper is stretched over a flat rubber or felt pad, which vibrates rapidly, evenly sanding a large area with no danger of cutting the scallops or troughs produced by the other sanders. Its base extends beyond the body so that sanding is possible right into corners. The finishing sander is an excellent tool, but once again it is worth buying a heavy duty one, preferably of industrial quality as then on large projects it can be used continuously for hours with no fear of overheating or other damage. Some makes of orbital sander vibrate their pads in larger circles than others. These can leave crescent-shaped marks when used on hardwood, which show up after varnishing. Better results are obtained from sanders with a fine, tightly controlled action.

Sanding curved surfaces by machine can be difficult. Convex curves, particularly gentle ones such as those found on a hull can be tackled with an ordinary finishing sander, but concave surfaces are more awkward. Often they have to be done by hand, although in some cases a *foam drum sander,* attached to an electric drill, can be very effective.

Abrasive Paper

Abrasive papers are available with different types of grit and backing material, and a wide range of degrees of coarseness.

The normal sheet size is 11 in x 9 in (280 x 230 mm) but sheets are specially prepared to fit all the types of sander mentioned above. For larger workshops it is economical to buy the 165 ft rolls (50 m) which can be obtained in widths to suit any make of finishing sander.

The paper backings are graded in weight from 'A' to 'E', although some special backing materials are made for heavy industrial purposes. 'A' is very light and for hand sanding only, 'C' or 'D' can be used for either hand or machine use, while 'E' is designed for use with sanding machines and is too stiff for use with hand blocks.

The degree of fineness or coarseness of the paper is measured by the grit size, which refers to the mesh of a screen through which the grit can pass. For example '100 grit' can pass through a mesh with 100 rectangular holes to the inch (or 25 mm). Grit sizes range from 16 to 1200, but for most finishing work 100 to 240 is adequate. Coarser papers can be useful for shaping timber, and finer ones are used in fibreglass work.

If the grit completely covers the backing paper it is called 'closed coat'; if it only provides a seventy-five percent covering it is called 'open coat'. Closed coat paper cuts more quickly, but the tighter packed grains clog easily. Open coat paper should be used on resinous wood, and for sanding varnish and paintwork.

Abrasive papers are often referred to as sand paper although this is a misnomer as sand is never used. The yellow coloured paper that appears to be sand is in fact glass. Glass is a fairly soft type of grit and although this is the cheapest type of paper it also loses its bite most quickly. It is only suitable for hand sanding, as it dulls too quickly for machine use.

Garnet is a reddish brown grit that retains its sharpness longer. It is an excellent paper for hand sanding, and can be used with machines, although for these the best choice is aluminium oxide paper. This is a light grey coloured grit that is exceptionally hard and tough.

Silicon carbide is a dark, almost black grit which is also extremely hard, but its brittleness makes it less suitable for machine use. It is not often used for rubbing down bare wood, but is suitable for rubbing down paint or varnish between coats. It is backed by a waterproof paper so that it can be used with water as a lubricant, which is why it is sometimes called 'wet and dry' paper. Particularly when using the very fine grades for polishing, using it wet has the advantage that clogging is reduced: the paper should be continually dipped in water to remove dust from the pores, and the slurry of water and dust wiped from the work with a damp cloth before it has time to dry. A squirt of washing-up liquid in the water reduces clogging even further. A type of silicon carbide paper is available called 'Lubrisil', that is used dry, but actually has its own lubricant in the paper.

Emery cloth is not intended for wood or paint work, but is designed to be used to finish metal.

Table 15 shows the available grit sizes for each of the above types of abrasive.

Table 15 Availability of abrasive papers (as supplied by English Abrasives Ltd)

Type of grit	Backing weight	Grit sizes available															
		500	400	360	320	280	240	220	180	150	120	100	80	70	60	50	40
Glass (closed coat)	C						✓	✓		✓	✓	✓		✓			✓
Garnet (open coat)	A				✓		✓	✓	✓	✓	✓	✓	✓				
Garnet (open coat)	C							✓	✓	✓	✓	✓	✓		✓	✓	✓
Aluminium oxide (open or closed coat)	C								✓	✓	✓	✓	✓		✓	✓	✓
Aluminium oxide (open or closed coat)	E						✓	✓	✓	✓	✓	✓	✓		✓		
Silicon carbide 'Wet and Dry' (closed coat)	A	✓	✓	✓	✓	✓	✓	✓									
Silicon carbide 'Wet and Dry' (closed coat)	C		✓	✓	✓	✓	✓	✓	✓	✓	✓	✓	✓		✓		
Silicon carbide 'Wet and Dry' (closed coat)	E		✓					✓	✓	✓	✓	✓	✓		✓	✓	✓
Silicon carbide 'Lubrisil' (open coat)	A				✓	✓	✓	✓	✓								
Silicon carbide 'Lubrisil' (open coat)	C									✓	✓	✓	✓				
Emery (closed coat)	Cloth					✓		✓		✓	✓	✓	✓		✓	✓	✓

Glossary

Amidship Middle part of the vessel, or the centre line.

Anneal Heating metal to a certain temperature range and allowing it to cool again; this alters the metal's physical properties — some are toughened, others softened.

Anode In an electrical cell the positive electrode is the anode, the negative electrode the cathode. When galvanic action occurs, the anode is corroded.

Apron Internal part of a two part stem corresponding to the hog of a two part keel.

Athwart Across the vessel, the opposite of fore and aft.

Ballast keel See *Keel*.

Batten Thin flexible length of wood used for fairing and drawing curved lines.

Bedding Mastic used under fittings to prevent leaks.

Bevel An edge surface that has been angled other than at right angles, either for appearance, or in order to fit it against another member.

Bilge (1) The space in a boat under the sole boards.

(2) The external curve of the hull where the bottom becomes the side; a 'hard bilge' curves tightly, and a 'soft bilge' is gently rounded.

Body plan The part of the lines plan that shows the transverse sections or station lines for making the moulds.

Boot top A stripe of contrasting paint just above the load water line that separates the bottom from the topsides.

Breasthook A wood or iron horizontal knee that links the gunwales or stringers at the stem.

Bulkhead A partition below decks. 'Main bulkheads' span the entire hull athwartships, 'half bulkheads' are only on one side of the hull.

Butt (1) The lower part of a tree trunk.

(2) The simplest joint, where two members meet squarely. A 'butt block' is the timber pad fastened inside a butt joint at the ends of two planks.

Buttock line A fore and aft vertical section of the boat, found on the sheer plan of the lines drawing.

Camber The curve of the deck athwartships.

Carling (Carline) A fore and aft member at the sides of any deck opening such as cabin, cockpit or hatches. It is dovetailed at each end into main deckbeams, side deckbeams being let into it.

Carvel A construction method where plank edges butt against each other.

Cast A metal object is cast if it is made by pouring molten metal into a mould and allowing it to cool, see *Wrought*.

Cathode See *Anode*.

Caulk To make a seam water-tight by driving in strands of cotton.

Ceiling Plank lining on inside of timbers usually only used on larger craft.

Chamfer A small bevel neatly finishing exposed timber edges.

Checks Splits in timber due to drying.

Chine (1) Construction method where transverse sections are not curved, but made up of a series of straight lines.

(2) The corner on this type of hull where two of the wide 'planks' meet at an angle.

(3) The supporting member that runs fore and aft inside this angle, sometimes called the 'chine log'.

Chopped strand matt Glass fibre reinforcing sheet consisting of fibres randomly arranged, not woven. Widely used in fibreglass construction.

Clamp(1) Steel or timber tool used for holding parts together or exerting pressure.

(2)Internal fore and aft member reinforcing the gunwale at the chain plates.

Clench Shape the end of a fastening so that it will not draw out. Usually means burring the end of a copper nail over a rove, but sometimes used when a nail is simply turned.

Clinker Construction method where planks overlap; 'lapstrake' in America.

Closed assembly period Time two glued faces are in contact before clamping pressure is applied.

Coachroof The deck or 'roof' covering a cabin that is raised above deck level to increase headroom below.

Coaming The raised side of a cockpit or hatch.

Cold moulded Construction method where the hull is laminated from several layers of veneers fastened to a jig.

Constant Camber   Construction method devised by multihull designer, Jim Brown, where the hull is made from prefabricated laminated timber sheets, each with a standard curve.

Covering board   Outermost deck plank that covers the edge of the sheer plank and timber ends.

Cramp   See *Clamp*, (1).

Crook   Timber with naturally curved grain used for making floors and knees.

Crop   The height the crown of the deck is above the sheer.

Crown   The highest point of the deck's camber, located on the centre line.

Deadwood   See *Keel*.

Dezincification   Loss of zinc from a copper zinc alloy such as brass due to immersion in salt water, resulting in a weak and porous copper residue.

Die   Tool for cutting the external thread on metal rod; a 'tap' cuts the corresponding internal thread in a hole.

Dolly   A metal tool used to support a nail while it is clenched.

Dowel   Round wooden pin used to hide fastenings.

Drift   Large metal fastening driven into a blind hole — like an outsized nail.

Dummy stick   Tool used to mark a standard distance when scribing or spiling.

Edge set   To bend a plank across its width, or edgeways.

Face   One surface of a piece of wood, the 'face side' and 'face edge' are the surfaces that will be seen when a piece of timber is in position; joiners true these sides first, then take all measurements from them.

Fair   A line is fair when it curves smoothly without bumps or hollows.

Fashion piece   Frame-like timber attached to inside of transom to provide a good support for the plank ends and their fastenings.

Feather edge   An edge that tapers to nothing.

Fiddles   Strips of wood fitted to tables and other surfaces to prevent objects sliding off.

Fillers   Any substances added to resin to change properties such as density, hardness, workability, or colour.

Flare   The outward curve of a vessel's topsides resulting in hollow sections.

Floor   A transverse structural member linking frames across the keel.

Frame   The rib of a vessel when it is either laminated or sawn from solid timber to the correct shape; ribs that are bent into place are called 'timbers'.

Futtock When a frame cannot be sawn from a single piece, it is made up of several futtocks, scarfed or bolted together.

Garboard The plank adjacent to the keel.

Graving piece A piece of wood let into a large member to repair a damaged or rotten section of timber.

Ground Timber cleat attached to a hull to allow fastening of bulkheads.

Gunwale Fore and aft structural member fitted inside the frames at the sheer; sometimes called an 'inwale'.

Half breadth plan The part of the lines plan that shows the vessel in plan view and water lines.

Hanging knee A vertical knee.

Hog (1) Distortion of a hull where the ends drop, see *Sag*.

(2) When the wood keel is made from two parts, each full length, the inner member is called the hog, and the outer the keel.

Horn A check for squareness by triangulation.

Horn timber Fore and aft structural member in a counter sterned craft, which extends from the sternpost to the transom.

Jig Any frame or apparatus used as a former to produce a required shape.

Keel The main fore and aft member on which the whole vessel is built. May be in two parts, see *Hog*, (2). A 'ballast keel' is a cast piece of iron or lead bolted beneath the wood keel, and a 'false keel' or 'deadwood' is timber fastened below the keel to produce the required profile, but of no structural importance.

Keelson A fore and aft member bolted over the timbers or floors to spread any vertical load, such as that from the mast. On larger craft the keelson may extend the full length of the hull.

Knee A timber or metal member connecting two others where they meet at an angle. They are used to strengthen all important 'corners' of the hull.

Laminate To make a curved shape by gluing thin strips of timber against a jig. Each strip is also called a laminate.

Laminated plastic Plastic sheets such as 'Formica'.

Lines plan The drawing that gives the external shape of the hull. It is in three parts, sheer plan, half breadth plan, and body plan.

Lining out Marking the position of all the planks on the moulds, so checking that the run of the planking will be fair.

Lloyd's Rules Comprehensive construction guidelines drawn up by Lloyd's.

Lodging knee Horizontal knee.

Loft floor Large flat area, painted white, for lofting. In the past it was literally in the loft of the boatshop.

Lofting Process of drawing the lines plan full size in order to check that lines are fair and to make the scrieve board and templates of main members.

Longitudinal Any fore and aft member.

Luting Mastic placed in a joint before it is fastened.

Margin boards Deck planks around deck openings such as hatches, cockpit, and cabin.

Moisture content Weight of water contained in timber expressed as a percentage of the timber's dry weight.

Monocoque In one part. Modern laminated hulls are monocoque structures, whereas traditional hulls are made from many pieces which can be dismantled and replaced.

Mortise A slot cut in a piece of timber to accept a pin cut on another, so making a mortise and tenon joint.

Mould (1) Female (or reverse) of hull shape from which fibreglass hulls are made; see *Plug*.

(2) Timber pattern corresponding to the shape of a station line on the body plan. Moulds are set up across the keel to provide a guide until planking is complete.

Moulded line The side of the mould when set up that corresponds to the station line.

Moulding (1) The height or depth of a member, measured normal to the centre line or hull planking; see *Siding*.

(2) A fibreglass hull as it is removed from the mould, before any further work is done to it.

Pay The process of filling deck seams after caulking.

Plug A male pattern, usually timber, from which a female mould is made in order to produce the finished article in another material. Examples are: (1), fibreglass boats are made from fibreglass moulds, themselves made from wooden plugs; (2), metal ballast keels are cast in sand moulds, made by ramming the sand around a wooden plug.

Polyester resin The resin normally used to produce glass fibre hulls.

Pot life The time resin or glue is usable after the two parts have been mixed.

Profile (1) The shape of the vessel as seen from the side.

(2) The outline of any member.

Quarter knee Knee connecting the gunwale (or stringer) to the transom.

Quench Rapidly cool metal after annealing by plunging into water; this can produce different results from allowing the hot metal to cool slowly.

Rebate (Rabbet) A groove cut in one member to accept another, so that it lies flush. In particular the triangular groove cut into the stem, keel, and stern post to accept the planking.

Rebate line The point where the planking meets the backbone on the outside of the hull.

Ribbands Long flexible pieces of wood used in carvel construction; they are fastened to the moulds to form a false hull against which the timbers can be bent.

Riser (Rising) Longitudinal member fastened inside the timbers to support thwarts, soles, and other transverse members.

Rubbing strake A fore and aft member fastened outside the planking at the sheer to provide protection when going alongside.

Run The shape of the hull underwater aft.

Run of the planking The appearance of all the planking laps or seams considered together.

Sacrificial anode A piece of base metal (zinc, magnesium, or aluminium) deliberately linked with another metal to protect it from galvanic action.

Sag Distortion of a hull where the middle part droops; see *Hog.*

Scantlings The dimensions of members.

Scarf A tapered joint designed to connect two similar sectioned pieces of wood end to end.

Scribe (1) To mark a line by cutting it into the timber.
(2) A tool for marking; scratch awl.

Scribing A method of marking a piece of timber that has to be fitted against a complicated shape.

Scrieve board Permanent full size record of the body plan.

Section The shape of a hull if it were cut at any point, normally taken to mean square to the centre line.

Shakes Faults in timber, see *Thunder shakes.*

Sheer The curve of the deck, where it meets the planking, as seen in profile.

Sheer plan The part of the lines plan that shows the vessel's profile, and buttock lines.

Sheer strake The topmost plank.

Shelf life Time that materials can be stored before they become ineffective.

Shore A beam used to prop up a hull, or to apply pressure from a distant strong point.

298

Shutter When carvel planking is proceeding from both the sheer down and the garboard up simultaneously, the shutter is the last plank fitted, closing the gap.

Siding The width of a member, measured parallel to the centre line, or hull planking; see *Moulding*, (1).

Sole The floor of the cabin, cockpit, or other area.

Spiling Method of marking a piece of timber that has to be fitted against a complicated shape.

Spring (1) Bending a piece of wood into place cold.

(2) The movement of timber after it has been rip sawn, due to tensions within the wood.

Station Position on the keel of a section marked on the half breadth plan. The 'station lines' are all the sections shown on that plan.

Stealer A strake that does not run the full length of the hull, so gaining or losing a plank where the plank ends would otherwise be too wide, or too narrow.

Stem The forward member of the centre line structure, to which the plank ends are fastened. It can be made in two parts, see *Apron*.

Stopping Putty, or other sealant, worked into seams after caulking.

Stopwater A softwood dowel driven through joints in the main frame. They prevent the ingress of water by swelling against the adjacent hardwood.

Strake One run of planking from stem to stern; it may consist of a single plank, or two or more scarfed or butt jointed together.

Stringer A longitudinal strengthening member fastened inside the timbers, and reaching from stem to stern.

Strip planking A construction method using thin planks glued together; they are not fitted but edge set into position.

Tap See *Die*.

Template A semi-permanent pattern of stem, transom, or other members made from thin plywood.

Tenon A rectangular pin cut in the end of a piece of timber to make half of a mortise and tenon joint; see *Mortise*.

Thunder shake Fault in timber that runs across the grain. They are hard to see but make the wood useless as it literally falls apart. Commonly found in mahogany.

Thwart A transverse board used as a seat.

Timber A rib steam-bent into position; see *Frame*.

Toe rail A length of wood fastened around the edge of the deck to prevent the loss of small items.

Topsides The sides of a hull above the water when the vessel is afloat and upright.

Transom The transverse board at the stern, fastened to the stern post, and to which the planks are fastened.

Trenail (Trunnel) Wooden dowel used as a fastening by wedging one or both ends.

Tuck The reverse curve in the after planking of a deep keeled yacht.

Tumblehome The inward curve of the topsides found on some designs.

Turn of the bilge See *Bilge*, (2).

Veneer Thin strips of timber used when laminating.

Wale A strake thicker than the others.

Water line Section through the hull parallel to the surface of the water when afloat. 'Load water line' is the section at the water line to which she is designed to float.

Web A supporting member whose strength is obtained by having a large moulded dimension, although very little siding. Usually made from plywood, they can be used for frames, knees, and other structural members.

Wrought Metal is wrought when it is worked into shape by force, either when hot or cold. Examples are wire, plate, rod, even extruded mast sections; see *Cast*.

Yield stress The point beyond which a metal ceases to behave elastically.

Bibliography

Design Considerations

The design requirements of a good boat, and the compromises inevitable in any boat, are discussed in the large number of design and cruising handbooks. Two of the classics are:

Kinney, F S, *Skene's Elements of Yacht Design*, Putnam, 1989.
Hiscock, E C, *Cruising Under Sail*, Adlard Coles Nautical, 1985.

Scantling Advice

Scantling rules for small craft are published by the major ship classification organisations, such as the American Bureau of Shipping in the United States and Det norske Veritas in Scandinavia. The rules produced by the equivalent British based organisation are used worldwide:

Lloyd's Register of Shipping, *Lloyd's Rules for Yachts and Small Craft.*

Formulations for traditional wooden yachts were devised by the American designer:

Herreshoff: Herreshoff's Rule in Kinney, F S (see above).

For working craft, information in a more accessible form is provided by:

Sea Fish Industry Authority, *Rules for the Construction of Wooden Fishing Vessels*, SFIA.

Additional information concerning rigging and equipment sizes, standard furniture dimensions, etc has been collated by:

Nicolson, I, *Boat Data Book*, 2nd ed, Adlard Coles Nautical 1985.

Construction

Traditional boatbuilding is described in greatest detail by Chapelle. Culler's book, although comparatively lightweight, provides many worthwhile insights:

Chapelle, H E, *Boatbuilding*, Norton, 1980.
Culler, R D, *Skiffs and Schooners*, International Marine, 1990.

Several books deal solely with clinker (lapstrake) construction. McKee's booklet provides a simple explanation of the method while the others mentioned below are construction manuals:

McKee, E, *Clenched Lap or Clinker*, National Maritime Museum, 1972.
Leather, J, *Clinker Boatbuilding*, Adlard Coles Nautical, 1987.
Simmons, W J, *Lapstrake Boatbuilding*, International Marine, 1983.

Modern construction methods are covered in greatest detail by the Gougeon brothers. Guzzwell and Nicolson provide detailed information on the cold moulding method:

Gougeon, *The Gougeon Brothers on Boat Construction*, 2nd ed, Pendell Publishing, 1980.
Guzzwell, J, *Modern Wooden Yacht Construction*, International Marine, 1979 (out of print).
Nicolson, I, *Cold-moulded and Strip-planked Wood Boatbuilding*, Adlard Coles Nautical, 1983

Additional information specifically concerned with fitting out and repair projects is provided by:

Bingham, F P, *Practical Yacht Joinery: Tools, Tips, Techniques*, International Marine, 1983.
Scarlett, J, *Wooden Boats: Restoration and Maintenance Manual*, David & Charles, 1987.

Lofting is dealt with in chapters in the books by Chapelle, the Gougeon brothers, and Guzzwell (detailed above) and by:

Vaitses, A H, *Lofting*, International Marine, 1987.

Timber

The properties of timbers are found in:

Building Research Establishment, *Handbook of Hardwoods*, HMSO, 1973.
Building Research Establishment, *Handbook of Softwoods*, HMSO, 1977.

A series of booklets, each dealing with one geographical region, contain similar information. If only two or three volumes are required, they are much cheaper:

Brown, W H (ed), *Timbers of the World Vols 1–9*, TRADA, 1978.

Information sheets issued by TRADA may prove adequate:

Timber Research and Development Association, *Timbers – Their Properties and Uses*, Information Sheet No.2/3–10, TRADA, 1991.

Timber Research and Development Association, *Wood Decorative and Practical*, Information Sheet No.2/3–6, TRADA, 1985.

Although mostly dealing with harbour and marina construction, more detailed information on timbers for use in the marine environment is provided by:

Brown, W H (ed), *Timber for Marine and Freshwater Construction*, TRADA, 1974.

Fascinating information on methods of shaping wood, either on a small or industrial scale, is provided by:

Stevens, W C and Turner, N, *The Woodbending Handbook*, HMSO and Woodcraft (out of print).

Preservative treatments are described and discussed by:

Timber Research and Development Association, *Timber Preservation*, TRADA, 1986.

Marine Metals

The technical literature on metals is vast, but one book that deals specifically with metals in relation to small boats is by:

Warren, N, *Metal Corrosion in Boats*, Adlard Coles Nautical, 1991.

Adhesives

Advice on the use of adhesives is given by:

Lees, W A, *Adhesives in Engineering Design*, Design Council, 1984.

Manufacturers provide technical information sheets about their products giving details of pot life, clamping times, curing temperatures etc, and those provided by Borden UK are particularly informative.

Tools

Several dictionaries of tools are available. Of the two mentioned here, the first is exceptionally comprehensive and informative, while the second is pleasingly illustrated:

Salaman, R A (ed), *Dictionary of Woodworking Tools*, Unwin Hyman, 1989.

Blackburn, G, *Illustrated Encyclopaedia of Woodworking Handtools*, Globe Pequot, 1991.

An even larger number of books offer advice and instruction on the use of tools, but the one mentioned here is notably clear and precise:

McDonnel, L P and Kaumeheiwa, A I, *The Use of Hand Woodworking Tools*, 2nd ed, Delmar, 1978.

Brief Details of Boats Featured in Illustrations

Arethusa: a 72 ft (22 m) ketch designed by D M Cannell. The hull was built at Fox's yard, Ipswich, Suffolk, England, then fitted out at the International Boatbuilding Training Centre, Oulton Broad, Lowestoft, Suffolk, England. The hull construction is cold moulded laminations on top of strip planking. (Plate 0.7.) *Arethusa's* two 12 ft (3.7 m) tenders were also designed by D M Cannell and built at the International Boatbuilding Training Centre. They are cold moulded, with two diagonal laminations, and one fore and aft. (Plate 0.6.)

Crestadonna: a 32 ft (9.7 m) sloop designed by C Patchett and built at his Martham Ferry Boatyard, Martham, Norfolk, England. She is strip planked, with steam bent timbers. (Plate 0.5.)

Naja: a 29 ft (8.8 m) sloop designed by S Langevin and built at Whisstock's Boatyard, Woodbridge, Suffolk, England. A hard chine design built of plywood on laminated 'ring' frames, that incorporate deck beams, cabin sides, and coach roof. (Plates 0.3, 0.8 and 1.34.)

Osea Jol: a 25 ft (7.6 m) gaff sloop, drawn by A H Robinson but based on a Polish fishing boat design. Clinker built by Janwillem Pick on Osea Island, Maldon, Essex, England. (Plate 1.28.)

Sandyloo: a 9 ft (2.7 m) rowing skiff built without plans 'by guess and by God' by Allan Wilson, Culswick, Shetland Isles. Flat bottomed with clinker sides. (Plate 0.4.)

RNLI Boarding boat: a 16 ft (4.9 m) tender built from RNLI plans by the International Boatbuilding Training Centre; clinker construction. (Plates 1.12–1.15 and 1.51–1.54.)

Tara: a 33 ft (10 m) ketch of the 'Ocean Dog' class designed by R Freeman and built at the International Boatbuilding Training Centre. She is of traditional carvel construction. (Plates 0.2 and 1.31.)

Tirrick: a 25 ft (7.7 m) clinker Folkboat, designed by T Sunden and built by the Author. (Plates 0.1 and 1.48.)

Addresses of Organisations Cited in the Text

British Wood Preserving Association
1 Gleneagles House
Vernon Gate
Derby
DE1 1UP
England

BSI (British Standards Institute)
389 Chiswick High Road
London
W4 4AH
England

Building Research Establishment
Garston
Watford
WD25 9XX
England

HMSO (Her Majesty's Stationary Office) Publishing Services
St. Clements House
2 - 16 Colgate
Norwich
NR3 1BQ
England

International Boatbuilding Training Centre
Sea Lake Road
Lowestoft
Suffolk
NR32 3LQ
England

Lloyd's Register of Shipping
71 Fenchurch Street
London
EC3M 4BS
England

National Maritime Museum
Greenwich
London
SE10 9NF
England

SBBNF (now the BMF, the British Marine Federation)
Marine House
Thorpe Lea Road
Egham
Surrey
TW20 8BF
England

Sea Fish Industry Authority
18 Logie Mill
Edingurgh
EH7 4HS
Scotland

TRADA (Timber Research and Development Association)
Stocking Lane
Hughendon Valley
High Wycombe
Buckinghamshire
HP14 4ND
England

Index

Figure numbers are in *italics,* and Plate numbers in **bold type.**